P9-DFJ-040

BEST-EVER RECIPES
EVERY DAY SOUP

BEST-EVER RECIPES
EVERY DAY SOUP

SENSATIONAL SOUPS FOR ALL OCCASIONS: 135 INSPIRING AND DELICIOUS
IDEAS FOR ALL THE CLASSICS SHOWN IN 230 STUNNING PHOTOGRAPHS

ANNE SHEASBY

JG
PRESS

Published by World Publications Group, Inc.
140 Laurel Street
East Bridgewater, MA 02333
www.wrldpub.net

Produced by Anness Publishing Ltd
Hermes House
88–89 Blackfriars Road, London SE1 8HA
tel. 020 7401 2077; fax 020 7633 9499

www.annesspublishing.com

If you like the images in this book and would like to
investigate using them for publishing, promotions or
advertising, please visit our website
www.practicalpictures.com for more information.

Publisher: Joanna Lorenz
Senior Managing Editor: Conor Kilgallon
Editor: Anne Hildyard
Production Controller: Claire Rae
Designed and edited for Anness Publishing Ltd by
the Bridgewater Book Company Ltd

ETHICAL TRADING POLICY
At Anness Publishing we believe that business should be
conducted in an ethical and ecologically sustainable
way, with respect for the environment and a proper
regard to the replacement of the natural resources we
employ.
As a publisher, we use a lot of wood pulp to make high-
quality paper for printing, and that wood commonly
comes from spruce trees. We are therefore currently
growing more than 750,000 trees in three Scottish
forest plantations: Berrymoss (130 hectares/320 acres),
West Touxhill (125 hectares/305 acres) and Deveron
Forest (75 hectares/185 acres). The forests we manage
contain more than 3.5 times the number of trees
employed each year in making paper for the books we
manufacture.
Because of this ongoing ecological investment
programme, you, as our customer, can have the pleasure
and reassurance of knowing that a tree is being
cultivated on your behalf to naturally replace the
materials used to make the book you are holding.
Our forestry programme is run in accordance with the
UK Woodland Assurance Scheme (UKWAS) and will be
certified by the internationally recognized Forest
Stewardship Council (FSC). The FSC is a non-
government organization dedicated to promoting
responsible management of the world's forests.
Certification ensures forests are managed in an
environmentally sustainable and socially responsible
way. For further information about this scheme, go to
www.annesspublishing.com/trees

© Anness Publishing Ltd 2008, 2009

All rights reserved. No part of this publication may be
reproduced, stored in a retrieval system, or transmitted
in any way or by any means, electronic, mechanical,
photocopying, recording or otherwise, without the prior
written permission of the copyright holder.

ISBN-10: 1-57215-589-2
ISBN-13: 978-1-57215-589-3

Printed and bound in Singapore

Many of the recipes in this book previously appeared in
The New Book of Soups by Anne Sheasby

PUBLISHER'S NOTE
Although the advice and information in this book are
believed to be accurate and true at the time of going to
press, neither the authors nor the publisher can accept
any legal responsibility or liability for any errors or
omissions that may be made.

NOTES
For all recipes, quantities are given in both
metric and imperial measures and, where
appropriate, in standard cups and spoons. Follow
one set of measures, but not a mixture, because
they are not interchangeable.
Standard spoon and cup measures are level.
1 tsp = 5ml, 1 tbsp = 15ml, 1 cup = 250ml/8fl oz.
Australian standard tablespoons are 20ml.
Australian readers should use 3 tsp in place of
1 tbsp for measuring small quantities.
American pints are 16fl oz/2 cups. American
readers should use 20fl oz/2.5 cups in place of
1 pint when measuring liquids.
Electric oven temperatures in this book are for
conventional ovens. When using a fan oven, the
temperature will probably need to be reduced by
about 10–20°C/20–40°F. Since ovens vary, you
should check with your manufacturer's
instruction book for guidance.
The nutritional analysis given for each recipe is
calculated per portion (i.e. serving or item),
unless otherwise stated. If the recipe gives a
range, such as Serves 4–6, then the nutritional
analysis will be for the smaller portion size, i.e.
6 servings. Measurements for sodium do not
include salt added to taste.
Medium (US large) eggs are used unless
otherwise stated.
Front cover shows Beef and Lamb Soup – for
recipe, see pages 188–9.

Contents

Introduction

Soups are very versatile and can be made using many different ingredients. One of the great things about soup is that you can use a selection of fresh, raw and sometimes cooked ingredients and a well-flavoured stock to create a delicious, home-made meal with very little effort.

Many soups are quick and easy to make and simply combine vegetables or meat with added flavourings, such as herbs or spices, whereas other soups – perhaps those suitable for a special occasion – may require a little more preparation. Some soups make good starters to a meal, and they are always a popular choice, while other soups are substantial dishes and only need some bread rolls as an accompaniment. There are many types of soups to choose from. Chilled, light and refreshing soups are perfect for summer dining al fresco. Choose from light and refreshing soups such as Vichyssoise, or Chilled Avocado Soup with Cumin from Spain. Chunky vegetable, legume,

pasta and noodle soups are ideal winter warmers. You could try classic Tuscan Bean Soup, North African Spiced Soup, or Malaysian Prawn Laksa.

Soups that are made with chicken, meat, fish or shellfish are full of nourishment and make a complete meal served with chunks of crusty bread. Here the choice is wide and varied – from traditional Irish Bacon Broth for family lunches to the more exotic Moroccan Chicken Soup with Charmoula Butter. Lobster Bisque, Scallop and Jerusalem Artichoke Soup or Cream of Duck Soup with Blueberry Relish are perfect for entertaining friends. Whichever kind you choose, fresh and

flavourful soups are always worth the time and effort.

An essential ingredient in most soups is a well-flavoured stock. Stock (bouillon) cubes and stock powder save time, but it is hard to beat the flavour and quality of home-made stocks, and they are relatively easy and inexpensive to make. Once you have a basic stock, there is a huge range of soups that you can create.

However, remember that your stock will only be as good as the

ABOVE: *Mexican Beef Chilli Soup with Monterey Jack Nachos is a hearty meal.*

ABOVE: *Pasta Soup with Meatballs and Basil makes a substantial main course.*

ABOVE: *Corn and Red Chilli Chowder is for those who enjoy hot and spicy food.*

quality of ingredients used to make it – you cannot produce a tasty stock from limp, past-their-best vegetables! If you are really short of time, you could choose one of the chilled fresh stock products that are available from some supermarkets and delicatessens.

Very little specialist equipment is needed to make soups, although you will find that a food processor or blender will save time and effort when you want to purée soup mixtures before serving. However, pressing the soup through a sieve (strainer) or using a hand-held blender are perfectly good alternatives to get a smooth soup. You will probably already have in your kitchen a good-quality, heavy pan, a sharp knife and chopping board, and a vegetable peeler.

For a finishing touch, an attractive garnish, perhaps a sprinkling of fresh herbs, some julienne vegetables, or a swirl of cream added at the last minute, will enhance the simplest of soups. Soups may be served on their own or topped with a few crunchy croûtons or grilled croûtes.

Soups feature in every cuisine around the world – whether they are called gumbos, potages, broth, chowders or consommées. Now that once-unfamiliar ingredients are readily available in specialist food shops and many supermarkets, there is absolutely no reason why you cannot make these delicious soups in your own home.

USING THIS BOOK

Few dishes give more all-round pleasure than a good home-made soup, and in this wonderful collection of recipes the world of soups is yours to explore. Each recipe in this book has easy-to-follow step-by-step instructions and a beautiful colour photograph to show the finished dish. The final chapter supplies detailed information on a range of ingredients that you may use in soups, advice on essential equipment and guidance on preparation and cooking techniques.

Light and refreshing soups

Chilled soups can be enjoyed on hot days and Gazpacho with Avocado Salsa is a perfect start to a summer meal. Refreshing soups can be clear or creamy and may contain fragrant or fruity ingredients such as mango or lemons, or stimulating, tangy flavours such as lemon grass and lime leaves. Avgolemono is an example of a lemon flavoured soup and Thai Hot and Sour Soup has typical flavours of coriander and Thai chillies.

Cucumber and salmon soup with salsa

Charred salmon brings a hint of heat to the refreshing flavours of this chilled soup. Good-looking and beautifully light, it makes the perfect opener for an al fresco *meal.*

SERVES 4

3 medium cucumbers

**300ml/¹/₂ pint/1¹/₄ cups Greek
   (US strained plain) yogurt**

**250ml/8fl oz/1 cup vegetable stock,
   chilled**

120ml/4fl oz/¹/₂ cup crème fraîche

15ml/1 tbsp chopped fresh chervil

15ml/1 tbsp chopped fresh chives

**15ml/1 tbsp chopped fresh flat leaf
   parsley**

**1 small fresh red chilli, seeded and very
   finely chopped**

a little oil, for brushing

**225g/8oz salmon fillet, skinned and cut
   into eight thin slices**

salt and ground black pepper

fresh chervil or chives, to garnish

1 Peel two of the cucumbers and halve them lengthways. Scoop out and discard the seeds, then roughly chop the flesh. Purée the chopped flesh in a food processor or blender.

2 Add the yogurt, stock, crème fraîche, chervil, chives and seasoning, and process until smooth. Pour the mixture into a bowl, cover and chill.

3 Peel, halve and seed the remaining cucumber. Cut the flesh into small neat dice. Mix with the chopped

parsley and chilli in a bowl. Cover the salsa and chill until required.

4 Brush a griddle or frying pan with oil and heat until very hot. Add the salmon slices and sear them for 1–2 minutes, then turn over carefully and sear the other side until tender and charred.

5 Ladle the chilled soup into soup bowls. Top each portion with two slices of salmon, then pile a portion of salsa in the centre. Garnish with the chervil or chives and serve.

Nutritional information per portion: Energy 314Kcal/1299kJ; Protein 17.8g; Carbohydrate 3.9g, of which sugars 3.7g; Fat 26.1g, of which saturates 13.1g; Cholesterol 62mg; Calcium 183mg; Fibre 1.2g; Sodium 92mg.

Vichyssoise

This classic, chilled summer soup was first created in the 1920s by Louis Diat, chef at the New York Ritz-Carlton. He named it after Vichy, near his home in France.

SERVES 4–6

50g/2oz/¼ cup unsalted butter

450g/1lb leeks, white parts only, thinly sliced

3 large shallots, sliced

250g/9oz floury potatoes (such as King Edward or Maris Piper), peeled and cut into chunks

1 litre/1¾ pints/4 cups light chicken stock or water

300ml/½ pint/1¼ cups double (heavy) cream

iced water (optional)

a little lemon juice (optional)

salt and ground black pepper

chopped fresh chives, to garnish

1 Melt the butter in a heavy pan and cook the leeks and shallots gently, covered, for 15–20 minutes, until soft but not browned.

2 Add the potatoes and cook, uncovered, for a few minutes.

3 Stir in the chicken stock or water, 5ml/1 tsp salt and pepper to taste. Bring to the boil, then reduce the heat and partly cover the pan. Simmer for 15 minutes, or until the potatoes are soft.

4 Cool, then process the soup until smooth in a food processor or blender. Strain the soup into a bowl and stir in the cream. Taste and adjust the seasoning and add a little iced water if the consistency of the soup seems too thick.

5 Chill the soup for at least 4 hours or until very cold. Check the seasoning and add a squeeze of lemon juice, if required. Pour the soup into bowls and sprinkle with chopped chives. Serve immediately.

Nutritional information per portion: Energy 547Kcal/2260kJ; Protein 4.6g; Carbohydrate 17.7g, of which sugars 6.8g; Fat 51.4g, of which saturates 31.7g; Cholesterol 129mg; Calcium 79mg; Fibre 3.6g; Sodium 103mg.

Gazpacho with avocado salsa

Tomatoes, cucumber and peppers form the basis of this classic chilled soup. Add a spoonful of chunky, fresh avocado salsa and a scattering of croûtons, and serve for a light lunch or simple supper on a warm summer day.

SERVES 4

2 slices day-old white bread, cubed
600ml/1 pint/2¹/₂ cups chilled water
1kg/2¹/₄lb fresh tomatoes
1 cucumber
1 red (bell) pepper, halved, seeded and
   chopped
1 fresh green chilli, seeded and chopped
2 garlic cloves, chopped
30ml/2 tbsp extra virgin olive oil
juice of 1 lime and 1 lemon
a few drops of Tabasco sauce
salt and ground black pepper
8 ice cubes, to garnish
a handful of basil leaves, to garnish

FOR THE CROÛTONS

2 slices day-old bread, crusts removed
1 garlic clove, halved
15ml/1 tbsp olive oil

FOR THE AVOCADO SALSA

1 ripe avocado
5ml/1 tsp lemon juice
2.5cm/1in piece cucumber, diced
¹/₂ red chilli, seeded and finely chopped

1 Place the cubed bread in a large bowl and pour over 150ml/¹/₄pint/²/₃ cup of the water. Leave to soak for 5 minutes.

2 Meanwhile, place the tomatoes in a bowl and cover with boiling water. Leave for 30 seconds, then peel off the skin, remove the seeds and finely chop the flesh.

3 Thinly peel the skin off the cucumber, cut it in half lengthways and scoop out all the seeds with a teaspoon. Discard the inner part and chop the flesh into a fine dice.

4 Place the bread, tomatoes, cucumber, red pepper, chilli, garlic, olive oil, citrus juices and Tabasco in a food processor or blender with the remaining 450ml/ ³/₄ pint/scant 2 cups chilled water and blend until well combined but still chunky. Season to taste and chill for 2–3 hours.

5 To make the croûtons, rub the slices of bread with the garlic clove. Cut the bread into cubes and place in a plastic bag with the olive oil. Seal the bag and shake until the bread cubes are coated with the oil.

6 Heat a large non-stick frying pan and fry the croûtons over a medium heat until crisp and golden.

7 Just before serving, make the avocado salsa. Halve the avocado, remove the stone (pit), then peel and dice. Toss the avocado in the lemon juice to prevent it from browning, then place it in a serving bowl and add the cucumber and chilli. Mix well.

8 Ladle the soup into four chilled bowls and add a couple of ice cubes to each one. Top each portion with a good spoonful of avocado salsa. Garnish with the basil and sprinkle the croûtons over the top of the salsa.

Nutritional information per portion: Energy 278Kcal/1166kJ; Protein 6.4g; Carbohydrate 32.2g, of which sugars 12.1g; Fat 14.6g, of which saturates 2.6g; Cholesterol 0mg; Calcium 80mg; Fibre 5.1g; Sodium 209mg.

Chilled tomato and sweet pepper soup

This is a recipe inspired by the Spanish gazpacho, in which raw ingredients are combined to make a chilled soup. For this dish, the ingredients are cooked first and then cooled down.

SERVES 4

2 red (bell) peppers, halved
45ml/3 tbsp olive oil
1 onion, finely chopped
2 garlic cloves, crushed
675g/1½lb ripe, well-flavoured
   tomatoes, cut into chunks
150ml/¼ pint/⅔ cup red wine
600ml/1 pint/2½ cups vegetable stock
salt and ground black pepper
chopped fresh chives, to garnish

FOR THE CROÛTONS
2 slices day-old white bread, crusts
   removed
60ml/4 tbsp olive oil

1 Cut each pepper half into quarters and seed. Place skin-side up on a grill (broiler) rack and cook until the skins have charred. Transfer to a bowl and cover with a plate.

2 Heat the oil in a large pan. Add the onion and garlic, and cook until soft. Skin the peppers and roughly chop. Add the peppers and tomatoes to the pan, then cover and cook gently for 10 minutes. Add the red wine and cook for 5 minutes. Add the stock and salt and pepper, and simmer for 20 minutes.

3 To make the croûtons, cut the bread into cubes. Heat the oil in a small frying pan, add the bread and fry until golden. Drain on paper towels, cool, then store in an airtight box.

4 Process the soup in a food processor or blender until smooth. Pour into a clean glass or ceramic bowl and leave to cool thoroughly before chilling for at least 3 hours. When the soup is cold, season to taste. Serve the soup in bowls, topped with the croûtons and garnished with chopped chives.

Nutritional information per portion: Energy 292Kcal/1216kJ; Protein 3.4g; Carbohydrate 18.8g, of which sugars 11.8g; Fat 20.4g, of which saturates 3g; Cholesterol 0mg; Calcium 40mg; Fibre 3.5g; Sodium 92mg.

Chilled tomato and basil-flower soup

This is a really fresh-tasting soup, packed with the complementary flavours of tomato and basil, and topped with pretty pink and purple sweet basil flowers.

SERVES 4

15ml/1 tbsp olive oil
1 onion, finely chopped
1 garlic clove, crushed
600ml/1 pint/2¹/₂ cups vegetable stock
900g/2lb tomatoes, roughly chopped
20 fresh basil leaves
a few drops of balsamic vinegar
juice of ¹/₂ lemon
150ml/¹/₄ pint/²/₃ cup natural (plain)
    yogurt
granulated (white) sugar and salt, to taste

FOR THE GARNISH

30ml/2 tbsp natural (plain) yogurt
8 small basil leaves
10ml/2 tsp basil flowers, all green parts
    removed

1 Heat the oil in a pan and add the onion and garlic. Fry for 2–3 minutes until soft and transparent, stirring occasionally.

2 Add 300ml/¹/₂ pint/1¹/₄ cups of the vegetable stock and the chopped tomatoes to the pan. Bring to the boil. Lower the heat and simmer for 15 minutes. Stir occasionally to prevent it from sticking to the base of the pan.

3 Allow to cool slightly, then transfer to a food processor or blender and process until smooth. Press through a sieve (strainer) to remove tomato skins and seeds.

4 Return the mixture to the food processor and add the remainder of the stock, half the basil leaves, the vinegar, lemon juice and yogurt. Season with sugar and salt to taste. Process until smooth. Pour into a bowl and chill.

5 Finely shred the remaining basil leaves and add to the soup. Pour into individual bowls. Garnish with yogurt topped with a few basil leaves and a sprinkling of basil flowers.

Nutritional information per portion: Energy 89Kcal/377kJ; Protein 3.7g; Carbohydrate 11g, of which sugars 10.6g; Fat 3.8g, of which saturates 0.8g; Cholesterol 1mg; Calcium 91mg; Fibre 2.5g; Sodium 52mg.

Chilled avocado soup with cumin

The Andalusian region in Spain is home to both avocados and gazpacho, so it is not surprising that this chilled avocado soup, which is also known as green gazpacho, was invented there.

SERVES 4

3 ripe avocados

1 bunch spring onions (scallions), white parts only, trimmed and roughly chopped

2 garlic cloves, chopped

juice of 1 lemon

1.5ml/¼ tsp ground cumin

1.5ml/¼ tsp paprika

450ml/¾ pint/scant 2 cups fresh chicken stock, cooled and all fat skimmed off

300ml/½ pint/1¼ cups iced water

salt and ground black pepper

roughly chopped fresh flat leaf parsley, to garnish

1 Starting half a day ahead, put the flesh of one avocado in a food processor or blender. Add the spring onions, garlic and lemon juice and purée until smooth. Add the second avocado and purée, then the third, with the spices and seasoning. Purée until smooth.

2 Gradually add the chicken stock. Pour the soup into a bowl and chill.

3 To serve, stir in the iced water, then season to taste with plenty of salt and black pepper. Garnish with chopped fresh flat leaf parsley and serve immediately.

Nutritional information per portion: Energy 242Kcal/1001kJ; Protein 2.8g; Carbohydrate 3g, of which sugars 1.3g; Fat 24.2g, of which saturates 5.2g; Cholesterol 0mg; Calcium 22mg; Fibre 4.6g; Sodium 9mg.

Spiced mango soup with yogurt

This delicious, light soup comes from Chutney Mary's, an Anglo-Indian restaurant in London. To fully appreciate the delicious flavours, it is best when served lightly chilled.

SERVES 4

2 ripe mangoes
15ml/1 tbsp gram flour
120ml/4fl oz/1/2 cup natural (plain) yogurt
900ml/11/2 pints/33/4 cups cold water
2.5ml/1/2 tsp grated fresh root ginger
2 red chillies, seeded and finely chopped
30ml/2 tbsp olive oil
2.5ml/1/2 tsp mustard seeds
2.5ml/1/2 tsp cumin seeds
8 curry leaves
salt and ground black pepper
fresh mint leaves, shredded, to garnish
natural yogurt, to serve

1 Peel the mangoes, remove the stones and cut the flesh into chunks. Purée in a food processor or blender until smooth.

2 Pour into a pan and stir in the gram flour, yogurt, water, ginger and chillies. Bring to the boil, stirring occasionally. Simmer for 4–5 minutes until thickened slightly, then set aside off the heat.

3 Heat the oil in a frying pan. Add the mustard seeds and cook for a few seconds until they begin to pop, then add the cumin seeds.

4 Add the curry leaves and then cook for 5 minutes.

5 Stir the spice mixture into the soup, return it to the heat and cook for 10 minutes.

6 Press through a mouli-legume (food mill) or a sieve (strainer), if you like, then season to taste. Leave the soup to cool completely, then chill for at least 1 hour.

7 Ladle the soup into bowls, and top each with yogurt. Garnish with shredded mint leaves and serve.

Nutritional information per portion: Energy 121Kcal/508kJ; Protein 2.8g; Carbohydrate 14.7g, of which sugars 12.7g; Fat 6.2g, of which saturates 1g; Cholesterol 0mg; Calcium 73mg; Fibre 2.4g; Sodium 28mg.

Iced melon soup with sorbet

Use different melons for the cool soup and ice sorbet to create a subtle contrast in flavour and colour. Try a combination of Charentais, Ogen or cantaloupe melon.

SERVES 6–8

2.25kg/5–5¼lb very ripe melon
45ml/3 tbsp orange juice
30ml/2 tbsp lemon juice
mint leaves, to garnish

FOR THE SORBET (SHERBET)

25g/1oz/2 tbsp granulated (white) sugar
120ml/4fl oz/½ cup water
2.25kg/5–5¼lb very ripe melon
juice of 2 limes
30ml/2 tbsp chopped fresh mint

1 To make the melon and mint sorbet, put the sugar and water into a pan and heat gently until the sugar dissolves. Bring to the boil and simmer for 4–5 minutes, then remove from the heat and leave to cool.

2 Halve the melon. Scrape out the seeds, then scoop out the flesh. Purée in a food processor or blender with the cooled syrup and lime juice.

3 Stir in the mint and pour the mixture into an ice-cream maker. Churn, following the manufacturer's instructions, until the sorbet is smooth and firm. Or, pour the mixture into a suitable container and freeze until icy around the edges. Transfer to a food processor or blender and process until smooth.

4 Repeat the freezing and processing two or three times or until the mixture is smooth and holding its shape, then freeze until firm.

5 To make the chilled melon soup, prepare the melon as in step 2 and purée it in a food processor or blender. Pour the purée into a bowl and stir in the orange and lemon juice. Place the soup in the refrigerator for 30–40 minutes, but do not chill it for too long as this will dull its flavour.

6 Ladle the soup into bowls and add a large scoop of the melon and mint sorbet to each. Garnish with mint leaves and serve at once.

Nutritional information per portion: Energy 117Kcal/494kJ; Protein 3.1g; Carbohydrate 26g, of which sugars 26g; Fat 0.8g, of which saturates 0g; Cholesterol 0mg; Calcium 101mg; Fibre 5.3g; Sodium 39mg.

Pea soup with prosciutto

This quick and simple soup is light and refreshing and deliciously creamy. Using frozen peas cuts out the labour involved in shelling fresh peas, without compromising the flavour.

SERVES 6

25g/1oz/2 tbsp butter
1 leek, sliced
1 garlic clove, crushed
450g/1lb/4 cups frozen petits pois
    (baby peas)
1.2 litres/2 pints/5 cups vegetable stock
small bunch of fresh chives, coarsely
    chopped

300ml/$^{1}/_{2}$ pint/1$^{1}/_{4}$ cups double
    (heavy) cream
90ml/6 tbsp Greek (US strained plain)
    yogurt
4 slices prosciutto, roughly chopped
salt and ground black pepper
fresh chives, to garnish

1 Melt the butter in a pan. Add the leek and garlic, cover and cook gently for 4–5 minutes, until softened.

2 Stir in the petits pois, vegetable stock and chives. Bring slowly to the boil, then simmer for 5 minutes. Set aside to cool slightly.

3 Process the soup in a food processor or blender until smooth. Pour into a bowl, stir in the cream and season to taste with salt and black pepper. Chill in the refrigerator for at least 2 hours.

4 When ready to serve, ladle the soup into bowls and add a spoonful of Greek yogurt to the centre of each bowl. Scatter the chopped prosciutto over the top of the soup and garnish with chives before serving.

Nutritional information per portion: Energy 378Kcal/1561kJ; Protein 9.7g; Carbohydrate 10.6g, of which sugars 3.7g; Fat 33.5g, of which saturates 20g; Cholesterol 85mg; Calcium 71mg; Fibre 4.2g; Sodium 198mg.

Chilled cucumber and prawn soup

If you've never served a chilled soup before, this is the one to try. Delicious and light with plenty of fresh herbs, it's the perfect dish for a summer celebration.

SERVES 4

25g/1oz/2 tbsp butter
2 shallots, finely chopped
2 garlic cloves, crushed
1 cucumber, peeled, seeded and diced
300ml/½ pint/1¼ cups milk
225g/8oz cooked peeled prawns (shrimp)
15ml/1 tbsp each finely chopped fresh
    mint, dill, chives and chervil
300ml/½ pint/1¼ cups whipping cream
salt and ground white pepper

FOR THE GARNISH

30ml/2 tbsp crème fraîche (optional)
4 large, cooked prawns (shrimp), peeled
    with tail intact
fresh dill and chives

1 Melt the butter in a pan and cook the shallots and garlic over a low heat until soft but not coloured. Add the cucumber and cook gently, stirring frequently, until tender.

2 Stir in the milk, bring almost to boiling point, then simmer for 5 minutes. Purée the soup in a food processor or blender. Season.

3 Pour the soup into a large bowl and leave to cool then stir in the prawns, chopped herbs and cream. Cover, transfer to the refrigerator and chill for at least 2 hours.

4 To serve, ladle the soup into four bowls, top each portion with a dollop of crème fraîche, if using, and garnish with a prawn over the edge of each dish. Scatter over a little extra chopped dill and tuck two or three chives under the prawns on the edge of the bowls to garnish. Serve the soup at once.

Nutritional information per portion: Energy 412Kcal/1704kJ; Protein 14.2g; Carbohydrate 6g, of which sugars 6g; Fat 37g, of which saturates 23g; Cholesterol 206mg; Calcium 184mg; Fibre 0.2g; Sodium 197mg.

Avgolemono

This is a great favourite in Greece. The key to success with this soup is to use a well-flavoured stock. Add as little or as much rice as you like.

SERVES 4

900ml/1½ pints/3¾ cups chicken stock, preferably home-made
50g/2oz/generous ⅓ cup long grain rice
3 egg yolks
30–60ml/2–4 tbsp lemon juice
30ml/2 tbsp finely chopped fresh parsley
salt and freshly ground black pepper
lemon slices and parsley sprigs, to garnish

1 Pour the stock into a pan, bring to simmering point, then add the drained rice. Half cover and cook for about 12 minutes until the rice is just tender. Season with salt and pepper.

2 Whisk the egg yolks in a bowl, then add about 30ml/2 tbsp of the lemon juice, whisking constantly until the mixture is smooth and bubbly. Add a ladleful of soup and whisk again.

3 Remove the soup from the heat and add the egg mixture in a slow but steady stream, whisking all the time. The soup will turn a pretty lemon colour and will thicken slightly.

4 Taste and add more lemon juice if necessary. Stir in the parsley. Serve at once, without reheating, garnished with lemon slices and parsley sprigs.

Nutritional information per portion: Energy 96Kcal/404kJ; Protein 3.3g; Carbohydrate 10.9g, of which sugars 0.2g; Fat 4.7g, of which saturates 1.2g; Cholesterol 151mg; Calcium 39mg; Fibre 0.4g; Sodium 10mg.

Winter melon soup with tiger lilies

This refreshing soup is made with traditional South-east Asian ingredients. Winter melon absorbs the herbal flavours and tiger lilies impart a light, floral scent.

SERVES 4

350g/12oz winter melon
25g/1oz light golden tiger lilies,
    soaked in hot water for 20 minutes
salt and ground black pepper
1 small bunch each coriander
    (cilantro) and mint, to serve

FOR THE STOCK
25g/1oz dried shrimp, soaked in water
    for 15 minutes
500g/1¼lb pork ribs
1 onion, peeled and quartered
175g/6oz carrots, peeled and cut
    into chunks
15ml/1 tbsp nuoc mam (fish sauce)
15ml/1 tbsp soy sauce
4 black peppercorns

1 To make the stock, drain and rinse the dried shrimp. Put the pork ribs in a large pan and cover with 2 litres/3½ pints/8 cups water. Bring the water to the boil, skim off any fat, and add the dried shrimp and the remaining stock ingredients. Cover and simmer for 1½ hours, then skim off any foam or fat. Continue simmering, uncovered, for about another 30 minutes. Strain and check the seasoning. You should have about 1.5 litres/2½ pints/6¼ cups.

2 Halve the winter melon lengthways and remove the seeds and inner membrane. Finely slice the flesh into half-moons. Squeeze the soaked tiger lilies dry and tie them in a knot.

3 Bring the stock to the boil in a deep pan or wok. Reduce the heat and add the winter melon and tiger lilies. Simmer for 15–20 minutes, or until the winter melon is tender. Season to taste, and scatter the herbs over the top.

Nutritional information per portion: Energy 46Kcal/198kJ; Protein 2g; Carbohydrate 9g, of which sugars 4g; Fat 0g, of which saturates 0g; Cholesterol 0mg; Calcium 90mg; Fibre 1.4g; Sodium 400mg

Hot and sweet vegetable and tofu soup

This soothing, nutritious soup takes only minutes to make as the spinach and silken tofu are simply placed in bowls and covered with the flavoured hot stock.

SERVES 4

1.2 litres/2 pints/5 cups vegetable stock

5–10ml/1–2 tsp Thai red curry paste

2 kaffir lime leaves, torn

40g/1¹/₂oz/3 tbsp palm sugar or light muscovado (brown) sugar

30ml/2 tbsp soy sauce

juice of 1 lime

1 carrot, cut into thin batons

50g/2oz baby spinach leaves, any coarse stalks removed

225g/8oz block silken tofu, diced

1 Heat the stock in a large pan, then add the red curry paste. Stir constantly over a medium heat until the paste has dissolved. Add the lime leaves, sugar and soy sauce and bring to the boil.

2 Add the lime juice and carrot to the pan. Reduce the heat and simmer for 5–10 minutes. Place the spinach and tofu in four individual serving bowls and pour the hot stock on top to serve.

Nutritional information per portion: Energy 105Kcal/439kJ; Protein 5.3g; Carbohydrate 13.2g, of which sugars 12.8g; Fat 3.8g, of which saturates 0.5g; Cholesterol 0mg; Calcium 320mg; Fibre 0.7g; Sodium 559mg.

Thai hot and sour soup

This invigorating soup, with its finely balanced combination of flavours, is best served at the beginning of a meal to stimulate the appetite.

SERVES 4

2 carrots
900ml/1½ pints/3¾ cups vegetable
    stock
2 Thai chillies, seeded and finely sliced
2 lemon grass stalks, outer leaves
    removed and each stalk cut into
    3 pieces
4 kaffir lime leaves

2 garlic cloves, finely chopped
4 spring onions (scallions), finely sliced
5ml/1 tsp sugar
juice of 1 lime
45ml/3 tbsp chopped fresh coriander
    (cilantro)
salt
130g/4½oz/1 cup Japanese tofu, sliced

1 To make carrot flowers, cut each carrot in half crossways, then cut four V-shaped channels lengthways. Slice into thin rounds and set aside.

2 Pour the stock into a large pan. Reserve 2.5ml/½ tsp of the chillies and add the rest to the pan with the lemon grass, lime leaves, garlic and half the spring onions. Bring to the boil, reduce the heat and simmer for 20 minutes.

3 Strain the stock and discard the flavourings. Return the stock to the pan, add the reserved chillies and spring onions, the sugar, lime juice, coriander and salt to taste.

4 Simmer over a gentle heat for 5 minutes, then add the carrot flowers and the tofu, and cook for a further 2 minutes until the carrot is just tender. Ladle into bowls and serve hot.

Nutritional information per portion: Energy 40Kcal/169kJ; Protein 3.3g; Carbohydrate 3.4g, of which sugars 3.1g; Fat 1.6g, of which saturates 0.2g; Cholesterol 0mg; Calcium 197mg; Fibre 1.2g; Sodium 11mg.

Pear and Roquefort soup with caramelized pears

Like most fruit-based soups, this is best served in small portions. The caramelized pears make this an unusual and seasonal appetizer for an autumn dinner party.

SERVES 4

30ml/2 tbsp sunflower oil
1 onion, chopped
3 pears, peeled, cored and chopped into
    1cm/$\frac{1}{2}$in chunks
400ml/14fl oz/1$\frac{2}{3}$ cups vegetable stock
2.5ml/$\frac{1}{2}$ tsp paprika
juice of $\frac{1}{2}$ lemon
175g/6oz Roquefort cheese

salt and ground black pepper
watercress sprigs, to garnish

FOR THE CARAMELIZED PEARS
50g/2oz/$\frac{1}{4}$ cup butter
2 pears, halved, cored and cut into
    wedges

1 Heat the oil in a pan. Add the onion and cook for 4–5 minutes until soft.

2 Add the pears and stock. Bring to the boil and cook for 8–10 minutes, until the pears are soft. Stir in the paprika, lemon juice, cheese and seasoning.

3 Cool the soup slightly and purée it in a food processor or blender until smooth, then pass it through a fine sieve (strainer). Return the soup to the pan.

4 To make the caramelized pears, melt the butter in a frying pan and add the pears. Cook for 8–10 minutes, turning occasionally, until golden.

5 Reheat the soup gently, then ladle into small, shallow bowls and add a few caramelized pear wedges to each portion. Garnish with tiny sprigs of watercress and serve at once.

Nutritional information per portion: Energy 381Kcal/1579kJ; Protein 10.1g; Carbohydrate 21.8g, of which sugars 20.9g; Fat 28.7g, of which saturates 15.6g; Cholesterol 59mg; Calcium 246mg; Fibre 4.7g; Sodium 616mg.

Vegetable soups

A bowl of vegetable soup served with some

crusty bread makes an excellent appetizer

or light meal at any time of year. Choose

fresh vegetables in season – tomatoes and

herbs in the summer, pumpkins and squash

for the autumn and leeks and root

vegetables during the winter months. The

soups in this section are vegetable-based

but some contain meat or poultry stock.

Carrot and orange soup

This bright and summery soup is always popular for its wonderfully creamy consistency and vibrantly fresh citrus flavour. Use a good, home-made chicken or vegetable stock if you can.

SERVES 4

50g/2oz/¼ cup butter
3 leeks, sliced
450g/1lb carrots, sliced
1.2 litres/2 pints/5 cups chicken or
　vegetable stock
rind and juice of 2 oranges
2.5ml/½ tsp freshly grated nutmeg
150ml/¼ pint/⅔ cup Greek (strained
　plain) yogurt
salt and ground black pepper
fresh sprigs of coriander (cilantro), to
　garnish

1 Melt the butter in a large pan. Add the leeks and carrots and stir well, coating them with the butter. Cover and cook for about 10 minutes, until the vegetables are beginning to soften but not colour.

2 Pour in the stock and the orange rind and juice. Add the nutmeg and season to taste with salt and pepper. Bring to the boil, lower the heat, cover and simmer for about 40 minutes, or until the vegetables are tender. Leave to cool slightly, then purée the soup in a food processor or blender until smooth.

3 Return the soup to the pan and add 30ml/2 tbsp of the yogurt, then taste the soup and adjust the seasoning, if necessary. Reheat gently.

4 Ladle the soup into warm bowls and put a swirl of yogurt in the centre of each. Garnish with fresh sprigs of coriander and serve immediately.

Nutritional information per portion: Energy 206Kcal/856kJ; Protein 5g; Carbohydrate 15.8g, of which sugars 14.2g; Fat 14.4g, of which saturates 8.3g; Cholesterol 27mg; Calcium 111mg; Fibre 5.8g; Sodium 131mg.

Irish potato soup

This most Irish of all soups is not only excellent as it is, but versatile too, as it can be used as a base for numerous other soups. Use a floury potato, such as Golden Wonder.

SERVES 6–8

50g/2oz/¼ cup butter
2 large onions, peeled and finely chopped
675g/1½lb potatoes, diced
about 1.75 litres/3 pints/7½ cups hot
   chicken or vegetable stock
sea salt and ground black pepper
a little milk, if necessary
chopped fresh chives, to garnish

1 Melt the butter in a large, heavy-based pan and add the onions, turning them in the butter until well coated. Cover and leave to sweat over a very low heat for about 10 mintues.

2 Add the potatoes to the pan, and mix well with the butter and onions. Season with salt and pepper, cover and cook without colouring over a gentle heat for about 10 minutes. Add the stock, bring to the boil and simmer for 25 minutes, or until the vegetables are tender.

3 Remove from the heat and allow to cool slightly. Purée the soup in batches in a food processor or blender.

4 Reheat the soup over a low heat and adjust the seasoning. If the soup seems too thick, add a little chicken stock or milk. Serve the soup very hot, sprinkled with chopped chives.

Nutritional information per portion: Energy 167Kcal/699kJ; Protein 2.9g; Carbohydrate 23.5g, of which sugars 5.3g; Fat 7.5g, of which saturates 4.5g; Cholesterol 18mg; Calcium 26mg; Fibre 2.1g; Sodium 201mg.

Creamy parsnip soup

This lightly spiced soup is popular in Ireland, and many variations abound. Parsnips taste sweetest after the first frost as the cold converts their starches to sugar.

SERVES 6

**900g/2lb parsnips, peeled and
    thinly sliced**
50g/2oz/¼ cup butter
1 onion, chopped
2 garlic cloves, crushed
10ml/2 tsp ground cumin
5ml/1 tsp ground coriander
**about 1.2 litres/2 pints/5 cups hot
    chicken stock**
**150ml/¼ pint/⅔ cup single
    (light) cream**
salt and ground black pepper
**chopped fresh chives or parsley and/or
    croûtons, to garnish**

1 Heat the butter in a large heavy-based pan and add the thinly sliced parsnips and chopped onion with the crushed garlic. Cook until softened but not coloured, stirring occasionally.

2 Add the cumin and coriander to the vegetables and cook, stirring, for 1–2 minutes, and then gradually blend in the hot chicken stock.

3 Cover and simmer for about 20 minutes, or until the parsnip is soft. Purée the soup, adjust the texture with extra stock or water if it seems too thick, and check the seasoning. Add the cream and reheat without boiling.

4 Serve immediately, sprinkled with chopped chives or parsley and/or croûtons, to garnish.

Nutritional information per portion: Energy 215Kcal/899kJ; Protein 3.9g; Carbohydrate 21.3g, of which sugars 10.6g; Fat 13.3g, of which saturates 7.7g; Cholesterol 32mg; Calcium 92mg; Fibre 7.3g; Sodium 74mg.

Curried parsnip soup with croûtons

The mild sweetness of parsnips and mango chutney in this simple soup is given an exciting lift with a blend of spices, and is garnished with unusual sesame naan croûtons.

SERVES 4

30ml/2 tbsp olive oil
1 onion, chopped
1 garlic clove, crushed
1 small green chilli, seeded and chopped
15ml/1 tbsp grated fresh root ginger
5 large parsnips, diced
5ml/1 tsp cumin seeds
5ml/1 tsp ground coriander
2.5ml/½ tsp ground turmeric
30ml/2 tbsp mango chutney
1.2 litres/2 pints/5 cups water
juice of 1 lime
salt and ground black pepper
60ml/4 tbsp natural (plain) yogurt and
    mango chutney, to serve

FOR THE NAAN CROÛTONS

45ml/3 tbsp olive oil
1 large naan
15ml/1 tbsp sesame seeds

1 Heat the oil in a large pan and add the onion, garlic, chilli and ginger. Cook for 4–5 minutes, until the onion has softened. Add the parsnips and cook for 2–3 minutes. Sprinkle in the cumin seeds, coriander and turmeric and cook for 1 minute, stirring constantly.

2 Add the chutney and the water. Season well and bring to the boil. Reduce the heat and simmer for 15 minutes, until the parsnips are soft.

3 Cool the soup slightly, then process it in a food processor or blender until smooth, then return it to the saucepan. Stir the lime juice into the soup.

4 For the naan croûtons, cut the naan into small dice. Heat the oil in a large frying pan and cook until golden all over. Remove from the heat and drain off any excess oil. Add the sesame seeds and return to the heat for 30 seconds, until the seeds are golden.

5 Ladle the soup into bowls. Add a little yogurt and top with mango chutney and naan croûtons.

Nutritional information per portion: Energy 189Kcal/792kJ; Protein 4g; Carbohydrate 26.6g, of which sugars 15.5g; Fat 8.2g, of which saturates 1.2g; Cholesterol 0mg; Calcium 101mg; Fibre 7.5g; Sodium 110mg.

Creamy hearts of palm soup

This delicate soup has a luxurious, creamy, almost velvety texture. The subtle yet distinctive flavour of palm hearts is like no other, although it is mildly reminiscent of artichokes and asparagus. Serve with fresh bread for a satisfying lunch.

SERVES 4

25g/1oz/2 tbsp butter

10ml/2 tsp olive oil

1 onion, finely chopped

1 large leek, finely sliced

15ml/1 tbsp plain (all-purpose) flour

1 litre/1¾ pints/4 cups chicken stock

350g/12oz potatoes, peeled and cubed

2 x 400g/14oz cans hearts of palm, drained and sliced

250ml/8fl oz/1 cup double (heavy) cream

salt and ground black pepper

cayenne pepper and chopped fresh chives, to garnish

1 Heat the butter and oil in a large pan over a low heat. Add the onion and leek and stir well until coated in butter. Cover and cook for 5 minutes until softened and translucent.

2 Sprinkle over the flour. Cook, stirring, for 1 minute.

3 Pour in the chicken stock and add the potatoes. Bring the mixture to the boil, then lower the heat and simmer gently for 10 minutes. Stir in the hearts of palm and the double cream, and simmer gently for 10 minutes.

4 Process in a food processor or blender until smooth. Return the soup to the pan and heat gently, adding a little water if necessary. The consistency should be thick but not too heavy. Season with salt and ground black pepper.

5 Ladle the soup into heated bowls and garnish each with a pinch of cayenne pepper and a scattering of fresh chives. Serve immediately.

VARIATION

For a richer, buttery flavour, add the flesh of a ripe avocado when blending.

Nutritional information per portion: Energy 486Kcal/2016kJ; Protein 4.9g; Carbohydrate 25.9g, of which sugars 3g; Fat 41.1g, of which saturates 24.4g; Cholesterol 99mg; Calcium 127mg; Fibre 3.7g; Sodium 97mg.

Artichoke soup with anchovy and artichoke bruschetta

Jerusalem artichokes are perfect in soups, gratins or purées. Globe artichokes, which are not related to Jerusalem artichokes, are typically eaten in salads with a piquant dressing.

SERVES 6

squeeze of lemon juice

450g/1lb Jerusalem artichokes, peeled and diced

65g/2½oz/5 tbsp butter

175g/6oz potatoes, roughly diced

1 small onion, chopped

1 garlic clove, chopped

1 celery stick, chopped

1 small fennel bulb, halved, cored and chopped

1.2 litres/2 pints/5 cups vegetable stock

300ml/½ pint/1¼ cups double (heavy) cream

pinch of freshly grated nutmeg

salt and ground black pepper

basil leaves, to garnish

FOR THE ARTICHOKE AND ANCHOVY BRUSCHETTA

6 thick slices French bread

1 garlic clove

50g/2oz/¼ cup unsalted (sweet) butter

400g/14oz can artichoke hearts, drained and halved

45ml/3 tbsp tapenade

9 salted anchovy fillets, halved lengthways

1 Prepare a large bowl of cold water with a squeeze of lemon juice added. Add the artichokes to the water as soon as each one is prepared. This will prevent them from discolouring.

2 Melt the butter in a large, heavy-based saucepan. Drain the artichokes and add to the pan with the potatoes, onion, garlic, celery and fennel. Stir well and cook for 10 minutes, stirring occasionally, until beginning to soften.

3 Pour in the stock and bring to the boil, then simmer for 10–15 minutes, until all the vegetables are softened. Cool the soup slightly, then process in a food processor or blender until smooth. Press the soup through a sieve (strainer) into a clean pan. Then add the cream and nutmeg, and season well.

4 To make the bruschetta, lightly toast the bread slices on both sides. Rub each one with the garlic clove and set aside. Melt the butter in a pan. Add the artichoke hearts and cook for 3–4 minutes.

5 Spread the tapenade on the toast and arrange pieces of artichoke heart on top. Top with anchovy fillets and garnish with basil leaves. Reheat the soup without allowing it to boil, then ladle it into bowls. Serve the bruschetta with the soup.

Nutritional information per portion: Energy 790Kcal/3303kJ; Protein 14.3g; Carbohydrate 85.6g, of which sugars 16.4g; Fat 45.8g, of which saturates 27.3g; Cholesterol 111mg; Calcium 232mg; Fibre 7.6g; Sodium 1030mg.

Potato and fennel soup
with warm rosemary scones

The simple flavours in this fine soup are enhanced by the delicate perfume of herb flowers, and complemented by rosemary-seasoned scones.

SERVES 4

75g/3oz/6 tbsp butter

2 onions, chopped

5ml/1 tsp fennel seeds, crushed

3 fennel bulbs, coarsely chopped

900g/2lb potatoes, thinly sliced

1.2 litres/2 pints/5 cups chicken stock

150ml/¼ pint/⅔ cup double (heavy)
   cream

salt and ground black pepper

fresh herb flowers and 15ml/1 tbsp
   chopped fresh chives, to garnish

**FOR THE ROSEMARY SCONES
(BISCUITS)**

225g/8oz/2 cups self-raising (self-rising)
   flour

2.5ml/½ tsp salt

5ml/1 tsp baking powder

10ml/2 tsp chopped fresh rosemary

50g/2oz/¼ cup butter

150ml/¼ pint/⅔ cup milk

1 egg, beaten, to glaze

1 Melt the butter in a pan. Add the onions and cook gently for 10 minutes, stirring occasionally, until very soft. Add the fennel seeds and cook for 2–3 minutes. Stir in the fennel and potatoes.

2 Cover the pan with a sheet of wet baking parchment and put a lid on top. Cook gently for 10 minutes until very soft. Remove the baking parchment. Pour in the stock, bring to the boil, cover and simmer for 35 minutes.

3 Meanwhile, make the scones. Preheat the oven to 230°C/450°F/Gas 8 and grease a baking tray. Sift the flour, salt and baking powder into a bowl. Stir in the rosemary, then rub in the butter. Add the milk and mix to a soft dough. Knead very lightly on a floured surface. Roll out to 2cm/¾in thick. Stamp out 12 rounds with a cutter. Brush with the egg and bake on the baking tray for 8–10 minutes, until risen and golden. Cool on a wire rack until warm.

4 Leave the soup to cool slightly, then purée it in a food processor or blender. Press through a sieve (strainer) into the rinsed-out pan. Stir in the cream with seasoning then reheat gently but do not boil. Ladle the soup into bowls and scatter with the herb flowers and chives. Serve with the scones.

Nutritional information per portion: Energy 797Kcal/3332kJ; Protein 12.3g; Carbohydrate 84.1g, of which sugars 8.8g; Fat 48.1g, of which saturates 29.6g; Cholesterol 120mg; Calcium 316mg; Fibre 7.6g; Sodium 703mg.

Curried cauliflower soup

This is a very simple soup to make and its spicy, creamy taste makes it perfect for lunch on a cold winter's day served with crusty bread and garnished with fresh coriander.

SERVES 4

750ml/1¼ pints/3 cups milk
1 large cauliflower, cut into florets
15ml/1 tbsp garam masala
coriander (cilantro) leaves, to garnish
salt and ground black pepper

1 Heat the milk over a medium heat. Add the cauliflower florets to the milk with the garam masala and season with salt and pepper.

2 Bring the milk to the boil, then reduce the heat, partially cover the pan with a lid and simmer for about 20 minutes, or until the cauliflower is tender.

3 Let the mixture cool for a few minutes, then transfer to a food processor or blender and process in two batches until smooth.

4 Return the purée to the pan and heat gently without boiling, adjusting the seasoning to taste. Serve immediately, garnished with fresh coriander leaves if liked.

Nutritional information per portion: Energy 143Kcal/601kJ; Protein 12g; Carbohydrate 13.9g, of which sugars 12.6g; Fat 4.8g, of which saturates 2.3g; Cholesterol 11mg; Calcium 271mg; Fibre 3.2g; Sodium 104mg.

Roasted garlic and butternut squash soup with tomato salsa

This is a wonderful, richly flavoured dish. A spoonful of the hot and spicy tomato salsa gives bite to the sweet-tasting squash and garlic soup.

SERVES 4–5

2 garlic bulbs, outer skin removed
75ml/5 tbsp olive oil
a few fresh thyme sprigs
1 large butternut squash, halved
   and seeded
2 onions, chopped
5ml/1 tsp ground coriander
1.2 litres/2 pints/5 cups vegetable or
   chicken stock
   30–45ml/2–3 tbsp chopped fresh
   oregano or marjoram
salt and ground black pepper

FOR THE TOMATO SALSA

4 large ripe tomatoes, halved and seeded
1 red (bell) pepper, halved and seeded
1 large fresh red chilli, halved and seeded
30–45ml/2–3 tbsp extra virgin olive oil
15ml/1 tbsp balsamic vinegar
pinch of caster (superfine) sugar

1 Preheat the oven to 220°C/425°F/Gas 7. Place the garlic bulbs on a piece of foil and pour over half the olive oil. Add the thyme sprigs, then fold the foil around the garlic bulbs to enclose them completely. Place the foil parcel on a baking sheet with the butternut squash and brush the squash with 15ml/ 1 tbsp of the remaining olive oil. Add the tomatoes, red pepper and fresh chilli for the salsa.

2 Roast the vegetables for 25 minutes, then remove the tomatoes, pepper and chilli. Reduce the temperature to 190°C/375°F/Gas 5 and cook the squash and garlic for 20–25 minutes more, or until the squash is tender.

3 Heat the remaining oil in a large, heavy-based pan and cook the onions and ground coriander gently for about 10 minutes, or until softened.

4 To make the salsa, skin the pepper and chilli and process in a food processor or blender with the tomatoes and 30ml/2 tbsp olive oil. Stir in the balsamic vinegar and seasoning to taste, adding a pinch of caster sugar. Add the remaining oil if you think the salsa needs it.

5 Squeeze the roasted garlic out of its papery skin into the onions and scoop the squash out of its skin, adding it to the pan. Add the stock, 5ml/1 tsp salt and plenty of black pepper. Bring to the boil and simmer for 10 minutes. Stir in half the oregano or marjoram and cool the soup slightly, then process it in a food processor or blender. Alternatively, press the soup through a fine sieve (strainer).

6 Reheat the soup without allowing it to boil, then taste for seasoning before ladling it into warmed bowls. Top each with a spoonful of salsa and sprinkle over the remaining chopped oregano or marjoram. Serve immediately.

Nutritional information per portion: Energy 303Kcal/1256kJ; Protein 4.2g; Carbohydrate 20.7g, of which sugars 16.6g; Fat 23.2g, of which saturates 3.5g; Cholesterol 0mg; Calcium 107mg; Fibre 5.7g; Sodium 15mg.

Spicy roasted pumpkin soup
with pumpkin crisps

The pumpkin is roasted whole, then split open and scooped out to make this delicious soup. Topped with crisp strips of fried pumpkin, it is a real treat.

SERVES 6–8

1.5kg/3–3¹/₂lb pumpkin
90ml/6 tbsp olive oil
2 onions, chopped
3 garlic cloves, chopped
7.5cm/3in piece fresh root ginger, grated
5ml/1 tsp ground coriander
2.5ml/¹/₂ tsp ground turmeric
pinch of cayenne pepper

1 litre/1³/₄ pints/4 cups vegetable stock
salt and ground black pepper
15ml/1 tbsp sesame seeds and fresh
    coriander (cilantro) leaves, to garnish

FOR THE PUMPKIN CRISPS
wedge of fresh pumpkin, seeded
120ml/4fl oz/¹/₂ cup olive oil

1 Preheat the oven to 200°C/400°F/Gas 6. Prick the pumpkin around the top several times with a fork. Brush with plenty of the oil and bake for 45 minutes or until tender. Leave until cool enough to handle then scoop out and discard the seeds. Scoop out and chop the flesh.

2 Heat 60ml/4 tbsp of the remaining oil (you may not have to use all of it) in a large pan and add the onions, garlic and ginger, then cook gently for 4–5 minutes. Add the coriander, turmeric and cayenne, and cook for 2 minutes. Stir in the pumpkin flesh and stock. Bring to the boil, reduce the heat and simmer for 20 minutes.

3 Cool the soup slightly, then purée it in a food processor or blender until smooth. Return the soup to the rinsed-out pan and season well.

4 Meanwhile, prepare the pumpkin crisps. Using a swivel-bladed potato peeler, pare off long thin strips. Heat the oil in a small pan and fry the strips in batches for 2–3 minutes, until crisp. Drain on kitchen paper.

5 Reheat the soup and ladle it into bowls. Top with the pumpkin crisps and garnish each portion with sesame seeds and coriander leaves.

Nutritional information per portion: Energy 271Kcal/1119kJ; Protein 3.1g; Carbohydrate 11.1g, of which sugars 8.2g; Fat 24.1g, of which saturates 3.6g; Cholesterol 0mg; Calcium 110mg; Fibre 3.8g; Sodium 3mg.

Tomato soup with black olive ciabatta toasts

Tomato soup is everybody's favourite, particularly when made with fresh sun-ripened tomatoes. This delicious soup is wonderfully warming and has an earthy richness.

SERVES 6

450g/1lb very ripe fresh tomatoes
30ml/2 tbsp olive oil
1 onion, chopped
1 garlic clove, crushed
30ml/2 tbsp sherry vinegar
30ml/2 tbsp tomato purée (paste)
15ml/1 tbsp cornflour (cornstarch) or
    potato flour
300ml/$\frac{1}{2}$ pint/1$\frac{1}{4}$ cups passata
    (bottled strained tomatoes)
1 bay leaf
900ml/1$\frac{1}{2}$ pints/3$\frac{3}{4}$ cups vegetable or
    chicken stock
200ml/7fl oz/scant 1 cup crème fraîche
salt and ground black pepper
basil leaves, to garnish

**FOR THE BLACK OLIVE
CIABATTA TOASTS**
1 plain or black olive ciabatta
1 small red (bell) pepper
3 whole garlic cloves, skins on
225g/8oz black olives (preferably
    a wrinkly Greek variety)
30–45ml/2–3 tbsp salted capers or capers
    in vinegar
12 drained canned anchovy fillets or
    1 small can tuna in oil, drained
about 150ml/$\frac{1}{4}$ pint/$\frac{2}{3}$ cup good
    quality olive oil
fresh lemon juice and ground black
    pepper, to taste
45ml/3 tbsp chopped fresh basil

1 Make the toasts first. Preheat the oven to 200°C/400°F/Gas 6. Split the ciabatta in half and cut each half into nine pieces. Place on a baking sheet and bake for 10–15 minutes until crisp.

2 Place the whole pepper and garlic cloves under a hot grill (broiler) and cook for 15 minutes, turning, until charred all over. If you prefer, you can bake them in the oven for about 25 minutes. Once charred, put the garlic and pepper in a plastic bag, seal and leave to cool for 10 minutes.

3 When the pepper is cool, peel off the skin and remove the stalk and seeds. Peel the skin off the garlic. Stone (pit) the olives. Rinse the capers under running water. Place the prepared ingredients in a food processor or blender with the anchovies or tuna and process until roughly chopped.

4 With the machine running, slowly add the olive oil until you have a fairly smooth dark paste. Alternatively, just stir in the olive oil. Season to taste with lemon juice and pepper. Stir in the basil.

5 Spread the paste on the finger toasts, or, if not using immediately, transfer to a jar, cover with a layer of olive oil and keep in the refrigerator for up to three weeks.

6 For the soup, cut the tomatoes in half and remove the seeds and pulp using a lemon squeezer. Press the pulp through a sieve (strainer) and reserve the liquid.

7 Heat the oil in a pan and add the onion, garlic, sherry vinegar, tomato purée and the tomato halves. Stir, then cover the pan and cook over a low heat for 1 hour, stirring occasionally. When done, process the soup in a food processor or blender. Pass through a sieve then return to the pan.

8 Mix the cornflour or potato flour with the reserved tomato pulp. Stir into the soup with the passata, bay leaf and stock. Simmer for 30 minutes. Stir in the crème fraîche and garnish with the basil leaves. Serve piping hot, with the ciabatta toasts.

Nutritional information per portion: Energy 532Kcal/2211kJ; Protein 11.9g; Carbohydrate 29.3g, of which sugars 7.6g; Fat 41.7g, of which saturates 13.2g; Cholesterol 50mg; Calcium 120mg; Fibre 3.5g; Sodium 1352mg.

Tortilla tomato soup

There are several tortilla soups. This one is an aguada *– or liquid – version, and is served as an appetizer or light meal. The tortilla pieces add interest and give the soup an unusual texture.*

SERVES 4

4 corn tortillas

15ml/1 tbsp vegetable oil, plus extra for frying

1 small onion, chopped

2 garlic cloves, crushed

350g/12oz ripe plum tomatoes

400g/14oz can plum tomatoes, drained

1 litre/1¾ pints/4 cups chicken stock

small bunch of fresh coriander (cilantro)

50g/2oz/½ cup grated mild Cheddar cheese

salt and ground black pepper

1 Using a sharp knife, cut each tortilla into four or five strips, each measuring about 2cm/¾in wide. Pour vegetable oil to a depth of 2cm/¾in into a frying pan. Heat until a small piece of tortilla, added to the oil, floats on the top and bubbles at the edges.

2 Add a few tortilla strips to the hot oil and fry until crisp and golden brown. Remove the tortilla chips with a slotted spoon and drain on kitchen paper. Cook the remaining tortilla strips in the same way.

3 Heat the 15ml/1 tbsp vegetable oil in a large pan. Add the onion and garlic and cook over a medium heat for 2–3 minutes, until the onion is soft and translucent.

4 Skin the fresh tomatoes by plunging them into boiling water for 30 seconds, refreshing them in cold water, draining them and then peeling off the skins with a sharp knife.

5 Chop the fresh and canned tomatoes and add them to the onion mixture. Pour in the chicken stock. Bring to the boil, then lower the heat and simmer for 10 minutes. Stir occasionally. Roughly chop or tear the coriander into pieces. Add to the soup and season with salt and pepper to taste.

6 Place a few of the crisp tortilla pieces in each of four large heated soup bowls. Ladle the soup on top. Sprinkle each portion with some of the grated mild Cheddar cheese and serve immediately.

Nutritional information per portion: Energy 270Kcal/1135kJ; Protein 8.3g; Carbohydrate 36.9g, of which sugars 7.2g; Fat 10.7g, of which saturates 3.6g; Cholesterol 12mg; Calcium 164mg; Fibre 3.3g; Sodium 248mg.

Tomato, ciabatta and basil oil soup

Throughout Europe, bread is a popular ingredient for thickening soup, and this recipe with its fabulous Mediterranean flavours shows how wonderfully quick and easy this method can be.

SERVES 4

45ml/3 tbsp olive oil
1 red onion, chopped
6 garlic cloves, chopped
300ml/½ pint/1¼ cups white wine
150ml/¼ pint/⅔ cup water
12 plum tomatoes, quartered
2 x 400g/14oz cans plum tomatoes
2.5ml/½ tsp sugar
½ ciabatta loaf
salt and ground black pepper
basil leaves, to garnish

FOR THE BASIL OIL

115g/4oz basil leaves
120ml/4fl oz/½ cup olive oil

1 For the basil oil, process the basil leaves and olive oil in a food processor or blender to make a paste. Line a bowl with muslin (cheesecloth) and scrape the basil paste into it. Gather up the muslin and squeeze very firmly until the oil has been extracted. Set aside the basil oil.

2 Heat the olive oil in a large pan and cook the onion and garlic for 4–5 minutes until softened.

3 Add the wine, water, fresh and canned tomatoes. Bring to the boil, reduce the heat and cover the pan, then simmer for 3–4 minutes. Add the sugar and season well with salt and black pepper.

4 Break the bread into bitesize pieces and stir into the soup.

5 Ladle the soup into bowls. Garnish with basil and drizzle the basil oil over each portion.

Nutritional information per portion: Energy 332Kcal/1396kJ; Protein 7.8g; Carbohydrate 35.4g, of which sugars 16.3g; Fat 13.4g, of which saturates 2g; Cholesterol 0mg; Calcium 98mg; Fibre 5g; Sodium 306mg.

Roasted pepper soup with Parmesan toast

The secret of this delicious soup is to serve it just cold, rather than over-chilled, topped with hot Parmesan toast dripping with cheese and melted butter.

SERVES 4

1 onion, quartered

4 garlic cloves, unpeeled

2 red (bell) peppers, seeded and
    quartered

2 yellow (bell) peppers, seeded and
    quartered

30–45ml/2–3 tbsp olive oil

grated rind and juice of 1 orange

200g/7oz can chopped tomatoes

600ml/1 pint/2¹/₂ cups cold water

salt and ground black pepper

30ml/2 tbsp chopped fresh chives, to
    garnish (optional)

**FOR THE HOT PARMESAN
TOAST**

1 medium baguette

50g/2oz/¹/₄ cup butter

175g/6oz Parmesan cheese

1 Preheat the oven to 200°C/400°F/Gas 6. Put the onion, garlic and peppers in a roasting tin (pan). Drizzle over the oil and mix well, then turn the pieces of pepper skin sides up. Roast for 25–30 minutes, then allow to cool slightly.

2 Squeeze the garlic flesh into a food processor or blender. Add the orange rind and juice, tomatoes, water and vegetables. Process until smooth then press through a sieve (strainer) into a bowl. Season and chill for 30 minutes.

3 Make the Parmesan toasts when you are ready to serve the soup. Preheat the grill (broiler) to high. Cut the baguette in half lengthways, then tear or cut it across to give four large pieces. Spread with butter.

4 Pare most of the Parmesan into shavings, then finely grate the rest. Arrange the sliced Parmesan on the toasts, then dredge with the grated cheese. Transfer the baguette pieces to a baking sheet or grill (broiler) rack and toast under the grill for a few minutes until the topping is well browned.

5 Ladle the soup into shallow bowls and sprinkle with the chives, if using, and plenty of freshly ground black pepper. Serve with the hot Parmesan toast.

Nutritional information per portion: Energy 124Kcal/516kJ; Protein 2.4g; Carbohydrate 15g, of which sugars 14.2g; Fat 6.4g, of which saturates 1g; Cholesterol 0mg; Calcium 23mg; Fibre 3.5g; Sodium 13mg.

Sherried onion and almond soup with saffron

The Spanish combination of onions, sherry and saffron gives this pale yellow soup a beguiling flavour that is perfect as the opening course of a special meal.

SERVES 4

40g/1¹/₂oz/3 tbsp butter
2 large yellow onions, thinly sliced
1 small garlic clove, finely chopped
good pinch of saffron threads (about 12 threads)
50g/2oz blanched almonds, toasted and finely ground

750ml/1¹/₄ pints/3 cups good chicken or vegetable stock
45ml/3 tbsp dry sherry
salt and ground black pepper
30ml/2 tbsp flaked or slivered almonds, toasted and chopped, and chopped fresh parsley, to garnish

1 Melt the butter in a heavy-based pan over a low heat. Add the onions and garlic, stirring to coat them thoroughly in the butter, then cover the pan and cook very gently, stirring frequently, for 15–20 minutes, until the onions are a soft texture and golden yellow in colour.

2 Add the saffron threads and cook, uncovered, for 3–4 minutes, then add the blanched almonds and cook, stirring constantly, for another 2–3 minutes. Pour in the stock and sherry and stir in 5ml/1 tsp salt. Season with plenty of black pepper. Bring to the boil, then lower the heat and simmer gently for about 10 minutes.

3 Process the soup in a food processor or blender until smooth, then return it to the rinsed-out pan. Reheat slowly, stirring occasionally, but do not allow the soup to boil. Taste for seasoning, adding more salt and pepper if required.

4 Ladle the soup into heated bowls, garnish with the toasted flaked or slivered almonds and a little parsley, and serve immediately.

Nutritional information per portion: Energy 255Kcal/1054kJ; Protein 5.8g; Carbohydrate 11.5g, of which sugars 8.1g; Fat 19.6g, of which saturates 6.1g; Cholesterol 21mg; Calcium 82mg; Fibre 3.2g; Sodium 68mg.

Summer herb soup with chargrilled radicchio

The sweetness of shallots and leeks in this soup is balanced beautifully by the slightly acidic sorrel with its delicate hint of lemon, and a bouquet of summer herbs.

SERVES 4–6

30ml/2 tbsp dry white wine
2 shallots, finely chopped
1 garlic clove, crushed
2 leeks, sliced
1 large potato, about 225g/8oz, roughly chopped
2 courgettes (zucchini), chopped
600ml/1 pint/2¹⁄₂ cups water
115g/4oz sorrel, torn

large handful of fresh chervil
large handful of fresh flat leaf parsley
large handful of fresh mint
1 round (butterhead) lettuce, separated into leaves
600ml/1 pint/2¹⁄₂ cups vegetable stock
1 small head of radicchio
5ml/1 tsp groundnut (peanut) oil
salt and ground black pepper

1 Put the wine, shallots and garlic into a heavy-based pan and bring to the boil. Cook the mixture for 2–3 minutes, until softened.

2 Add the leeks, potato and courgettes with enough of the water to come about halfway up the vegetables. Lay a wetted piece of greaseproof (waxed) paper over the vegetables and put a lid on the pan, then cook for 10–15 minutes, until soft.

3 Remove the paper from the pan and add the sorrel, chervil, flat leaf parsley, fresh mint and lettuce. Cook for about 1–2 minutes, or until wilted.

4 Pour in the remaining water along with the stock and simmer for 10 minutes. Cool the soup slightly, then process it in a food processor or blender until smooth. Return the soup to the rinsed-out pan and season well.

5 Cut the radicchio into thin wedges that hold together, then brush the cut sides with the oil. Heat a ridged griddle or frying pan until very hot and add the radicchio wedges.

6 Cook the radicchio for 1 minute on each side until slightly charred. Reheat the soup over a low heat, then ladle it into warmed bowls. Serve with a wedge of radicchio.

Nutritional information per portion: Energy 102Kcal/428kJ; Protein 5g; Carbohydrate 15.1g, of which sugars 5.7g; Fat 2.2g, of which saturates 0.4g; Cholesterol 0mg; Calcium 135mg; Fibre 4.9g; Sodium 57mg.

Mushroom soup

Using a mixture of mushrooms gives this soup character. This makes a flavoursome light meal served with fresh crusty bread.

SERVES 4–6

20g/³/₄oz/1¹/₂ tbsp butter
15ml/1 tbsp oil
1 onion, roughly chopped
4 potatoes, about 250–350g/9–12oz, roughly chopped
350g/12oz mixed mushrooms, such as Paris Browns, field
    (portabello) and button (white), cleaned and roughly chopped
1 or 2 garlic cloves, crushed
150ml/¹/₄ pint/²/₃ cup white wine or dry (hard) cider
1.2 litres/2 pints/5 cups good chicken stock
bunch of fresh parsley, chopped
salt and ground black pepper
whipped or sour cream, to garnish

1 Heat the butter and oil in a pan over medium heat. Add the chopped onion, turning it in the butter until well coated. Stir in the potatoes. Cover and sweat over a low heat for 5–10 minutes until softened but not browned.

2 Add the mushrooms, garlic and white wine or cider and stock. Season, bring to the boil and cook for 15 minutes, until all the ingredients are tender.

3 Put the mixture through a mouli-legume (food mill), using the coarse blade, or liquidize (blend). Return the soup to the rinsed-out pan, and add three-quarters of the parsley. Bring back to the boil, season, and garnish with cream and the remaining parsley.

Nutritional information per portion: Energy 155Kcal/648kJ; Protein 3.2g; Carbohydrate 13.6g, of which sugars 3.4g; Fat 7.6g, of which saturates 3.2g; Cholesterol 11mg; Calcium 23mg; Fibre 2.1g; Sodium 44mg.

Garlic soup

This interesting and subtly flavoured Irish soup makes good use of an ancient ingredient that is believed to have health-giving properties.

SERVES 8

12 large garlic cloves, peeled and crushed
15ml/1 tbsp olive oil
15ml/1 tbsp melted butter
1 small onion, finely chopped
15g/¹/₂oz/2 tbsp plain (all-purpose) flour
15ml/1 tbsp white wine vinegar
1 litre/1³/₄ pints/4 cups chicken stock
1 litre/1³/₄ pints/4 cups water
2 egg yolks, lightly beaten
bread croûtons, fried in butter, to serve

1 Put the oil and butter into a pan, add the garlic and onion, and cook them gently for 20 minutes, until soft but not brown.

2 Add the flour and stir to make a roux. Cook for a few minutes, then stir in the wine vinegar, stock and water. Simmer for about 30 minutes.

3 When ready to serve the soup, whisk in the lightly beaten egg yolks. Put the croûtons into eight soup bowls and pour over the hot soup.

Nutritional information per portion: Energy 55Kcal/229kJ; Protein 1.6g; Carbohydrate 3.6g, of which sugars 0.6g; Fat 4g, of which saturates 1.3g; Cholesterol 53mg; Calcium 13mg; Fibre 0.4g; Sodium 11mg.

Garlic soup with egg and polenta croûtons

This delicious garlic soup, which originates from Andalusia in Spain, is married with Italian polenta and poached eggs to produce a filling and nutritious dish.

SERVES 4

15ml/1 tbsp olive oil
1 garlic bulb, unpeeled, broken into cloves
4 slices day-old ciabatta bread
1.2 litres/2 pints/5 cups chicken stock
pinch of saffron
15ml/1 tbsp white wine vinegar
4 eggs

salt and ground black pepper
chopped fresh parsley, to garnish

FOR THE POLENTA CROÛTONS
750ml/1¼ pints/3 cups milk
175g/6oz/1 cup quick-cook polenta
50g/2oz/¼ cup butter

1 Preheat the oven to 200°C/400°F/Gas 6. Brush the oil over a roasting tin (pan), then add the garlic and bread, and roast for about 20 minutes. Leave until cool.

2 Meanwhile, make the polenta. Bring the milk to the boil in a large pan and gradually pour in the polenta, stirring constantly. Cook for about 5 minutes, stirring frequently, until the polenta begins to come away from the side. Spoon the polenta on to a chopping board and spread out to 1cm/½in thick. Allow to cool and set, then cut into dice.

3 Squeeze the garlic cloves from their skins into a food processor or blender. Add the bread, broken into pieces, and 300ml/½ pint/1¼ cups of the stock, then process until smooth. Pour into a pan. Pound the saffron in a mortar and stir in a little of the stock, then add to the soup with enough of the remaining stock to thin the soup as required.

4 Melt the butter in a frying pan and cook the diced polenta over a high heat for 1–2 minutes, tossing until beginning to brown. Drain on kitchen paper.

5 Season the soup and reheat gently. Boil a large frying pan of water. Add the vinegar and reduce the heat to a simmer. Crack an egg on to a saucer. Swirl the water with a knife and drop the egg into the middle. Repeat with the other eggs and poach for 2–3 minutes until set. Lift out the eggs, then place one in each bowl. Ladle the soup over the eggs, and serve with the croûtons and parsley.

Nutritional information per portion: Energy 415Kcal/1731kJ; Protein 13.4g; Carbohydrate 43.9g, of which sugars 0.9g; Fat 20.8g, of which saturates 8.6g; Cholesterol 217mg; Calcium 57mg; Fibre 1.9g; Sodium 247mg.

Pea soup with garlic

This delicious soup has a wonderfully sweet taste and smooth texture, and is great served with crusty bread and garnished with mint.

SERVES 4

25g/1oz/2 tbsp butter
1 garlic clove, crushed
900g/2lb/8 cups frozen peas
1.2 litres/2 pints/5 cups chicken stock
salt and ground black pepper
mint, to garnish

1 Heat the butter in a large pan and add the garlic. Fry gently for about 2–3 minutes, until softened, then add the peas. Cook for 1–2 minutes more, then pour in the stock.

2 Bring the soup to the boil, then reduce the heat to a simmer. Cover and cook for 5–6 minutes, until the peas are tender. Leave to cool slightly, then transfer the mixture to a food processor or blender and process until smooth (you may have to do this in two batches).

3 Return the soup to the pan and heat through gently. Season with salt and pepper to taste. Garnish with mint.

Nutritional information per portion: Energy 233Kcal/965kJ; Protein 15.6g; Carbohydrate 25.5g, of which sugars 5.2g; Fat 8.5g, of which saturates 3.9g; Cholesterol 13mg; Calcium 49mg; Fibre 10.6g; Sodium 40mg.

Aubergine soup with mozzarella and gremolata

Gremolata is a classic Italian mixture of garlic, lemon rind and chopped fresh parsley which adds a flourish of tangy Mediterranean flavour to this rich creamy soup.

SERVES 6

30ml/2 tbsp olive oil
2 shallots, chopped
2 garlic cloves, chopped
1kg/2¼lb aubergines (eggplants), trimmed and roughly chopped
1 litre/1¾ pints/4 cups chicken stock
150ml/¼ pint/⅔ cup double (heavy) cream
30ml/2 tbsp chopped fresh parsley
175g/6oz buffalo mozzarella, sliced
salt and ground black pepper

FOR THE GREMOLATA
2 garlic cloves, finely chopped
grated rind of 2 lemons
15ml/1 tbsp chopped fresh parsley

1 Heat the oil in a large pan and add the chopped shallots and garlic. Cook for 4–5 minutes, until soft. Add the aubergines and cook for about 25 minutes, stirring occasionally, until soft and browned.

2 Pour in the stock and cook for about 5 minutes. Leave the soup to cool slightly, then purée in a food processor or blender until smooth. Return to the rinsed-out pan and season to taste with salt and black pepper. Add the cream and parsley and bring to the boil.

3 Mix the ingredients for the gremolata in a small bowl.

4 Ladle the soup into bowls and lay the mozzarella on top. Scatter with gremolata and serve.

Nutritional information per portion: Energy 261Kcal/1079kJ; Protein 7.5g; Carbohydrate 4.9g, of which sugars 4.3g; Fat 23.7g, of which saturates 13.1g; Cholesterol 51mg; Calcium 137mg; Fibre 3.5g; Sodium 124mg.

Cream of mushroom soup with goat's cheese crostini

Classic cream of mushroom soup takes on a new twist with the addition of luxuriously crisp and garlicky crostini.

SERVES 6

25g/1oz/2 tbsp butter

1 onion, chopped

1 garlic clove, chopped

450g/1lb/6 cups button (white), chestnut or brown cap (cremini) mushrooms, chopped

15ml/1 tbsp plain (all-purpose) flour

45ml/3 tbsp dry sherry

900ml/1½ pints/3¾ cups vegetable stock

150ml/¼ pint/⅔ cup double (heavy) cream

salt and ground black pepper

fresh chervil sprigs, to garnish

FOR THE CROSTINI

15ml/1 tbsp olive oil, plus extra for brushing

1 shallot, chopped

115g/4oz/1½ cups button (white) mushrooms, finely chopped

15ml/1 tbsp chopped fresh parsley

6 brown cap (cremini) mushrooms

6 slices baguette

1 small garlic clove

115g/4oz/1 cup soft goat's cheese

1 Melt the butter in a pan and cook the onion and garlic for 5 minutes. Stir in the button mushrooms, cover and cook for 10 minutes, stirring occasionally. Stir in the flour and cook for 1 minute. Stir in the sherry and stock then simmer for 15 minutes. Cool slightly, then purée the soup until smooth.

2 For the crostini, heat the oil in a pan. Add the shallot and mushrooms, and cook until softened. Drain well and chop finely with the parsley.

3 Preheat the grill (broiler). Brush the brown cap mushrooms with oil and cook for 5–6 minutes. Toast the slices of baguette, rub with the garlic and put a spoonful of cheese on each. Top the grilled (broiled) mushrooms with the mushroom mixture and place on the crostini.

4 Return the soup to the pan and stir in the cream. Season, then reheat gently. Float a crostini in each bowl of soup and garnish with chervil.

Nutritional information per portion: Energy 313Kcal/1305kJ; Protein 6.2g; Carbohydrate 26.8g, of which sugars 2.5g; Fat 20g, of which saturates 11g; Cholesterol 43mg; Calcium 75mg; Fibre 2.2g; Sodium 283mg.

Egg flower soup

This simple, healthy soup is flavoured with fresh root ginger and Chinese five-spice powder. It is quick and delicious and is perfect if you need a last-minute dish.

SERVES 4

1.2 litres/2 pints/5 cups fresh chicken
    or vegetable stock
10ml/2 tsp peeled, grated fresh root
    ginger
10ml/2 tsp light soy sauce
5ml/1 tsp sesame oil
5ml/1 tsp Chinese five-spice powder
15ml/1 tbsp cornflour (cornstarch)
2 eggs
salt and ground black pepper
1 spring onion (scallion), very finely sliced
    diagonally, and 15ml/1 tbsp roughly
    chopped coriander (cilantro) or flat
    leaf parsley, to garnish

1 Put the chicken or vegetable stock into a large pan with the ginger, soy sauce, oil and five-spice powder. Bring to the boil and allow to simmer gently for about 10 minutes.

2 Blend the cornflour in a measuring jug (pitcher) with 60–75ml/4–5 tbsp water and stir into the stock. Cook, stirring constantly, until the soup has slightly thickened. Season to taste with salt and pepper.

3 In a jug (pitcher), beat both the eggs together with 30ml/2 tbsp cold water until the mixture becomes frothy.

4 Bring the soup back just to the boil and drizzle in the egg mixture, stirring vigorously with chopsticks. Choose a jug (pitcher) with a fine spout to form a thin drizzle. Serve at once, sprinkled with the sliced spring onions and chopped coriander or parsley.

Nutritional information per portion: Energy 71Kcal/298kJ; Protein 3.3g; Carbohydrate 7.1g, of which sugars 0.2g; Fat 3.6g, of which saturates 0.9g; Cholesterol 95mg; Calcium 16mg; Fibre 0g; Sodium 217mg.

Egg and cheese soup

In this classic Roman soup, eggs and cheese are beaten into hot soup, which produces the slightly scrambled texture that is characteristic of this dish.

SERVES 6

3 eggs
45ml/3 tbsp fine semolina
90ml/6 tbsp freshly grated Parmesan
  cheese
pinch of nutmeg
1.5 litres/2½ pints/6¼ cups cold meat
  or chicken stock
salt and ground black pepper
12 rounds of country bread or ciabatta,
  to serve

1 Beat the eggs in a bowl, then beat in the semolina and the cheese. Add the nutmeg and beat in 250ml/8fl oz/1 cup of the meat or chicken stock. Pour the mixture into a measuring jug (pitcher).

2 Pour the remaining stock into a large pan and bring to a gentle simmer, stirring occasionally.

3 Just before you are ready to serve the soup, whisk the egg mixture into the hot stock. Raise the heat slightly, and bring it barely to the boil. Season and cook for 3 minutes.

4 To serve, toast the rounds of country bread or ciabatta, place two in each soup plate and ladle on the hot soup. Serve immediately.

Nutritional information per portion: Energy 245Kcal/1030kJ; Protein 14.1g; Carbohydrate 27.5g, of which sugars 1.3g; Fat 9.4g, of which saturates 4.1g; Cholesterol 110mg; Calcium 246mg; Fibre 1.1g; Sodium 424mg.

Corn and red chilli chowder

Corn and chillies often make good partners, and here the cool combination of creamed corn and milk tempers the raging heat of the chillies.

SERVES 6

2 tomatoes, skinned

1 onion, roughly chopped

375g/13oz can creamed corn

2 red (bell) peppers, halved and seeded

15ml/1 tbsp olive oil, plus extra for brushing

3 red chillies, seeded and sliced

2 garlic cloves, chopped

5ml/1 tsp ground cumin

5ml/1 tsp ground coriander

600ml/1 pint/2½ cups milk

350ml/12fl oz/1½ cups chicken stock

3 cobs of corn, kernels removed

450g/1lb potatoes, finely diced

60ml/4 tbsp double (heavy) cream

60ml/4 tbsp chopped fresh parsley

salt and ground black pepper

1 Process the tomatoes and onion in a food processor or blender to a smooth purée. Add the creamed corn and process again, then set aside. Preheat the grill (broiler) to high.

2 Put the peppers, skin sides up, on a grill rack and brush with oil. Grill (broil) for 8–10 minutes, until the skins blacken and blister. Transfer to a bowl and cover with clear film (plastic wrap), then leave to cool. Peel and dice the peppers, then set them aside.

3 Heat the oil in a pan and add the chillies and garlic. Cook, stirring, for 2–3 minutes, until softened. Add the cumin and coriander, and cook for a minute. Add the corn purée and cook for 8 minutes, stirring occasionally.

4 Pour in the milk and stock, then stir in the corn kernels, potatoes, red pepper and season to taste. Cook for 15–20 minutes, until the potatoes and corn are tender. Pour into bowls, add the cream, then sprinkle over the parsley.

Nutritional information per portion: Energy 343Kcal/1448kJ; Protein 9.4g; Carbohydrate 55.4g, of which sugars 23.2g; Fat 10.9g, of which saturates 5.1g; Cholesterol 20mg; Calcium 147mg; Fibre 4g; Sodium 383mg.

Corn and potato chowder

This creamy yet chunky soup is rich with the sweet taste of corn. It's excellent served with thick crusty bread and topped with some melted Cheddar cheese.

SERVES 4

1 onion, chopped

1 garlic clove, crushed

1 medium baking potato, chopped

2 celery sticks, sliced

1 small green (bell) pepper, seeded,
  halved and sliced

30ml/2 tbsp sunflower oil

25g/1oz/2 tbsp butter

600ml/1 pint/2½ cups stock or water

300ml/½ pint/1¼ cups milk

200g/7oz can flageolet (small
  cannellini) beans

300g/11oz can corn kernels

good pinch dried sage

salt and ground black pepper

Cheddar cheese, grated, to serve

1 Put the onion, garlic, potato, celery and green pepper into a large heavy-based pan with the oil and butter.

2 Heat the ingredients until sizzling then reduce the heat to low. Cover and cook gently for about 10 minutes, shaking the pan occasionally to prevent the ingredients sticking.

3 Pour in the stock or water, season with salt and pepper to taste and bring to the boil. Reduce the heat, cover again and simmer gently for about 15 minutes until the vegetables are tender.

4 Add the milk, beans and corn – including their liquids – and the sage. Simmer, uncovered, for 5 minutes. Check the seasoning and serve hot, sprinkled with grated cheese.

Nutritional information per portion: Energy 251Kcal/1052kJ; Protein 9.7g; Carbohydrate 25.9g, of which sugars 9.3g; Fat 12.9g, of which saturates 4.9g; Cholesterol 18mg; Calcium 128mg; Fibre 5.5g; Sodium 1154mg.

Leek and oatmeal soup

This traditional Irish soup is known as brotchán foltchep *or* brotchán roy, *and combines leeks, oatmeal and milk – three ingredients that have been staple foods in Ireland for centuries.*

SERVES 4–6

about 1.2 litres/2 pints/5 cups chicken
   stock and milk, mixed
30ml/2 tbsp medium pinhead oatmeal
25g/1oz/2 tbsp butter
6 large leeks, sliced into 2cm/³⁄₄in pieces
   and washed
sea salt and ground black pepper
pinch of ground mace
30ml/2 tbsp chopped fresh parsley
single (light) cream and chopped fresh
   parsley leaves or chives, to garnish

1 Bring the stock and milk mixture to the boil over medium heat and sprinkle in the oatmeal. Stir well to prevent lumps forming, and then simmer gently.

2 Melt the butter in a separate pan and cook the leeks over a gentle heat until softened slightly, then add them to the stock. Simmer for 15–20 minutes, until the oatmeal is cooked.

3 Season with salt, pepper and mace, stir in the parsley and serve in warmed bowls. Decorate with a swirl of cream and some chopped fresh parsley or chives, if you like.

Nutritional information per portion: Energy 121Kcal/505kJ; Protein 4.2g; Carbohydrate 11.3g, of which sugars 4.5g; Fat 6.8g, of which saturates 3.5g; Cholesterol 13mg; Calcium 53mg; Fibre 4.9g; Sodium 44mg.

Leek and blue cheese soup

The blue cheese is an integral part of this substantial soup because of its buttery piquant flavour. Adding it to a soup can be a good way to use up leftover cheese.

SERVES 6

3 large leeks
50g/2oz/¼ cup butter
30ml/2 tbsp oil
115g/4oz Irish blue cheese, such as Cashel Blue, coarsely grated
15g/½oz/2 tbsp plain (all-purpose) flour
15ml/1 tbsp wholegrain Irish mustard, or to taste
1.5 litres/2½ pints/6¼ cups chicken stock
ground black pepper
50g/2oz/½ cup grated cheese and chopped chives or spring onion (scallion) greens, to garnish

1 Slice the leeks thinly. Heat the butter and oil together in a large heavy pan and gently cook the leeks in it, covered, for 10–15 minutes, or until just softened but not brown.

2 Add the cheese to the pan, stirring over a low heat until it is melted. Add the flour and cook for 2 minutes, stirring constantly with a wooden spoon, then add ground black pepper and mustard to taste.

3 Gradually add the stock, stirring constantly and blending it in well, then bring the soup to the boil. Reduce the heat, cover and simmer very gently for about 15 minutes. Check the seasoning.

4 Serve the soup garnished with the extra grated cheese and the chopped chives or spring onion greens, and hand fresh bread around separately.

Nutritional information per portion: Energy 205Kcal/852kJ; Protein 8.2g; Carbohydrate 7.9g, of which sugars 2.2g; Fat 15.7g, of which saturates 9.9g; Cholesterol 40mg; Calcium 188mg; Fibre 2.2g; Sodium 347mg.

French onion soup with Gruyère croûtes

This is perhaps the most famous of all onion soups. Traditionally, it was served as a sustaining early morning meal to the workers of Les Halles market in Paris.

SERVES 6

50g/2oz/¼ cup butter
15ml/1 tbsp olive oil
2kg/4½lb yellow onions, peeled and
    sliced
5ml/1 tsp chopped fresh thyme
5ml/1 tsp caster (superfine) sugar
15ml/1 tbsp sherry vinegar
1.5 litres/2½ pints/6¼ cups good beef,
    chicken or duck stock
25ml/1½ tbsp plain (all-purpose) flour
150ml/¼ pint/⅔ cup dry white wine

45ml/3 tbsp brandy
salt and ground black pepper

FOR THE CROÛTES
6–12 thick slices day-old French stick or
    baguette, about 2.5cm/1in thick
1 garlic clove, halved
15ml/1 tbsp French mustard
115g/4oz/1 cup coarsely grated Gruyère
    cheese

1 Melt the butter with the oil in a large pan. Stir in the onions and cook over a medium heat for 5–8 minutes until the onions soften. Stir in the thyme. Reduce the heat to very low, cover the pan and cook the onions for 20–30 minutes, stirring frequently, until they are very soft and golden yellow.

2 Uncover the pan and increase the heat slightly. Stir in the sugar and cook for 5–10 minutes, until the onions start to brown. Add the sherry vinegar and increase the heat again, then continue cooking, stirring frequently, until the onions turn a deep, golden brown – this could take up to 20 minutes.

3 In another pan, bring the stock to the boil. Stir the flour into the onions and cook for 2 minutes, then gradually pour in the stock. Add the wine and brandy and season. Simmer for 10–15 minutes.

4 For the croûtes, preheat the oven to 150°C/300°F/Gas 2. Place the slices of bread on a greased baking tray and bake for 15–20 minutes, until dry and lightly browned. Rub the bread with the cut surface of the garlic and spread with the mustard, then sprinkle the Gruyère cheese over the slices.

5 Preheat the grill (broiler) on the hottest setting. Ladle the soup into a large flameproof pan or six flameproof bowls. Float the croûtes on the soup, then grill until the cheese bubbles. Serve at once.

Nutritional information per portion: Energy 484Kcal/2030kJ; Protein 15.3g; Carbohydrate 67.2g, of which sugars 21.5g; Fat 15.1g, of which saturates 8.7g; Cholesterol 36mg; Calcium 314mg; Fibre 6.4g; Sodium 611mg.

Roast vegetable soup with sun-dried tomato bread

Winter meets summer in this soup recipe for chunky roasted roots. Serve it with bread baked with a hint of added flavour in the form of sun-dried tomatoes.

SERVES 4

4 parsnips, quartered lengthways

2 red onions, cut into thin wedges

4 carrots, thickly sliced

2 leeks, thickly sliced

1 small swede (rutabaga), cut into
    bitesize pieces

4 potatoes, cut into chunks

60ml/4 tbsp olive oil

few sprigs of fresh thyme

1 garlic bulb, broken into cloves, unpeeled

1 litre/1¾ pints/4 cups vegetable stock

salt and ground black pepper

fresh thyme sprigs, to garnish

FOR THE SUN-DRIED TOMATO BREAD

1 ciabatta loaf (about 275g/10oz)

75g/3oz/6 tbsp butter, softened

1 garlic clove, crushed

4 sun-dried tomatoes, finely chopped

30ml/2 tbsp chopped fresh parsley

1 Preheat the oven to 200°C/400°F/Gas 6. Cut the thick ends of the parsnip quarters into four, then place them in a large roasting tin (pan). Add the other vegetables and spread them in an even layer. Drizzle over the olive oil then add the thyme sprigs and the unpeeled garlic cloves. Toss well and roast for about 45 minutes, until the vegetables are tender and slightly charred.

2 Meanwhile, to make the sun-dried tomato bread, cut diagonal slits along the loaf, taking care not to cut right through it. Mix the butter with the garlic, sun-dried tomatoes and parsley. Spread the mixture into each slit, then press the bread back together. Wrap the loaf in foil and bake for 15 minutes, opening the foil for the last 5 minutes.

3 Discard the thyme from the roasted vegetables. Squeeze the garlic cloves from their skins over the vegetables. Process about half the vegetables with the stock in a food processor or blender until almost smooth. Pour into a pan and add the remaining vegetables. Bring to the boil and season well.

4 Ladle the soup into bowls, garnish with thyme and serve with the bread.

Nutritional information per portion: Energy 511Kcal/2146kJ; Protein 13.9g; Carbohydrate 72.6g, of which sugars 18.9g; Fat 20.4g, of which saturates 10.6g; Cholesterol 40mg; Calcium 218mg; Fibre 12.1g; Sodium 521mg.

Butternut squash and blue cheese risotto soup

This is, in fact, a very wet risotto, but it bears more than a passing resemblance to soup and makes a very smart first course for a dinner party.

SERVES 4

25g/1oz/2 tbsp butter
30ml/2 tbsp olive oil
2 onions, finely chopped
½ celery stick, finely sliced
1 small butternut squash, peeled, seeded and cut into small cubes
15ml/1 tbsp chopped sage
300g/11oz/1½ cups risotto rice
1.2 litres/2 pints/5 cups hot chicken stock
30ml/2 tbsp double (heavy) cream
30ml/2 tbsp olive oil
4 large sage leaves
115g/4oz blue cheese, finely diced
salt and ground black pepper

1 Place the butter in a large pan with the oil and heat gently. Add the onions and celery, and cook for 4–5 minutes, until softened. Stir in the butternut squash and cook for 3–4 minutes, then add the sage.

2 Add the rice and cook for 1–2 minutes, stirring, until the grains are slightly translucent. Add the chicken stock a ladleful at a time. Cook until each ladleful of stock has been absorbed before adding the next. Continue adding the stock in this way until you have a very wet rice mixture. Season and stir in the cream.

3 Meanwhile, heat the oil in a frying pan and fry the sage leaves for a few seconds until crisp. Drain.

4 Stir the blue cheese into the risotto soup and ladle it into bowls. Garnish with a fried sage leaf.

Nutritional information per portion: Energy 505Kcal/2100kJ; Protein 9.2g; Carbohydrate 63.7g, of which sugars 5.7g; Fat 23g, of which saturates 8.3g; Cholesterol 26mg; Calcium 110mg; Fibre 2.7g; Sodium 91mg.

Castilian garlic soup

This rich, dark garlic soup comes from the La Mancha region in central Spain, which is famous for its hot and dry summer sunshine. The strong taste of this soup matches the harsh climate.

SERVES 4

30ml/2 tbsp olive oil
4 large garlic cloves, peeled
4 slices stale country bread
20ml/4 tbsp paprika
1 litre/1³⁄₄ pints/4 cups beef stock
1.5ml/¹⁄₄ tsp ground cumin
4 free-range (farm-fresh) eggs
salt and ground black pepper
chopped fresh parsley, to garnish

1 Preheat the oven to 230°C/450°F/Gas 8. Heat the olive oil in a large pan. Add the whole peeled garlic cloves and cook until they are golden, then remove and set aside. Fry the slices of bread in the oil until golden, then set these aside.

2 Add 15ml/1 tbsp of the paprika to the pan, and fry for a few seconds. Stir in the beef stock, cumin and remaining paprika, then add the reserved garlic, crushing the cloves with the back of a wooden spoon. Season to taste, then cook for about 5 minutes.

3 Break up the slices of fried bread into bitesize pieces and stir them into the soup. Ladle the soup into four ovenproof bowls. Carefully break an egg into each bowl of soup and place in the oven for about 3 minutes, until the eggs are set. Sprinkle the soup with chopped fresh parsley and serve immediately.

Nutritional information per portion: Energy 202Kcal/843kJ; Protein 9.3g; Carbohydrate 15.3g, of which sugars 1.5g; Fat 12.2g, of which saturates 2.4g; Cholesterol 190mg; Calcium 69mg; Fibre 0.6g; Sodium 202mg.

Greek aubergine and courgette soup

A fusion of flavours from the sunny Greek islands creates this fabulous soup, which is served with tzatziki, the popular combination of cucumber and creamy yogurt.

SERVES 4

2 large aubergines (eggplants), roughly
    diced
4 large courgettes (zucchini), roughly
    diced
1 onion, roughly chopped
4 garlic cloves, roughly chopped
45ml/3 tbsp olive oil
1.2 litres/2 pints/5 cups vegetable stock
15ml/1 tbsp chopped fresh oregano
salt and ground black pepper
mint sprigs, to garnish

FOR THE TZATZIKI

1 cucumber, peeled, seeded and diced
10ml/2 tsp salt
2 garlic cloves, crushed
5ml/1 tsp white wine vinegar
225g/8oz/1 cup Greek (US strained plain)
    yogurt
small bunch of fresh mint leaves, chopped

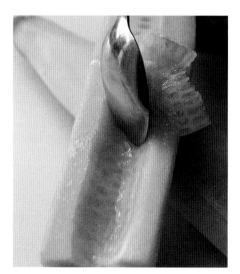

1 Preheat the oven to 200°C/400°F/Gas 6. Place the aubergines and courgettes in a roasting tin (pan). Add the onion and garlic, and then drizzle over the olive oil. Roast for 35 minutes, turning once, until they are tender and slightly charred.

2 Place half the roasted vegetables in a food processor or blender. Add the stock and process until almost smooth. Pour into a large pan and add the remaining vegetables. Bring to the boil, season and stir in the oregano.

3 For the tzatziki, place the cucumber flesh in a colander and sprinkle with salt. Leave for 30 minutes. Mix the garlic with the vinegar and stir into the yogurt. Pat the cucumber dry on kitchen paper and then fold it into the yogurt. Season to taste and stir in the mint. Chill until required.

4 Ladle the soup into bowls and garnish with mint sprigs. Hand round the bowl of tzatziki so that your guests can add a dollop or two to their soup.

Nutritional information per portion: Energy 188Kcal/778kJ; Protein 6.9g; Carbohydrate 8.5g, of which sugars 7.3g; Fat 14.9g, of which saturates 4.3g; Cholesterol 0mg; Calcium 134mg; Fibre 3.6g; Sodium 1027mg.

Balinese vegetable soup

The Balinese base this popular soup on beans, but any seasonal vegetables can be added or substituted. The recipe also includes shrimp paste, which is known locally as terasi.

SERVES 8

225g/8oz French beans
1.2 litres/2 pints/5 cups lightly
    salted water
1 garlic clove, roughly chopped
2 macadamia nuts or 4 almonds, finely
    chopped
1cm/$\frac{1}{2}$in cube shrimp paste
10–15ml/2–3 tsp coriander seeds,
    dry fried

30ml/2 tbsp vegetable oil
1 onion, finely sliced
400ml/14fl oz can coconut milk
2 bay leaves
225g/8oz/4 cups beansprouts
8 thin lemon wedges
30ml/2 tbsp lemon juice
salt and ground black pepper

1 Top and tail the beans, then cut them into small pieces. Bring the lightly salted water to the boil, add the beans to the pan and cook for 3–4 minutes. Drain, reserving the cooking water. Set the beans aside.

2 Finely grind the chopped garlic, macadamia nuts or almonds, shrimp paste and the coriander seeds to a paste using a mortar and pestle or in a food processor.

3 Heat the oil in a wok, and fry the onion until transparent. Remove with a slotted spoon. Add the nut paste to the wok and fry it for 2 minutes without allowing it to brown.

4 Pour in the reserved vegetable water. Spoon off 45–60ml/3–4 tbsp of the cream from the top of the coconut milk and set it aside. Add the remaining coconut milk to the wok, bring to the boil and add the bay leaves. Cook, uncovered, for 15–20 minutes.

5 Just before serving, reserve a few French beans, fried onions and beansprouts to garnish and stir the rest into the soup. Add the lemon wedges, reserved coconut cream, lemon juice and seasoning and stir well. Pour into individual soup bowls and serve, garnished with the reserved beans, onion and beansprouts.

Nutritional information per portion: Energy 54Kcal/224kJ; Protein 2.1g; Carbohydrate 5.2g, of which sugars 4.2g; Fat 2.8g, of which saturates 0.4g; Cholesterol 0mg; Calcium 38mg; Fibre 1.3g; Sodium 57mg.

Sweet and sour cabbage, beetroot and tomato borscht

There are many variations of this classic Jewish soup, which may be served hot or cold. This version includes plentiful amounts of cabbage, tomatoes and potatoes.

SERVES 6

1 onion, chopped

1 carrot, chopped

4–6 raw or vacuum-packed (cooked, not pickled) beetroot (beets), 3–4 diced and 1–2 coarsely grated

400g/14oz can tomatoes

4–6 new potatoes, cut into bitesize pieces

1 small white cabbage, thinly sliced

1 litre/1¾ pints/4 cups vegetable stock

45ml/3 tbsp sugar

30–45ml/2–3 tbsp white wine, cider vinegar or citric acid (sour salt)

45ml/3 tbsp chopped fresh dill, plus extra to garnish

salt and ground black pepper

sour cream, to garnish

buttered rye bread, to serve

1 Put the onion, carrot, diced beetroot, tomatoes, potatoes, cabbage and stock in a large pan. Bring to the boil, reduce the heat and simmer for 30 minutes, or until the potatoes are tender.

2 Add the grated beetroot, sugar and wine, vinegar or citric acid to the soup and cook for 10 minutes. Taste for a good sweet-sour balance and add more sugar and/or vinegar if necessary. Season.

3 Stir the chopped dill into the soup and ladle into warmed bowls immediately. Garnish each bowl with a generous spoonful of sour cream and more dill and serve with buttered rye bread.

Nutritional information per portion: Energy 111Kcal/470kJ; Protein 3.2g; Carbohydrate 24.6g, of which sugars 17.8g; Fat 0.6g, of which saturates 0.1g; Cholesterol 0mg; Calcium 65mg; Fibre 3.8g; Sodium 52mg.

Thai vegetable soup

This is a surprisingly satisfying soup from Thailand that is very quick and easy to prepare. It is a versatile recipe, too, as you can vary the vegetables according to what is seasonally available.

SERVES 4

1 egg
15ml/1 tbsp groundnut (peanut) oil
900ml/1¹/₂ pints/3³/₄ cups vegetable
   stock
2 large carrots, finely diced
4 outer leaves Savoy cabbage, shredded
30ml/2 tbsp soy sauce
2.5ml/¹/₂ tsp granulated (white) sugar
2.5ml/¹/₂ tsp ground black pepper
fresh coriander (cilantro) leaves,
   to garnish

1 Put the egg in a bowl and beat lightly with a fork. Heat the oil in a small frying pan until it is hot, but not smoking. Pour in the egg and swirl the pan so that it coats the base evenly. Cook over a medium heat until the omelette has set and the underside is golden.

2 Slide it out of the pan and roll it up like a pancake. Slice into 5mm/¹/₄in rounds and set aside for the garnish.

3 Put the stock into a large pan. Add the carrots and cabbage and bring to the boil. Reduce the heat and simmer for 5 minutes, then add the soy sauce, granulated sugar and pepper.

4 Stir well, then pour into warmed bowls. Lay a few omelette rounds on the surface of each portion and complete the garnish with the coriander leaves.

Nutritional information per portion: Energy 64Kcal/264kJ; Protein 2.3g; Carbohydrate 4.3g, of which sugars 4.1g; Fat 4.3g, of which saturates 0.7g; Cholesterol 48mg; Calcium 27mg; Fibre 1.1g; Sodium 560mg.

Goan potato soup with spiced pea samosas

In Goa this soup would be served as a complete meal. Both the soup and the samosas are quick and simple to prepare, and make a substantial and tasty vegetarian lunch.

SERVES 4

60ml/4 tbsp sunflower oil
10ml/2 tsp black mustard seeds
1 large onion, chopped
1 red chilli, seeded and chopped
2.5ml/1/2 tsp ground turmeric
1.5ml/1/4 tsp cayenne pepper
900g/2lb potatoes, cut into cubes
4 fresh curry leaves
750ml/11/4 pint/3 cups water
225g/8oz spinach leaves, torn if large
400ml/14fl oz/12/3 cups coconut milk
handful of fresh coriander (cilantro) leaves
salt and ground black pepper

FOR THE SAMOSA DOUGH
275g/10oz/21/2 cups plain (all-purpose)
    flour
1.5ml/1/4 tsp salt
30ml/2 tbsp sunflower oil
150ml/1/4 pint/2/3 cup warm water

FOR THE SAMOSA FILLING
60ml/4 tbsp sunflower oil
1 small onion, finely chopped
175g/6oz/11/2 cups frozen peas, thawed
15ml/1 tbsp grated fresh root ginger
1 green chilli, seeded and finely chopped
45ml/3 tbsp water
350g/12oz cooked potatoes, finely diced
7.5ml/11/2 tsp ground coriander
5ml/1 tsp garam masala
7.5ml/11/2 tsp ground cumin
1.5ml/1/4 tsp cayenne pepper
10ml/2 tsp lemon juice
30ml/2 tbsp chopped fresh
    coriander (cilantro)
vegetable oil, for deep frying

1 Make the samosa dough. Mix the flour and salt in a bowl and make a well in the middle. Add the oil and water and mix in the flour to make a soft dough. Knead briefly on a lightly floured surface. Wrap in clear film (plastic wrap) and chill for 30 minutes.

2 To make the filling, heat the oil in a frying pan and add the onion. Cook for 6–7 minutes until golden. Add the peas, ginger, chilli and water. Cover and simmer for 5–6 minutes. Add the potatoes, spices and lemon juice. Cook over a low heat for 2–3 minutes. Stir in the coriander and season well. Leave to cool.

3 Divide the dough into eight. On a floured surface, roll out one piece into an 18cm/7in round. Keep the remaining dough covered. Cut the round in half and place 30ml/2 tbsp of the filling on each half towards one corner. Dampen the edges and fold the dough over the filling. Pinch the edges together to form triangles. Repeat with the remaining dough and filling.

4 Heat the oil for deep frying to 190°C/375°F, or until a cube of bread rises and sizzles in 30 seconds. Fry the samosas for 4–5 minutes, turning once. Drain on kitchen paper.

5 To make the soup, heat the oil in a large pan. Add the mustard seeds, cover and cook until they begin to pop. Add the onion and chilli and cook for 5–6 minutes, until softened. Stir in the turmeric, cayenne, potatoes, curry leaves and water. Cover and cook over a low heat for 15 minutes, stirring occasionally, until the potatoes are soft.

6 Add the spinach and cook for 5 minutes. Stir in the coconut milk and cook for a further 5 minutes. Season with salt and black pepper and add the coriander leaves before ladling the soup into bowls. Serve with the vegetable samosas.

Nutritional information per portion: Energy 836Kcal/3503kJ; Protein 16.7g; Carbohydrate 112g, of which sugars 8.6g; Fat 38.7g, of which saturates 4.9g; Cholesterol 0mg; Calcium 227mg; Fibre 8.9g; Sodium 117mg.

Shiitake mushroom laksa

The pronounced, almost meaty flavour of shiitake mushrooms contrasts with the blander flour noodles in this soup, which is based on the classic Malaysian soup known as Penang laksa.

SERVES 6

150g/5oz/2½ cups dried shiitake
  mushrooms
1.2 litres/2 pints/5 cups boiling vegetable
  stock
30ml/2 tbsp tamarind paste
250ml/8fl oz/1 cup hot water
6 large dried red chillies, stems removed
  and seeded
2 lemon grass stalks, finely sliced
5ml/1 tsp ground turmeric

15ml/1 tbsp grated fresh galangal
1 onion, chopped
5ml/1 tsp dried shrimp paste
30ml/2 tbsp oil
10ml/2 tsp palm sugar (jaggery)
175g/6oz rice vermicelli
1 red onion, peeled and very finely sliced
1 small cucumber, seeded and cut into
  strips
handful of fresh mint leaves, to garnish

1 Place the mushrooms in a bowl and pour in enough boiling stock to cover them. Set aside and leave to soak for 30 minutes.

2 Put the tamarind paste into a bowl and pour in the hot water. Mash the paste against the side of the bowl. Strain and reserve the liquid, discarding the pulp.

3 Soak the chillies in enough hot water to cover for 5 minutes, then drain, reserving the liquid. Process the lemon grass, turmeric, galangal, onion, chillies and shrimp paste in a food processor or blender, adding a little soaking water from the chillies to form a paste.

4 Heat the oil in a heavy-based pan and cook the paste over a low heat for 4–5 minutes until fragrant. Add the tamarind liquid and bring to the boil. Simmer for 5 minutes then remove from the heat.

5 Drain the mushrooms and reserve the stock. Discard the stems, then halve or quarter the mushrooms. Add the mushrooms to the pan with their soaking liquid, the remaining stock and the palm sugar. Simmer for 25–30 minutes or until tender.

6 Cook the rice vermicelli according to the packet instructions. Drain and put into six bowls. Top with onion and cucumber, then ladle in the soup. Add the mint leaves and serve.

Nutritional information per portion: Energy 152Kcal/635kJ; Protein 3.2g; Carbohydrate 25.9g, of which sugars 2.6g; Fat 4g, of which saturates 0.5g; Cholesterol 0mg; Calcium 14mg; Fibre 0.6g; Sodium 4mg.

Bean, pasta and noodle soups

Soups made with legumes – peas, beans and lentils – are very nutritious because they contain protein, fibre, minerals and B vitamins, and are low in fat. Hearty pasta soups are perfect served for a light supper or lunch. Noodles are a key ingredient in Asian soups and there is a choice of a huge range of shapes, sizes and flavours.

American red bean soup with guacamole salsa

This soup is in Tex-Mex style, and it is served with a cooling avocado and lime salsa. If you relish chillies, add a little more cayenne for a truly fiery experience.

SERVES 6

30ml/2 tbsp olive oil
2 onions, chopped
2 garlic cloves, chopped
10ml/2 tsp ground cumin
1.5ml/1/4 tsp cayenne pepper
15ml/1 tbsp paprika
15ml/1 tbsp tomato purée (paste)
2.5ml/1/2 tsp dried oregano
2 x 400g/14oz cans red kidney beans
400g/14oz can chopped tomatoes
900ml/1 1/2 pints/3 3/4 cups water
salt and ground black pepper
Tabasco sauce, to serve

FOR THE GUACAMOLE SALSA

2 avocados
1 small red onion, finely chopped
1 green chilli, seeded and chopped
15ml/1 tbsp chopped fresh coriander
  (cilantro)
juice of 1 lime

1 Heat the oil in a pan and add the onions and garlic. Cook for 4–5 minutes, until softened. Add the cumin, cayenne and paprika, and cook for 1 minute.

2 Stir in the tomato purée and cook for a few seconds, then stir in the oregano. Drain and rinse the kidney beans and add along with the chopped tomatoes and water. Bring to the boil and simmer for 15–20 minutes.

3 Cool the soup slightly, then purée it in a food processor or blender until smooth. Return to the pan and season.

4 To make the guacamole salsa, halve, stone (pit) and peel the avocados, then dice them finely. Place in a small bowl and gently, but thoroughly, mix with the finely chopped red onion and chilli, and the coriander and lime juice.

5 Reheat the soup and ladle into bowls. Spoon a little guacamole salsa into the middle of each and serve, offering Tabasco sauce separately.

Nutritional information per portion: Energy 244Kcal/1023kJ; Protein 10.5g; Carbohydrate 27.5g, of which sugars 7.4g; Fat 11g, of which saturates 2g; Cholesterol 0mg; Calcium 108mg; Fibre 10g; Sodium 535mg.

Butter bean, sun-dried tomato and pesto soup

This bean soup is incredibly quick and easy to make, and using plenty of pesto and sun-dried tomato purée gives it a rich, minestrone-like flavour.

SERVES 4

2 x 400g/14oz cans butter (lima) beans
900ml/1¹/₂ pints/3³/₄ cups chicken or vegetable stock
60ml/4 tbsp sun-dried tomato purée (paste)
75ml/5 tbsp pesto

1 Drain and rinse the butter beans. Put the drained beans in a large pan with the stock and bring just to the boil.

2 Reduce the heat and stir in the tomato purée and pesto. Cover, bring back to simmering point and cook gently for 5 minutes.

3 Transfer six ladlefuls of the soup to a food processor or blender, scooping up plenty of the beans. Process until smooth, then return to the pan.

4 Heat gently, stirring frequently, for 5 minutes, then season if necessary. Ladle into four warmed soup bowls.

Nutritional information per portion: Energy 264Kcal/1109kJ; Protein 14.8g; Carbohydrate 27.4g, of which sugars 3.6g; Fat 11.3g, of which saturates 2.7g; Cholesterol 6mg; Calcium 109mg; Fibre 9.5g; Sodium 932mg.

Spicy red lentil soup with onion

This light lentil soup is flavoured with tomatoes and subtly spiced. The garnishes play an important role and are sometimes served in a separate bowl.

SERVES 6

30–45ml/2–3 tbsp olive
1 large onion, finely chopped
2 garlic cloves, finely chopped
1 fresh red chilli, seeded and chopped
5–10ml/1–2 tsp cumin seeds
5–10ml/1–2 tsp coriander seeds
1 carrot, finely chopped
scant 5ml/1 tsp ground fenugreek
5ml/1 tsp sugar
15ml/1 tbsp tomato purée (paste)
250g/9oz/1 cup split red lentils
1.75 litres/3 pints/7^1/2 cups
    chicken stock
salt and ground black pepper

TO SERVE

1 small red onion, finely chopped
15ml/1 tbsp chopped fresh parsley
4–6 lemon wedges

1 Heat the oil in a heavy pan and stir in the onion, garlic, chilli, cumin and coriander seeds. When the onion begins to colour slightly, toss in the carrot and cook for 2–3 minutes. Add the fenugreek, sugar and tomato purée and stir in the lentils.

2 Pour in the stock, stir well and bring to the boil. Lower the heat, partially cover the pan with a lid and simmer for 30–40 minutes, until the lentils have broken up.

3 If the soup is too thick for your preference, thin it down to the desired consistency with a little water. Season with salt and pepper to taste.

4 Serve the soup as it is or, if you prefer a smooth texture, leave it to cool slightly, then whiz it in a food processor or blender and reheat. Ladle the soup into bowls and sprinkle liberally with the chopped onion and parsley. Serve with a wedge of lemon.

Nutritional information per portion: Energy 203kcal/856kJ; Protein 11.1g; Carbohydrate 31.8g, of which sugars 7.3g; Fat 4.4g, of which saturates 0.6g; Cholesterol 0mg; Calcium 45mg; Fibre 3.5g; Sodium 26mg.

Cannellini bean soup with cavolo nero

Cavolo nero is a very dark green type of kale (which is similar to cabbage). It is grown in Italy and it is an ideal vegetable for this traditional recipe.

SERVES 4

2 x 400g/14oz cans chopped tomatoes
    with herbs

250g/9oz cavolo nero leaves, or Savoy
    cabbage

400g/14oz can cannellini beans, drained
    and rinsed

60ml/4 tbsp extra virgin olive oil

salt and ground black pepper

1 Pour the tomatoes into a large pan and add a can of cold water. Season with salt and pepper and bring to the boil, then reduce the heat to a simmer.

2 Roughly shred the cabbage leaves and add them to the pan. Partially cover the pan and then simmer gently for about 15 minutes, or until the cabbage is tender.

3 Add the cannellini beans to the pan and warm through for a few minutes. Check and adjust the seasoning, then ladle the soup into bowls, drizzle each one with a little olive oil and serve.

Nutritional information per portion: Energy 227Kcal/950kJ; Protein 8.2g; Carbohydrate 22.3g, of which sugars 10.4g; Fat 12.2g, of which saturates 1.9g; Cholesterol 0mg; Calcium 60mg; Fibre 7.9g; Sodium 443mg.

Broad bean minestrone

The classic, wintry minestrone soup takes on a summer-fresh image in this light recipe. Any small pasta shapes can be used instead of the spaghettini if you prefer.

SERVES 6

30ml/2 tbsp olive oil

2 onions, peeled and finely chopped

2 garlic cloves, peeled and finely chopped

2 carrots, very finely chopped

1 celery stick, very finely chopped

1.27 litres/2¼ pints/5²/₃ cups boiling water

450g/1lb shelled fresh broad (fava) beans

225g/8oz mangetouts (snow peas), cut into fine strips

3 tomatoes, peeled and chopped

5ml/1 tsp tomato purée (paste)

50g/2oz spaghettini, broken into 4cm/1¹/₂in lengths

225g/8oz baby spinach

30ml/2 tbsp chopped fresh parsley

handful of fresh basil leaves

salt and ground black pepper

basil sprigs, to garnish

freshly grated Parmesan cheese, to serve

1 Heat the oil in a pan and add the chopped onions and garlic. Cook over a low heat for 4–5 minutes, until softened but not browned. Add the carrots and celery, and cook for 2–3 minutes. Add the boiling water and simmer for 15 minutes, until the vegetables are tender.

2 Cook the broad beans in boiling salted water for 4–5 minutes. Remove with a slotted spoon, refresh under cold water and set aside.

3 Bring the pan of water back to the boil, add the mangetouts and cook for 1 minute or until just tender. Drain, then refresh under cold water and set aside.

4 Add the tomatoes and the tomato purée to the soup. Cook for 1 minute. Purée two or three large ladlefuls of the soup and a quarter of the broad beans in a food processor or blender until smooth. Set aside.

5 Add the spaghettini to the remaining soup and cook for 6–8 minutes, until tender. Stir in the purée and spinach and cook for 2–3 minutes. Add the rest of the broad beans, the mangetouts and parsley, and season well. When you are ready to serve, stir in the basil leaves, ladle the soup into deep cups or bowls and garnish with sprigs of basil. Serve a little grated Parmesan with the soup.

Nutritional information per portion: Energy 162Kcal/682kJ; Protein 9.9g; Carbohydrate 20.8g, of which sugars 6.5g; Fat 4.9g, of which saturates 0.7g; Cholesterol 0mg; Calcium 137mg; Fibre 7.9g; Sodium 72mg.

Pasta, bean and vegetable soup

This is a Calabrian speciality known as Millecosedde. *The name comes from the Italian word* millecose, *meaning "a thousand things". Literally anything edible can go in this soup.*

SERVES 4–6

75g/3oz/scant ½ cup brown lentils
15g/½oz dried mushrooms
60ml/4 tbsp olive oil
1 carrot, diced
1 celery stick, diced
1 onion, finely chopped
1 garlic clove, finely chopped
a little chopped fresh flat leaf parsley
a good pinch of crushed red chillies
   (optional)

1.5 litres/2½ pints/6¼ cups vegetable
   stock
150g/5oz/scant 1 cup each canned red
   kidney beans, cannellini beans and
   chickpeas, rinsed and drained
115g/4oz/1 cup dried small pasta shapes,
   such as rigatoni, penne or penne rigate
salt and ground black pepper
freshly grated Pecorino cheese, to serve
chopped flat leaf parsley, to garnish

1 Put the lentils in a medium pan, add 475ml/16fl oz/ 2 cups water and bring to the boil over a high heat. Lower the heat to a gentle simmer and cook, stirring occasionally, for 15–20 minutes or until the lentils are just tender. Meanwhile, soak the dried mushrooms in 175ml/6fl oz/ ¾ cup warm water for 15–20 minutes.

2 Put the lentils in a sieve (strainer) to drain, then rinse under the cold tap. Drain the mushrooms and reserve the soaking liquid. Finely chop the mushrooms and set aside.

3 Heat the oil in a large pan and add the carrot, celery, onion, garlic, parsley and chillies, if using. Cook over a low heat, stirring constantly, for 5–7 minutes until the vegetables are soft.

4 Add the stock, then the mushrooms and their soaking liquid. Bring to the boil, then add the beans, chickpeas and lentils. Season to taste. Cover, and simmer gently for 20 minutes. Add the pasta and bring back to the boil, stirring. Simmer for 7–8 minutes, until the pasta is *al dente*. Season, then serve hot in soup bowls, with grated Pecorino and chopped parsley.

Nutritional information per portion: Energy 668Kcal/2831kJ; Protein 41.4g; Carbohydrate 100.8g, of which sugars 7.5g; Fat 14g, of which saturates 2g; Cholesterol 0mg; Calcium 178mg; Fibre 26.1g; Sodium 44mg.

Tuscan bean soup

This Italian soup is known as Ribollita. *It is rather like minestrone, but made with beans instead of pasta, and is traditionally ladled over a rich green vegetable, such as spinach.*

SERVES 6

45ml/3 tbsp olive oil
2 onions, chopped
2 carrots, sliced
4 garlic cloves, crushed
2 celery sticks, thinly sliced
1 fennel bulb, trimmed and chopped
2 large courgettes (zucchini), thinly sliced
400g/14oz can chopped tomatoes
30ml/2 tbsp home-made or bought pesto
900ml/1½ pints/3¾ cups vegetable
   stock
400g/14oz can haricot (navy) or borlotti
   beans, drained
salt and ground black pepper

FOR THE SPINACH BASE

15ml/1 tbsp extra virgin olive oil, plus
   extra for drizzling
450g/1lb fresh young spinach
ground black pepper

1 Heat the oil in a large pan. Add the onions, carrots, garlic, celery and fennel and fry gently for about 10 minutes. Add the courgettes and fry for a further 2 minutes.

2 Stir in the tomatoes, pesto, stock and beans and bring to the boil. Lower the heat, cover and simmer gently for 25–30 minutes, until the vegetables are completely tender. Season with salt and black pepper to taste.

3 For the base, heat the oil in a frying pan and fry the spinach for about 2 minutes, or until wilted. Spoon the spinach into heated soup bowls, then ladle the soup over the spinach. Just before serving, drizzle with olive oil and sprinkle with ground black pepper.

Nutritional information per portion: Energy 197Kcal/822kJ; Protein 6.8g; Carbohydrate 20.8g, of which sugars 10.3g; Fat 10.2g, of which saturates 1.5g; Cholesterol 0mg; Calcium 93mg; Fibre 7.7g; Sodium 287mg.

Bean and pistou soup

This hearty vegetarian soup is a typical Provençal-style soup, where the beans are richly flavoured with a home-made garlic and fresh basil pistou sauce.

SERVES 4–6

150g/5oz/scant 1 cup dried haricot
   (navy) beans, soaked overnight
150g/5oz/scant 1 cup dried flageolet or
   cannellini beans, soaked overnight
1 onion, chopped
1.2 litres/2 pints/5 cups hot vegetable
   stock
2 carrots, roughly chopped
225g/8oz Savoy cabbage, shredded
1 large potato, about 225g/8oz, diced
225g/8oz French (green) beans, chopped
salt and ground black pepper
basil leaves, to garnish

FOR THE PISTOU

4 garlic cloves
8 large sprigs basil leaves
90ml/6 tbsp olive oil
60ml/4 tbsp freshly grated Parmesan
   cheese

1 Heat the oven to 200°C/400°F/Gas 6. Drain the beans and place in an ovenproof casserole. Add the onion and pour over sufficient cold water to come 5cm/2in above the beans. Cover the casserole and place in the heated oven. Cook for about 1½ hours.

2 Drain the beans and onions. Transfer half the beans and onions to a food processor or blender and process to a paste. Return the beans and paste to the casserole.

3 Add the stock, carrots, cabbage, potato and French beans. Season, cover and return the pot to the oven. Reduce the oven temperature to 180°C/350°F/Gas 4 and cook for 1 hour.

4 Meanwhile place the garlic and basil in a mortar and pound with a pestle, then gradually beat in the oil. Stir in the grated Parmesan. Stir half the pistou into the soup and then ladle into warmed soup bowls. Top each bowl of soup with a spoonful of the remaining pistou and serve garnished with basil.

Nutritional information per portion: Energy 286Kcal/1214kJ; Protein 19.8g; Carbohydrate 50.9g, of which sugars 11.1g; Fat 1.8g, of which saturates 0.3g; Cholesterol 0mg; Calcium 142mg; Fibre 16.1g; Sodium 36mg.

Potage of lentils

This traditional Jewish soup is sometimes known as Esau's soup. Red lentils and vegetables are cooked and puréed, then sharpened with lots of lemon juice.

SERVES 4

45ml/3 tbsp olive oil
1 onion, chopped
2 celery sticks, chopped
1–2 carrots, sliced
8 garlic cloves, chopped
1 potato, peeled and diced
250g/9oz/generous 1 cup red lentils,
    picked over and rinsed
1 litre/1³/₄ pints/4 cups vegetable stock
2 bay leaves
1–2 lemons, halved
2.5ml/¹/₂ tsp ground cumin, or to taste
cayenne pepper or Tabasco sauce, to taste
salt and ground black pepper
lemon slices and chopped fresh flat leaf
    parsley, to serve

1 Heat the oil in a large pan. Add the onion and cook for about 5 minutes, or until softened. Stir in the celery, carrots, half the garlic and all the potato. Cook for a few minutes until beginning to soften.

2 Add the lentils and stock to the pan and bring to the boil. Reduce the heat, cover and simmer gently for about 30 minutes until the potato and lentils are tender.

3 Add the bay leaves, remaining garlic and half the lemons to the pan and cook the soup for a further 10 minutes. Remove the bay leaves. Squeeze the juice from the remaining lemons, then stir into the soup, to taste.

4 Pour the soup into a food processor or blender and process in batches until smooth. Return the soup to the pan, stir in the cumin, cayenne pepper or Tabasco sauce, and season with salt and pepper.

5 Ladle the soup into bowls and top with lemon slices and parsley.

Nutritional information per portion: Energy 330Kcal/1391kJ; Protein 16.3g; Carbohydrate 48.1g, of which sugars 4.7g; Fat 9.4g, of which saturates 1.4g; Cholesterol 0mg; Calcium 50mg; Fibre 4.5g; Sodium 44mg.

North African spiced soup

Classically known as **Harira**, *this soup is often served in the evening during Ramadan, the Muslim religious festival when followers fast during the daytime for a month.*

SERVES 6

1 large onion, chopped
1.2 litres/2 pints/5 cups stock
5ml/1 tsp ground cinnamon
5ml/1 tsp turmeric
15ml/1 tbsp grated ginger
pinch of cayenne pepper
2 carrots, diced
2 celery sticks, diced
400g/14oz can chopped tomatoes
450g/1lb floury potatoes, diced
5 threads saffron
400g/14oz can chickpeas, drained
30ml/2 tbsp chopped fresh coriander
    (cilantro)
15ml/1 tbsp lemon juice
salt and ground black pepper
fried wedges of lemon, to serve

1 Place the chopped onion in a large pot with 300ml/¹/₂ pint/1¹/₄ cups of the vegetable stock. Bring the mixture to the boil and simmer gently for about 10 minutes.

2 Meanwhile, mix together the cinnamon, turmeric, ginger, cayenne pepper and 30ml/2 tbsp of stock to form a paste. Stir into the onion mixture with the carrots, celery and remaining stock.

3 Bring the mixture to a boil, reduce the heat, then cover and gently simmer for 5 minutes.

4 Add the tomatoes and potatoes and simmer gently, covered, for 20 minutes.

5 Add the saffron, chickpeas, coriander and lemon juice. Season to taste and when piping hot serve with fried wedges of lemon.

Nutritional information per portion: Energy 158Kcal/668kJ; Protein 7.2g; Carbohydrate 28.4g, of which sugars 7g; Fat 2.5g, of which saturates 0.4g; Cholesterol 0mg; Calcium 64mg; Fibre 5.4g; Sodium 173mg.

Red lentil soup with onion

*Crispy shallots and a parsley cream top this rich and aromatic soup, which is inspired by the
dhals of Indian cooking. Chunks of smoked bacon add texture.*

SERVES 6

5ml/1 tsp cumin seeds
2.5ml/^{1}/$_2$ tsp coriander seeds
5ml/1 tsp ground turmeric
30ml/2 tbsp olive oil
1 onion, chopped
2 garlic cloves, chopped
1 smoked bacon hock
1.2 litres/2 pints/5 cups vegetable stock
275g/10oz/1^1/$_4$ cups red lentils

400g/14oz can chopped tomatoes
15ml/1 tbsp vegetable oil
3 shallots, thinly sliced

FOR THE PARSLEY CREAM

45ml/3 tbsp chopped fresh parsley
150ml/^{1}/$_4$ pint/^{2}/$_3$ cup Greek (strained
   plain) yogurt
salt and ground black pepper

1 Heat a frying pan and add the cumin and coriander seeds.
Roast them over a high heat for a few seconds, until they
smell aromatic. Transfer to a mortar and crush using a
pestle. Mix in the turmeric. Set aside.

2 Heat the oil in a large pan. Add the onion and garlic and
cook for 4–5 minutes, until softened. Add the spice mixture
and cook for 2 minutes, stirring continuously.

3 Place the bacon in the pan and pour in the stock. Bring to the boil, cover and simmer gently for
30 minutes. Add the red lentils and cook for 20 minutes or until the lentils and bacon hock are
tender. Stir in the tomatoes and cook for a further 5 minutes.

4 Remove the bacon from the pan and set aside until cool enough to handle. Leave the soup to cool
slightly, then process in a food processor or blender until almost smooth. Return it to the rinsed-out
pan. Cut the meat from the hock, discarding skin and fat, then stir it into the soup and reheat.

5 Heat the oil in a frying pan and fry the shallots for 10 minutes until crisp and golden. Remove and
drain on kitchen paper. Stir the chopped parsley into the yogurt and season well. Ladle the soup
into bowls and add a dollop of the parsley cream. Pile some shallots on to each portion and serve.

Nutritional information per portion: Energy 235Kcal/991kJ; Protein 13g; Carbohydrate 28.4g, of which sugars 3.7g; Fat 8.8g, of which saturates 2.2g;
Cholesterol 0mg; Calcium 66mg; Fibre 2.9g; Sodium 40mg.

Pasta soup with meatballs and basil

This rustic pasta soup is thickened with puréed cannellini beans. Home-made meatballs flavoured with orange and garlic are added to the soup to make a satisfying Italian classic.

SERVES 4

400g/14oz can cannellini beans
1 litre/1¾ pints/4 cups vegetable stock
45ml/3 tbsp olive oil
1 onion, finely chopped
2 garlic cloves, chopped
1 small red chilli, seeded and chopped
2 celery sticks, finely chopped
1 carrot, finely chopped
15ml/1 tbsp tomato purée (paste)
300g/11oz small pasta shapes
large handful of fresh basil, torn
salt and ground black pepper
basil leaves, to garnish
freshly grated Parmesan cheese, to serve

FOR THE MEATBALLS
1 thick slice white bread, crusts removed
    and broken into small pieces
60ml/4 tbsp milk
350g/12oz lean minced (ground) beef
    or veal
30ml/2 tbsp chopped fresh parsley
grated rind of 1 orange
2 garlic cloves, crushed
1 egg, beaten
30ml/2 tbsp olive oil

1 To prepare the meatballs, place the bread in a bowl with the milk and leave to soak for 10 minutes. Add the meat, parsley, orange rind and garlic, and season. Mix well then add enough egg to bind the mixture. Shape the mixture into balls about the size of a large olive. Heat the oil in a frying pan and fry the meatballs in batches for 6–8 minutes until browned all over. Remove them from the pan, and set them aside.

2 Purée the drained and rinsed cannellini beans with a little of the stock in a food processor or blender until smooth. Set aside.

3 Heat the olive oil in a large pan. Add the onion and garlic, chilli, celery and carrot, and cook for 4–5 minutes. Cover and cook gently for a further 5 minutes. Stir in the tomato purée, the bean purée and the remaining vegetable stock. Bring the soup to the boil and cook for about 10 minutes.

4 Add the pasta shapes and simmer for 8–10 minutes, until the pasta is tender. Add the meatballs and basil and cook for a further 5 minutes. Season and serve garnished with basil and Parmesan cheese.

Nutritional information per portion: Energy 718Kcal/3014kJ; Protein 35g; Carbohydrate 80.9g, of which sugars 10g; Fat 30.5g, of which saturates 8.5g; Cholesterol 53mg; Calcium 152mg; Fibre 9.7g; Sodium 529mg.

Black-eyed bean and tomato broth

This delicious soup – known as Lubiya *in Israel – is flavoured with tangy lemon and speckled with chopped fresh coriander. It is ideal for serving at parties. Multiply the quantities as required.*

SERVES 4

175g/6oz/1 cup black-eyed beans (peas)
15ml/1 tbsp olive oil
2 onions, chopped
4 garlic cloves, chopped
1 medium-hot or 2–3 mild fresh chillies, chopped
5ml/1 tsp ground cumin
5ml/1 tsp ground turmeric
250g/9oz fresh or canned tomatoes, diced
600ml/1 pint/2½ cups chicken, beef or vegetable stock
25g/1oz fresh coriander (cilantro) leaves, roughly chopped
juice of ½ lemon
pitta bread, to serve

1 Put the beans in a pan, cover with cold water, bring to the boil and cook for 5 minutes.

2 Remove from the heat, cover and leave to stand for 2 hours.

3 Drain the beans, return to the pan, cover with fresh cold water, then simmer for 35–40 minutes, or until the beans are tender. Drain and set aside.

4 Heat the oil in a pan, add the onions, garlic and chilli and cook for 5 minutes, or until the onion is soft.

5 Stir in the cumin, turmeric, tomatoes, stock, half the coriander and the beans and simmer for 20–30 minutes.

6 Stir in the lemon juice and remaining coriander and serve at once with pitta bread.

Nutritional information per portion: Energy 168Kcal/712kJ; Protein 10.7g; Carbohydrate 25g, of which sugars 2.3g; Fat 3.6g, of which saturates 0.6g; Cholesterol 0mg; Calcium 52mg; Fibre 4.1g; Sodium 10mg.

Old-fashioned chicken noodle soup

This is a really traditional soup – clear, golden and warming, and filled with lightly cooked pasta. It is guaranteed to make you feel better whenever you have a cold.

SERVES 4–6

2kg/4¹/₂lb boiling fowl (stewing chicken) with the giblets (except the liver)
1 large onion, peeled and halved
2 large carrots, halved lengthways
6 celery sticks, roughly chopped
1 bay leaf
175g/6oz vermicelli pasta
45ml/3 tbsp chopped fresh parsley or whole parsley leaves
salt and ground black pepper

1 Put the chicken into a pan with the vegetables and the bay leaf. Cover with 2.4 litres/4 pints/10 cups cold water. Bring slowly to the boil and skim off any scum. Add 5ml/1 tsp salt and some ground black pepper.

2 Turn down the heat and simmer for at least 2 hours, or until the fowl is tender. Do not allow the soup to boil or it will become cloudy.

3 When tender, remove the bird from the broth and strip the flesh off the carcass. (Use the meat in sandwiches or a risotto.) Return the bones to the soup and simmer for another hour.

4 Strain the soup into a bowl, cool, then chill overnight. The soup will set to a solid jelly with a layer of solidified chicken fat. Remove the fat.

5 Reheat the soup in a large pan. Add the vermicelli and parsley. Simmer for 6–8 minutes until the pasta is cooked. Taste and season.

Nutritional information per portion: Energy 176Kcal/748kJ; Protein 6.3g; Carbohydrate 37.5g, of which sugars 5.7g; Fat 1.2g, of which saturates 0.1g; Cholesterol 0mg; Calcium 66mg; Fibre 3.4g; Sodium 39mg.

Crab soup with coriander relish

Prepared fresh crab is readily available, high quality and convenient, which makes it perfect for creating an exotic seafood and noodle soup in minutes.

SERVES 4

45ml/3 tbsp olive oil

1 red onion, finely chopped

2 red chillies, seeded and finely chopped

1 garlic clove, finely chopped

450g/1lb fresh white crab meat

30ml/2 tbsp each chopped fresh parsley
   and coriander (cilantro)

juice of 2 lemons

1 lemon grass stalk

1 litre/1¾ pints/4 cups good fish or
   chicken stock

15ml/1 tbsp Thai fish sauce (nam pla)

150g/5oz vermicelli or angel hair pasta,
   broken into 5–7.5cm/ 2–3in lengths

salt and ground black pepper

FOR THE CORIANDER RELISH

2.5ml/½ tsp ground roasted cumin seeds

50g/2oz/1 cup coriander (cilantro) leaves

1 green chilli, seeded and chopped

15ml/1 tbsp sunflower oil

25ml/1½ tbsp lemon juice

1 Heat the oil in a pan and add the onion, chillies and garlic. Cook over a gentle heat for 10 minutes until the onion is very soft. Transfer to a bowl Stir in the crab meat, parsley, coriander and lemon juice. Set aside.

2 Lay the lemon grass on a chopping board and bruise it with a rolling pin or pestle. Pour the stock and fish sauce into a pan. Add the lemon grass and bring to the boil, then add the pasta. Simmer, uncovered, for 3–4 minutes.

3 Meanwhile, make the relish. Using a mortar and pestle, make a coarse paste with the cumin, fresh coriander, chilli, oil, and lemon juice.

4 Remove and discard the lemon grass. Stir the chilli and crab mixture into the soup and season it well. Bring to the boil, then reduce the heat and simmer for 2 minutes.

5 Ladle the soup into bowls and put a spoonful of the coriander relish in the centre of each. Serve at once.

Nutritional information per portion: Energy 425Kcal/1773kJ; Protein 26.7g; Carbohydrate 50.7g, of which sugars 1.4g; Fat 12.6g, of which saturates 1.6g; Cholesterol 81mg; Calcium 198mg; Fibre 1.3g; Sodium 632mg.

Malaysian prawn laksa

This spicy prawn and noodle soup tastes just as good when made with fresh crab meat or any flaked cooked fish instead of the prawns. If you are short of time, buy ready-made laksa paste.

SERVES 2–3

115g/4oz rice vermicelli
15ml/1 tbsp vegetable oil
600ml/1 pint/2¹/₂ cups fish stock
400ml/14fl oz/1²/₃ cups coconut milk
30ml/2 tbsp Thai fish sauce (nam pla)
¹/₂ lime
16–24 cooked peeled prawns (shrimp)
pinch of salt and cayenne pepper, to taste
60ml/4 tbsp fresh coriander (cilantro)
   sprigs and leaves, chopped, to garnish

FOR THE SPICY PASTE
2 lemon grass stalks, finely chopped
2 fresh red chillies, seeded and chopped
2.5cm/1in piece fresh root ginger, peeled
   and sliced
2.5ml/¹/₂ tsp shrimp paste
2 garlic cloves, chopped
2.5ml/¹/₂ tsp ground turmeric
30ml/2 tbsp tamarind paste

1 Cook the rice vermicelli in a large pan of boiling salted water for 3–4 minutes, or according to the instructions on the packet. Transfer the noodles to a large sieve (strainer), then rinse under cold water and drain. Set aside.

2 To make the spicy paste, place all the ingredients in a mortar and pound with a pestle. Alternatively, put in a food processor or blender until a smooth paste is formed.

3 Heat the vegetable oil in a large saucepan, add the spicy paste and fry, stirring constantly, for a few moments to release all the flavours. Be careful not to let it burn.

4 Add the fish stock and coconut milk and bring to the boil. Stir in the fish sauce, then simmer gently for 5 minutes. Season with salt and cayenne to taste, adding a squeeze of lime. Add the prawns and heat through for a few seconds.

5 Divide the noodles among two or three soup plates. Pour over the soup. Garnish with fresh coriander and serve piping hot.

Nutritional information per portion: Energy 436Kcal/1830kJ; Protein 36.9g; Carbohydrate 55.3g, of which sugars 10.2g; Fat 7.6g, of which saturates 1.2g; Cholesterol 341mg; Calcium 239mg; Fibre 0.8g; Sodium 562mg.

Thai cellophane noodle soup

The Thai noodles used in this soup have a variety of interesting names including glass noodles, cellophane noodles, bean thread or transparent noodles. They are made from mung bean flour, and are especially valued for their brittle texture.

SERVES 4

4 large dried shiitake mushrooms

15g/½oz dried lily buds

½ cucumber, coarsely chopped

2 garlic cloves, halved

90g/3½oz white cabbage, chopped

1.2 litres/2 pints/5 cups boiling water

115g/4oz cellophane noodles

30ml/2 tbsp soy sauce

15ml/1 tbsp palm sugar (jaggery) or light
  muscovado (brown) sugar

90g/3½oz block silken tofu, diced

fresh coriander (cilantro), to garnish

1 Soak the shiitake mushrooms and dried lily buds in two separate bowls of warm water for 30 minutes.

2 Meanwhile, put the chopped cucumber, garlic and cabbage in a food processor or blender and process to a smooth paste. Scrape the mixture into a large pan and add the measured boiling water.

3 Bring to the boil, then reduce the heat and cook for 2 minutes, stirring the mixture occasionally. Strain this warm stock into another pan, return to a low heat and gently bring to simmering point.

4 Drain the soaked lily buds, rinse under cold running water, then drain again. Cut off any hard ends. Add the lily buds to the stock with the noodles, soy sauce and sugar and cook for 5 minutes more.

5 Strain the liquid from the soaked mushrooms into the soup. Discard the mushroom stems, then slice the caps. Divide them and the tofu among four bowls. Pour the soup over, garnish with fresh coriander leaves and serve.

Nutritional information per portion: Energy 143Kcal/598kJ; Protein 4.9g; Carbohydrate 28.3g, of which sugars 5.6g; Fat 1.1g, of which saturates 0.1g; Cholesterol 0mg; Calcium 137mg; Fibre 0.6g; Sodium 362mg.

Thai chicken noodle soup with crab cakes

This soup is a meal in itself. Look for stores that sell bunches of coriander with the roots still attached, as they add excellent flavour to the stock.

SERVES 6

8 garlic cloves
bunch of coriander (cilantro), with roots
1.2–1.4kg/2¹/₂–3lb chicken
2 star anise
2 carrots, chopped
2 celery sticks, chopped
1 onion, chopped
30ml/2 tbsp soy sauce
150g/5oz egg noodles
30ml/2 tbsp vegetable oil
60ml/4 tbsp Thai fish sauce (nam pla)
1.5ml/¹/₄ tsp chilli powder
150g/5oz/1¹/₂ cups beansprouts
2 spring onions (scallions), sliced

fresh coriander (cilantro)
herb sprigs, to garnish
salt and ground black pepper

FOR THE CRAB CAKES

5ml/1 tsp Thai red curry paste
5ml/1 tsp cornflour (cornstarch)
5ml/1 tsp Thai fish sauce (nam pla)
1 small egg yolk
15ml/1 tbsp chopped fresh
   coriander (cilantro)
175g/6oz white crab meat
50g/2oz/1 cup fresh white breadcrumbs
30ml/2 tbsp vegetable oil

1 Chop four garlic cloves, thinly slice the remainder and set aside. Cut the roots off the coriander stems and place in a large pan with the garlic. Pick the coriander leaves off the stems.

2 Put the chicken in the pan and add the star anise, carrots, celery, onion and soy sauce. Pour in enough water to cover the chicken. Bring to the boil, reduce the heat, cover and simmer for 1 hour.

3 For the crab cakes, combine the curry paste, cornflour, fish sauce and egg yolk. Mix in the coriander, crab meat, breadcrumbs and seasoning. Divide the mixture into 12 portions and form into small cakes.

4 Cook the noodles according to the packet instructions. Drain and set aside.

5 Heat the oil in a pan and fry the sliced garlic until golden. Drain and set aside.

6 Remove the chicken and cool slightly. (Reserve the stock.) Discard the chicken skin, take the meat off the bones and tear it into large strips. Strain the stock and pour 1.2 litres/2 pints/5 cups into a pan. Stir in the fish sauce, chilli and seasoning, then bring to the boil. Keep hot.

7 To cook the crab cakes, heat the vegetable oil in a frying pan and fry the crab cakes for 2–3 minutes on each side until golden.

8 Divide the noodles, garlic slices, beansprouts, spring onions and chicken among six shallow soup bowls. Arrange two crab cakes on top, then ladle over the broth. Scatter coriander over the top and garnish with herbs.

Nutritional information per portion: Energy 250Kcal/1049kJ; Protein 10.9g; Carbohydrate 28.8g, of which sugars 3.5g; Fat 10.9g, of which saturates 1.8g; Cholesterol 62mg; Calcium 74mg; Fibre 1.9g; Sodium 638mg.

Tokyo-style ramen noodles in soup

Ramen noodles originated in China but are now popular in Japan, where ramen shops abound. Most counties have a version of the noodles and the soup; this is a legendary Tokyo version.

SERVES 4

250g/9oz dried ramen noodles

FOR THE SOUP STOCK
4 spring onions (scallions)
7.5cm/3in fresh root ginger, quartered
raw bones from 2 chickens, washed
1 large onion, quartered
4 garlic cloves, peeled
1 large carrot, roughly chopped
1 egg shell
120ml/4fl oz/$^1/_2$ cup sake
about 60ml/4 tbsp Japanese soy sauce
    (shoyu)
2.5ml/$^1/_2$ tsp salt

FOR THE *CHA-SHU* (POT-ROAST PORK)
500g/1$^1/_4$lb pork shoulder, boned
30ml/2 tbsp vegetable oil
2 spring onions (scallions), chopped
2.5cm/1in piece fresh root ginger, peeled
    and sliced
15ml/1 tbsp sake
45ml/3 tbsp Japanese soy sauce
15ml/1 tbsp caster (superfine) sugar

FOR THE TOPPINGS
2 hard-boiled eggs
$^1/_2$ nori sheet, broken into pieces
2 spring onions (scallions), chopped
ground white pepper
sesame oil or chilli oil

1 To make the soup stock, bruise the spring onions and ginger by hitting with the side of a large knife. Pour 1.5 litres/2$^1/_2$ pints/6$^1/_4$ cups water into a wok and bring to the boil. Add the chicken bones and boil until the meat changes colour. Discard the water and wash the bones.

2 Wash the wok, bring 2 litres/3$^1/_2$ pints/9 cups water to the boil and add the bones and other stock ingredients, except the soy sauce and salt. Reduce the heat to low, and simmer until the water has reduced by half, skimming off any scum. Strain into a bowl through a sieve (strainer) lined with muslin (cheesecloth). This will take 1–2 hours.

3 Make the *cha-shu*. Roll the meat up tightly, 8cm/3$^1/_2$in in diameter, and tie it with kitchen string.

4 Wash the wok and dry over a high heat. Heat the oil to smoking point in the wok. Add the spring onions and ginger. Cook briefly, then add the meat. Turn often to brown the outside evenly. Sprinkle with sake and add 400ml/14fl oz/1$^2/_3$ cups water, the soy sauce and sugar. Boil, then reduce the heat to low and cover. Cook for 25–30 minutes, turning every 5 minutes. Remove from the heat.

5 Slice the pork into 12 fine slices. Use any leftover pork for another recipe. Shell and halve the boiled eggs, and sprinkle some salt on to the yolks.

6 Pour 1 litre/1¾ pints/4 cups soup stock from the bowl into a large pan. Boil and add the soy sauce and salt. Check the seasoning and add more sauce if required.

7 Wash the wok again and bring 2 litres/3½ pints/9 cups water to the boil. Cook the ramen noodles according to the packet instructions until just soft. Stir constantly to prevent sticking. If the water bubbles up, pour in 50ml/2fl oz/¼ cup cold water. Drain well and divide among four bowls.

8 Pour the soup over the noodles to cover. Arrange half a boiled egg, pork slices, nori on top, and sprinkle with spring onions. Serve with pepper and sesame or chilli oil. Season with salt.

Nutritional information per portion: Energy 466Kcal/1947kJ; Protein 35.1g; Carbohydrate 49.9g, of which sugars 0.9g; Fat 13.9g, of which saturates 3.2g; Cholesterol 175mg; Calcium 43mg; Fibre 0.3g; Sodium 489mg.

Soba noodles in hot soup with tempura

This soup uses classic Japanese soba noodles, which are made from buckwheat. Shichimi togarashi or seven-spice powder is often used as a flavouring for this type of soup.

SERVES 4

400g/14oz dried soba noodles
1 spring onion (scallion), sliced
shichimi togarashi (optional)

FOR THE SOUP
150ml/1/4 pint/2/3 cup mirin (sweet
   rice wine)
150ml/1/4 pint/2/3 cup shoyu (soy sauce)
900ml/11/2 pints/33/4 cups water
25g/1oz kezuri-bushi (dried fish flakes) or
   2 x 15g/1/2oz packets
15ml/1 tbsp caster (superfine) sugar
5ml/1 tsp salt

900ml/11/2 pints/33/4 cups first dashi
   stock (fish stock) or the same amount
   of water and 12.5ml/21/2 tsp dashi-
   no-moto (freeze-dried stock granules)

FOR THE TEMPURA
16 raw king prawns (jumbo shrimp),
   heads and shells removed, tails intact
400ml/14fl oz/12/3 cups ice-cold water
1 large (US extra large) egg, beaten
200g/7oz/scant 2 cups plain (all-
   purpose) flour
vegetable oil, for deep-frying

1 To make the soup, put the mirin in a large pan. Bring to the boil, then add the rest of the soup ingredients apart from the dashi stock. Bring back to the boil, then reduce the heat to low. Skim off the scum and cook for 2 minutes. Strain the soup into a clean pan with the dashi stock.

2 Remove the vein from each prawn, then make five cuts into each prawn's belly. Clip the tip of the tail with scissors and squeeze out any moisture.

3 Pour the water into a bowl and mix in the egg. Sift in the flour and stir briefly. It should remain lumpy. Heat the oil in a wok or deep-fryer to 180°C/350°F. Hold the tails of two prawns, dunk them in the batter, then plunge them into the oil. Deep-fry until crisp and golden. Drain and keep warm.

4 Put the noodles in a large pan with at least 2 litres/31/2 pints/9 cups boiling water, and stir to stop them sticking. When the water foams, add 50ml/2fl oz/1/4 cup water. Repeat when the water foams again. The noodles should be softer than *al dente* pasta. Rinse the noodles in a sieve (strainer).

5 Heat the soup. Warm the noodles with hot water, and divide among bowls. Add the prawns and soup. Sprinkle with spring onion and shichimi togarashi, if you like. Serve.

Nutritional information per portion: Energy 728Kcal/3053kJ; Protein 30.7g; Carbohydrate 121.8g, of which sugars 5.3g; Fat 14g, of which saturates 1.9g; Cholesterol 218mg; Calcium 173mg; Fibre 1.6g; Sodium 728mg.

Pot-cooked udon in miso soup

Udon is a white wheat noodle eaten with various hot and cold soups. In this Japanese dish, known as Miso Nikomi Udon, *the noodles are cooked in a clay pot with a rich miso soup.*

SERVES 4

200g/7oz chicken breast portion, boned and skinned

10ml/2 tsp sake

2 abura-age (fried tofu)

900ml/1¹/₂ pints/3³/₄ cups second dashi stock, or the same amount of water and 7.5ml/1¹/₂ tsp dashi-no-moto

6 large fresh shiitake mushrooms, stalks removed, quartered

4 spring onions (scallions), trimmed and chopped into 3mm/¹/₈in lengths

30ml/2 tbsp mirin (sweet rice wine)

about 90g/3¹/₂oz aka miso or hatcho miso (dark brown soybean paste)

300g/11oz dried udon noodles (thick wheat noodles)

4 eggs

shichimi togarashi (optional)

1 Cut the chicken into bitesize pieces. Sprinkle with sake and leave to marinate for 15 minutes.

2 Put the abura-age in a sieve (strainer) and thoroughly rinse with hot water. Drain on kitchen paper and cut each abura-age into 4 squares.

3 For the soup, heat the second dashi stock in a pan. When it has come to the boil, add the chicken, shiitake mushrooms and abura-age and cook for 5 minutes. Remove from the heat and add the spring onions. Put the mirin and miso paste into a bowl. Scoop 30ml/2 tbsp soup from the pan and mix in.

4 To cook the udon, boil at least 2 litres/3¹/₂ pints/9 cups water in a large pan. The water should not come higher than two-thirds of the depth of the pan. Cook the udon for 6 minutes and drain.

5 Divide the udon among four small flameproof dishes. Mix the miso paste into the soup and check the taste. Add more miso if required. Ladle in enough soup to each dish to cover the udon, and arrange the soup ingredients on top of the udon. Heat each flameproof dish over a medium heat and break an egg on top of each. When the soup bubbles, wait for 1 minute, then cover and remove from the heat. Leave to stand for 2 minutes. Serve with shichimi togarashi, if you like.

Nutritional information per portion: Energy 431Kcal/1819kJ; Protein 28.6g; Carbohydrate 54.7g, of which sugars 2.2g; Fat 12.6g, of which saturates 3.5g; Cholesterol 248mg; Calcium 60mg; Fibre 2.9g; Sodium 594mg.

Fish and shellfish soups

Traditional hearty dishes such as

Bouillabaisse or Provençal Seafood Soup

are ideal for a substantial lunch or supper.

If you want a more sophisticated soup for

entertaining, Salmon Soup with Salsa and

Rouille is the perfect choice. To ring the

changes, try Thai Fish Broth, with its

delicious flavourings of lemon grass,

galangal and lime leaves.

Fisherman's soup

This chunky French soup is traditionally made from freshwater fish, including eel. Any firm fish can be used, such as monkfish and haddock, and a robust dry white or red wine adds extra flavour.

SERVES 6

1kg/2¼ lb mixed fish, including 450g/1lb
    conger eel if possible
50g/2oz/¼ cup butter
1 onion, thickly sliced
2 celery sticks, thickly sliced
2 carrots, thickly sliced
1 bottle dry white or red wine
1 fresh bouquet garni containing parsley,
    bay leaf and chervil
2 cloves
6 black peppercorns
beurre manié for thickening
salt and cayenne pepper

FOR THE GARNISH
25g/1oz/2 tbsp butter
12 baby onions, peeled
12 button (white) mushrooms
chopped flat leaf parsley

1 Cut all the fish into thick slices, removing any bones. Melt the butter in a large pan, add the fish and vegetables and stir over a medium heat until lightly browned.

2 Pour in the wine and cold water to cover. Add the bouquet garni and spices and season. Bring to the boil, then simmer for 20–30 minutes.

3 For the garnish, heat the butter in a frying pan and sauté the onions until golden and tender. Add the mushrooms and fry until golden.

4 Strain the soup through a large sieve (strainer) into a clean pan. Discard the herbs and spices in the sieve, then divide the fish among six deep soup plates (you can skin the fish if you wish) and keep hot.

5 Reheat the soup until it boils. Lower the heat and whisk in the *beurre manié* little by little until the soup thickens. Season and pour some soup over the fish in each bowl. Garnish each with fried baby onions and mushrooms and sprinkle with chopped parsley.

Nutritional information per portion: Energy 323Kcal/1346kJ; Protein 31.4g; Carbohydrate 2.3g, of which sugars 1.9g; Fat 11.6g, of which saturates 6.7g; Cholesterol 103mg; Calcium 35mg; Fibre 0.8g; Sodium 192mg.

Bouillabaisse

Authentic bouillabaisse comes from the south of France and includes rascasse (scorpion fish) as a characteristic ingredient. It is, however, perfectly possible to make this soup with other fish.

SERVES 4

45ml/3 tbsp olive oil

2 onions, chopped

2 leeks, white parts only, cleaned and
   chopped

4 garlic cloves, chopped

450g/1lb ripe tomatoes, peeled and
   chopped

3 litres/5 pints/12 cups boiling fish stock
   or water

15ml/1 tbsp tomato purée (paste)

large pinch of saffron threads

1 fresh bouquet garni, containing 2 thyme
   sprigs, 2 bay leaves and 2 fennel sprigs

3kg/6$\frac{1}{2}$ lb white fish, cleaned and cut
   into large chunks

4 potatoes, peeled and thickly sliced

salt, pepper and cayenne pepper

rouille and aioli, to serve

FOR THE GARNISH

16 slices of French bread, toasted and
   rubbed with garlic

30ml/2 tbsp chopped parsley

1 Heat the oil in a large pan. Add the onions, leeks, garlic and tomatoes. Cook until softened.

2 Stir in the stock or water, tomato purée and saffron. Add the bouquet garni and boil until the oil is amalgamated.

3 Lower the heat, add the fish and potatoes. Simmer the soup for 5–8 minutes, removing each type of fish when cooked. Continue to cook until the potatoes are tender. Season with salt, pepper and cayenne.

4 Divide the fish and potatoes among individual soup plates. Strain the soup and ladle it over the fish. Garnish with toasted French bread and parsley, and serve with rouille and aioli.

Nutritional information per portion: Energy 888Kcal/3748kJ; Protein 105.5g; Carbohydrate 88g, of which sugars 14g; Fat 14.8g, of which saturates 2.3g; Cholesterol 230mg; Calcium 217mg; Fibre 7.3g; Sodium 953mg.

Thai fish broth

*Lemon grass, chillies, coriander, lime and galangal are among the
flavourings used in this delicious and fragrant soup.*

SERVES 2–3

1 litre/1³⁄₄ pints/4 cups fish or light
   chicken stock
4 lemon grass stalks
3 limes
2 small fresh hot red chillies, seeded and
   thinly sliced
2cm/³⁄₄in piece fresh galangal, peeled
   and thinly sliced
6 coriander (cilantro) stalks and leaves

2 kaffir lime leaves, coarsely chopped
   (optional)
350g/12oz monkfish fillet, skinned and
   cut into 2.5cm/1in pieces
15ml/1 tbsp rice vinegar
45ml/3 tbsp Thai fish sauce (nam pla)
30ml/2 tbsp chopped coriander leaves,
   to garnish

1 Pour the stock into a large pan and bring it to the boil. Meanwhile, slice the
bulb end of each lemon grass stalk diagonally into pieces about 3mm/¹⁄₈in
thick. Peel off four wide strips of lime rind with a potato peeler, taking care to
avoid the white pith underneath which would make the soup bitter. Squeeze
the limes and reserve the juice.

2 Add the sliced lemon grass, lime rind, chillies, galangal and coriander stalks
to the stock, with the kaffir lime leaves, if using. Simmer for 1–2 minutes.

3 Add the monkfish, rice vinegar and fish sauce, with half the reserved lime
juice. Simmer for about 3 minutes, until the fish is just cooked. Lift out and
discard the coriander stalks, taste the broth and add more lime juice if
necessary; the soup should taste quite sour. Sprinkle with the coriander
leaves and serve very hot.

VARIATIONS
*Prawns (shrimp), scallops, squid or sole can be substituted for the monkfish. If you use
kaffir lime leaves, you will need the juice of only 2 limes.*

Nutritional information per portion: Energy 124Kcal/529kJ; Protein 28.3g; Carbohydrate 0.7g, of which sugars 0.6g; Fat
1g, of which saturates 0.2g; Cholesterol 25mg; Calcium 64mg; Fibre 1.3g; Sodium 40mg.

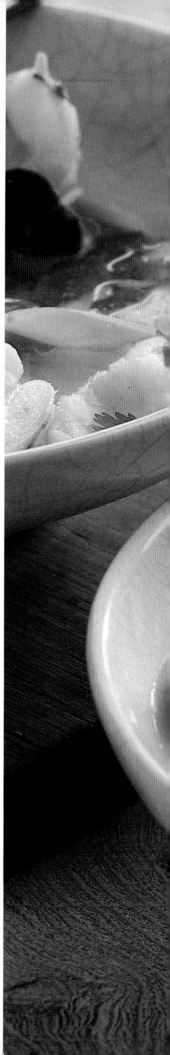

Fish soup with tomatoes and mushrooms

With some fresh crusty home-made brown bread or garlic bread, this quick and easy soup can be served like a stew and will make a delicious first course or supper.

SERVES 6

25g/1oz/2 tbsp butter
1 onion, finely chopped
1 garlic clove, crushed
1 small red (bell) pepper, chopped
salt and ground black pepper
2.5ml/½ tsp sugar
a dash of Tabasco sauce
25g/1oz/¼ cup plain (all-purpose) flour
600ml/1 pint/2½ cups fish stock
400g/14oz can chopped tomatoes
115g/4oz/1½ cups mushrooms, chopped
about 300ml/½ pint/1¼ cups milk
225g/8oz white fish, cut into cubes
115g/4oz smoked haddock or cod,
    skinned, and cut into bitesize cubes
12–18 mussels, cleaned (optional)
chopped fresh parsley, to garnish

1 Melt the butter in a large pan and cook the onion and garlic gently until soft but not browned. Add the chopped red pepper.

2 Season with salt and pepper, the sugar and Tabasco sauce. Sprinkle the flour over and cook gently for 2 minutes, stirring.

3 Stir in the stock and add the canned tomatoes and mushrooms.

4 Bring to the boil over a medium heat, stir, then reduce the heat and simmer until the vegetables are soft.

5 Add the milk to the pan and bring back to the boil. Add the fish and simmer for 3 minutes.

6 Add the mussels, if using, and cook for another 3–4 minutes, or until the fish is just tender but not breaking up. Discard any mussels that remain closed. Adjust the consistency with a little extra fish stock or milk, if necessary. Check the seasoning and adjust if needed.

7 Ladle the soup into six warmed bowls and serve piping hot, garnished with parsley.

Nutritional information per portion: Energy 132Kcal/556kJ; Protein 15.6g; Carbohydrate 8g, of which sugars 4.5g; Fat 4.4g, of which saturates 2.4g; Cholesterol 40mg; Calcium 29mg; Fibre 1.6g; Sodium 341mg.

Fish soup with rouille

Quick and simple to prepare, this soup is delicious, particularly with the addition of rouille. This garlicky mayonnaise sauce is the traditional accompaniment to French fish soup.

SERVES 6

1kg/2¼ lb mixed fish
30ml/2 tbsp olive oil
1 onion, chopped
1 carrot, chopped
1 leek, chopped
2 large ripe tomatoes, chopped
1 red (bell) pepper, seeded and chopped
2 garlic cloves, peeled
150g/5oz/²/₃ cup tomato purée (paste)
1 large fresh bouquet garni
300ml/½ pint/1¼ cups dry white wine
salt and ground black pepper

FOR THE ROUILLE

2 garlic cloves, roughly chopped
5ml/1 tsp coarse salt
1 thick slice of white bread, crust
    removed, soaked in water and
    squeezed dry
1 fresh red chilli, seeded and chopped
45ml/3 tbsp olive oil
salt and cayenne pepper

FOR THE GARNISH

12 slices of baguette, toasted in the oven
50g/2oz Gruyère cheese, finely grated

1 Cut the fish into 7.5cm/3in chunks, removing any bones. Heat the oil in a large pan, then add the fish and vegetables. Stir until these begin to colour.

2 Add all the other soup ingredients, with cold water to cover. Season and bring to just below boiling point, then lower the heat to a simmer, cover and cook for 1 hour.

3 Make the rouille. Put the garlic and salt in a mortar and crush to a paste with a pestle. Add the bread and chilli and pound until smooth. Whisk in the olive oil, drop by drop.

4 Season the sauce with salt and add a pinch of cayenne if you like a fiery taste. Set the rouille aside.

5 Lift out and discard the bouquet garni. Purée the soup in batches in a food processor or blender, then strain through a fine sieve (strainer) placed over a clean pan.

6 Reheat the soup gently. Check the seasoning and adjust if necessary, then ladle into bowls. Top each serving with two slices of toasted baguette, a spoonful of the rouille and some grated Gruyère. Serve the soup immediately.

Nutritional information per portion: Energy 518Kcal/2179kJ; Protein 41.5g; Carbohydrate 49g, of which sugars 10.8g; Fat 14.9g, of which saturates 3.6g; Cholesterol 85mg; Calcium 193mg; Fibre 4.3g; Sodium 665mg.

Salmon soup with salsa and rouille

This smart fish soup is the perfect choice for summer entertaining. To lower the fat content, use half-fat cream and reduce the amount of olive oil. Dill or fennel can be used instead of sorrel.

SERVES 4

90ml/6 tbsp olive oil
1 onion, chopped
1 leek, chopped
1 celery stick, chopped
1 fennel bulb, roughly chopped
1 red (bell) pepper, seeded and sliced
3 garlic cloves, chopped
grated rind and juice of 2 oranges
1 bay leaf
400g/14oz can chopped tomatoes
1.2 litres/2 pints/5 cups fish stock
pinch of cayenne pepper
800g/1¾lb salmon fillet, skinned
300ml/½ pint/1¼ cups double
   (heavy) cream

salt and ground black pepper
4 thin slices baguette, to serve

FOR THE RUBY SALSA
2 tomatoes, peeled, seeded and diced
½ small red onion, very finely chopped
15ml/1 tbsp cod's roe
15ml/1 tbsp chopped fresh sorrel

FOR THE ROUILLE
120ml/4fl oz/½ cup mayonnaise
1 garlic clove, crushed
5ml/1 tsp sun-dried tomato purée (paste)

1 Heat the oil in a pan and add the onion, leek, celery, fennel, pepper and garlic. Cover and cook for 20 minutes or until the vegetables have softened. Add the orange rind and juice, bay leaf and tomatoes. Cover and cook for 4–5 minutes. Add the stock and cayenne, cover and simmer for 30 minutes.

2 Add the salmon and cook gently for 8–10 minutes, until just cooked. Using a slotted spoon, remove the salmon and place it on a plate. Flake the salmon into large pieces, and remove any stray bones, then set aside.

3 To make the salsa, combine all of the ingredients.

4 To make the rouille, combine all of the ingredients. Let the soup cool slightly, then discard the bay leaf. Purée the soup in a food processor or blender until smooth, then strain it into the rinsed pan. Stir in the cream and season, then add the salmon. Toast the baguette slices on both sides. Reheat the soup. Add some rouille and salsa to each baguette. Ladle the soup into bowls and top with the baguette.

Nutritional information per portion: Energy 1153Kcal/4772kJ; Protein 44.9g; Carbohydrate 13.7g, of which sugars 12.5g; Fat 102.5g, of which saturates 34.9g; Cholesterol 225mg; Calcium 127mg; Fibre 4.7g; Sodium 268mg.

Soup niçoise with seared tuna

Ingredients for the famous salad from Nice in the South of France are transformed into a simple yet elegant soup by adding a hot garlic-infused stock.

SERVES 4

12 bottled anchovy fillets, drained
30ml/2 tbsp milk
115g/4oz French beans, halved
4 plum tomatoes
16 black olives, stoned (pitted) and
    quartered
1 litre/1¾ pints/4 cups vegetable stock
3 garlic cloves, crushed
30ml/2 tbsp lemon juice
15ml/1 tbsp olive oil
4 tuna steaks, about 75g/3oz each
small bunch of spring onions (scallions),
    shredded lengthways
handful of fresh basil leaves, finely
    shredded
salt and ground black pepper
fresh crusty bread, to serve

1 Soak the anchovies in the milk for 10 minutes. Drain and pat dry.

2 Cook the beans for 2–3 minutes. Drain, refresh under cold water and drain. Split thick beans diagonally lengthways. Peel, halve and seed the tomatoes, then cut into wedges. Set aside.

3 Bring the stock to the boil in a large pan. Add the garlic, reduce the heat and simmer for 10 minutes. Season and add the lemon juice.

4 Meanwhile, brush a griddle or frying pan with the oil and heat until very hot. Season the tuna and cook for 2 minutes on each side.

5 Gently toss together the French beans, tomatoes, spring onions, anchovies, olives and basil.

6 Put the tuna steaks into bowls and pile the vegetable mixture on top. Carefully ladle the stock around the ingredients. Serve at once, with crusty bread.

Nutritional information per portion: Energy 217Kcal/909kJ; Protein 27.4g; Carbohydrate 3g, of which sugars 2.7g; Fat 10.7g, of which saturates 2.2g; Cholesterol 34mg; Calcium 76mg; Fibre 2g; Sodium 829mg.

Red mullet and fennel soup

This delicious fish soup from Provence in France is made with fresh mayonnaise. The secret of success is to cook the soup gently so that the mayonnaise does not curdle.

SERVES 4

25ml/1½ tbsp olive oil

1 onion, chopped

3 garlic cloves, chopped

2 fennel bulbs, halved, cored and
    thinly sliced

4 tomatoes, chopped

1 bay leaf

1 fresh thyme sprig

1.2 litres/2 pints/5 cups fish stock

675g/1½lb red mullet or snapper,
    gutted, scaled and filleted

8 slices baguette

1 garlic clove

30ml/2 tbsp sun-dried tomato purée
    (paste)

12 black olives, stoned and quartered

salt and ground black pepper

fresh fennel fronds, to garnish

FOR THE MAYONNAISE

2 egg yolks

10ml/2 tsp white wine vinegar

300ml/½ pint/1¼ cups extra virgin
    olive oil

1 Heat the olive oil in a large pan. Add the onion and garlic and cook for 5 minutes, until soft. Add the fennel and cook for 2–3 minutes. Stir in the tomatoes, bay leaf, thyme and stock. Bring to the boil, then simmer for 30 minutes.

2 Meanwhile, make the mayonnaise. Put the egg yolks and vinegar in a bowl. Season and whisk well. Whisk in the oil, a little at a time. Set aside.

3 Cut each mullet fillet into two or three pieces, then add to the soup and cook for 5 minutes. Set aside.

4 Strain the cooking liquid. Whisk a ladleful of the soup into the mayonnaise, then whisk in the rest of the soup. Return to a clean pan and cook gently, whisking, until the mixture is thick. Add the fish. Set aside.

5 Toast the baguette slices on both sides. Rub each slice with the garlic and spread with tomato purée. Divide the olives among the bread slices.

6 Reheat the soup, but do not allow it to boil. Serve each topped with two toasts. Garnish with fennel.

Nutritional information per portion: Energy 322Kcal/1354kJ; Protein 35.3g; Carbohydrate 17.5g, of which sugars 6.4g; Fat 12.9g, of which saturates 1g; Cholesterol 0mg; Calcium 173mg; Fibre 4.4g; Sodium 299mg.

Pad thai red monkfish soup

This light coconut soup is based on Thailand's classic stir-fried noodle dish. It is perfect served as part of a special dinner party. The spring onion and chilli garnish makes it look very attractive.

SERVES 4

175g/6oz flat rice noodles

30ml/2 tbsp vegetable oil

2 garlic cloves, chopped

15ml/1 tbsp red curry paste

450g/1lb monkfish tail, cut into bitesize
  pieces

300ml/1/2 pint/1 1/4 cups coconut milk

750ml/1 1/4 pints/3 cups hot chicken
  stock

45ml/3 tbsp Thai fish sauce (nam pla)

15ml/1 tbsp palm sugar (jaggery)

60ml/4 tbsp roughly chopped roasted
  peanuts

4 spring onions (scallions), shredded
  lengthways

50g/2oz beansprouts

large handful of fresh Thai basil leaves

salt and ground black pepper

1 red chilli, seeded and cut lengthways
  into slivers, to garnish

1 Soak the noodles in boiling water for 10 minutes, or according to the packet instructions. Drain.

2 Heat the oil in a wok or saucepan over a high heat. Add the garlic and cook for 2 minutes. Stir in the curry paste and cook for 1 minute.

3 Add the monkfish and stir-fry over a high heat for 4–5 minutes, until just tender. Pour in the coconut milk and stock. Stir in the fish sauce and sugar, and bring just to the boil. Add the drained noodles and cook for 1–2 minutes, until tender.

4 Stir in half the peanuts, half the spring onions, half the beansprouts, the basil and seasoning. Ladle the soup into deep bowls and scatter over the remaining peanuts. Garnish with the rest of the spring onions and the beansprouts, and the red chilli.

Nutritional information per portion: Energy 379Kcal/1589kJ; Protein 25.5g; Carbohydrate 41.2g, of which sugars 4.7g; Fat 12g, of which saturates 2g; Cholesterol 18mg; Calcium 49mg; Fibre 0.9g; Sodium 111mg.

Curried salmon soup

A hint of mild curry paste really enhances the flavour of this soup, without making it too spicy. Grated creamed coconut adds a touch of luxury, while helping to amalgamate the flavours.

SERVES 4

50g/2oz/¼ cup butter

2 onions, roughly chopped

10ml/2 tsp mild curry paste

475ml/16fl oz/2 cups water

150ml/¼ pint/²/₃ cup white wine

300ml/½ pint/1¼ cups double (heavy)
   cream

50g/2oz/½ cup creamed coconut,
   grated, or 120ml/4fl oz/½ cup
   coconut cream

2 potatoes, about 350g/12oz, cubed

450g/1lb salmon fillet, skinned and cut
   into bitesize pieces

60ml/4 tbsp chopped fresh flat leaf
   parsley

salt and ground black pepper

1 Melt the butter in a large pan, add the onions and cook for 3–4 minutes, until beginning to soften. Stir in the curry paste. Cook for 1 minute more.

2 Add the water, wine, cream and creamed coconut or coconut cream, with seasoning. Bring to the boil, stirring until the coconut has dissolved.

3 Add the potatoes to the pan. Simmer, covered, for about 15 minutes or until they are almost tender. Do not allow the potatoes to break down into the mixture.

4 Add the fish gently so as not to break it up. Simmer for 2–3 minutes until just cooked. Add the parsley and adjust the seasoning. Serve immediately.

Nutritional information per portion: Energy 837Kcal/3466kJ; Protein 26.3g; Carbohydrate 16.6g, of which sugars 3.6g; Fat 71.8g, of which saturates 41.2g; Cholesterol 186mg; Calcium 74mg; Fibre 0.9g; Sodium 158mg.

Salmon and dill chowder

Dill is the perfect partner for salmon in this creamy soup. It is best served immediately after cooking, when the salmon is just tender.

SERVES 4

20g/³⁄₄oz/1¹⁄₂ tbsp butter

1 onion, finely chopped

1 leek, finely chopped

1 small fennel bulb, finely chopped

25g/1oz/¹⁄₄ cup plain (all-purpose) flour

1.75 litres/3 pints/7 cups fish stock

2 medium potatoes, cut into 1cm/
¹⁄₂in cubes

450g/1lb salmon fillet, skinned and cut
into 2cm/³⁄₄in cubes

175ml/6fl oz/³⁄₄ cup milk

120ml/4fl oz/¹⁄₂ cup whipping cream

30ml/2 tbsp chopped fresh dill

salt and ground black pepper

1 Melt the butter in a large pan. Add the onion, leek and chopped fennel and cook for 6 minutes until softened. Stir in the flour. Reduce the heat to low and cook for 3 minutes, stirring occasionally with a wooden spoon.

2 Add the fish stock and potatoes to the mixture in the pan. Season with a little salt and ground black pepper. Bring to the boil, then reduce the heat, cover and simmer gently for about 20 minutes or until the potatoes are tender when tested with a fork.

3 Add the cubed salmon and simmer for 3–5 minutes until it is just cooked.

4 Stir the milk, cream and chopped dill into the contents of the pan. Cook until just warmed through, stirring occasionally, but do not allow to boil. Adjust the seasoning to taste, then ladle into warmed soup bowls to serve.

Nutritional information per portion: Energy 464Kcal/1934kJ; Protein 27.9g; Carbohydrate 22.1g, of which sugars 6.5g; Fat 30g, of which saturates 12.9g; Cholesterol 101mg; Calcium 131mg; Fibre 3.1g; Sodium 122mg.

Smoked haddock and squash chowder

Based on a traditional Scottish recipe, this soup has American-style sweetness from the sweet potatoes and butternut squash, and is flavoured with a hint of basil.

SERVES 6

400g/14oz sweet potatoes
   (pink-fleshed variety)
225g/8oz butternut squash
50g/2oz/¼ cup butter
1 onion, chopped
450g/1lb smoked haddock fillets

300ml/½ pint/1¼ cups water
600ml/1 pint/2½ cups milk
small handful of basil leaves
60ml/4 tbsp double (heavy) cream
salt and ground black pepper

1 Peel the sweet potatoes and butternut squash and cut into small, bitesize pieces. Cook them separately in boiling salted water for 15 minutes or until just tender. Drain both vegetables well.

2 Melt half the butter in a large, heavy-based pan. Add the onion and cook for 4–5 minutes, until soft.

3 Use a sharp knife to skin the smoked haddock fillets. Add the fillets and water to the pan. Bring to the boil, reduce the heat and simmer for 10 minutes, until the fish is cooked. Use a slotted spoon to lift the fish out of the pan, and leave to cool. Set the cooking liquid aside.

4 When cool enough to handle, carefully break the flesh into large flakes, discarding the skin and bones. Set the fish aside.

5 Press the sweet potatoes through a sieve (strainer) and beat in the remaining butter with seasoning to taste. Strain the reserved fish cooking liquid and return it to the rinsed-out pan, then whisk in the sweet potato. Stir in the milk and bring to the boil. Simmer for about 2–3 minutes.

6 Stir in the butternut squash, fish, Thai basil leaves and cream. Season the soup to taste and heat through without boiling. Ladle the soup into six warmed soup bowls and serve immediately.

Nutritional information per portion: Energy 285Kcal/1196kJ; Protein 19.1g; Carbohydrate 20.7g, of which sugars 9.9g; Fat 14.7g, of which saturates 8.9g; Cholesterol 64mg; Calcium 166mg; Fibre 2.1g; Sodium 173mg.

Smoked mackerel and tomato soup

All the ingredients for this soup are cooked in a single pan. Smoked mackerel gives the soup a robust flavour, but this is tempered by the citrus tones in the lemon grass and tamarind.

SERVES 4

200g/7oz smoked mackerel fillets
4 tomatoes
1 litre/1¾ pints/4 cups vegetable stock
1 lemon grass stalk, finely chopped
5cm/2in piece fresh galangal, finely diced
4 shallots, finely chopped
2 garlic cloves, finely chopped
2.5ml/½ tsp dried chilli flakes
15ml/1 tbsp Thai fish sauce (nam pla)
5ml/1 tsp palm sugar (jaggery) or light
    muscovado (brown) sugar
45ml/3 tbsp thick tamarind juice
small bunch of fresh chives or spring
    onions (scallions), to garnish

1 Prepare the smoked mackerel. Remove and discard the skin, if necessary, then chop the flesh into large pieces. Remove any stray bones.

2 Cut the tomatoes in half, squeeze out most of the seeds with your fingers, then finely dice the flesh with a sharp knife. Set aside.

3 Pour the stock into a pan and add the lemon grass, galangal, shallots and garlic. Bring to the boil, reduce the heat and simmer for 15 minutes.

4 Add the fish, tomatoes, chilli flakes, fish sauce, sugar and tamarind juice. Simmer for 4–5 minutes, until the fish and tomatoes are heated through. Serve garnished with chives or spring onions.

Nutritional information per portion: Energy 203Kcal/845kJ; Protein 10.3g; Carbohydrate 5.3g, of which sugars 5g; Fat 15.8g, of which saturates 3.3g; Cholesterol 53mg; Calcium 21mg; Fibre 1.2g; Sodium 385mg.

Cod, broad bean and spinach chowder

Fresh cod and vegetables are abundant in this thick and creamy soup, which is finished with crisp Granary croûtons to soak up the delicious liquid. Use young, sweet fresh beans.

SERVES 6

1 litre/1¾ pints/4 cups milk
150ml/¼ pint/⅔ cup double (heavy)
    cream
675g/1½lb cod fillet, skinned and boned
45ml/3 tbsp olive oil
1 onion, sliced
2 garlic cloves, finely chopped
450g/1lb potatoes, thickly sliced
450g/1lb fresh broad (fava) beans,
    podded
225g/8oz baby spinach leaves
pinch of grated nutmeg
30ml/2 tbsp chopped fresh chives
salt and ground black pepper
fresh chives, to garnish

FOR THE CROÛTONS
60ml/4 tbsp olive oil
6 slices Granary (whole-wheat) bread,
    crusts removed, cut into large cubes

1 Bring the milk and cream to the boil in a large pan. Add the cod and bring back to the boil. Reduce the heat and simmer for 3 minutes, then leave to stand for 6 minutes, until the fish is just cooked. Remove the fish from the cooking liquid. Flake the cod into chunks, removing any bones or skin. Set aside.

2 Heat the olive oil in a large pan and add the onion and garlic. Cook for 5 minutes, until softened, stirring. Add the potatoes, stir in the milk mixture and bring to the boil. Reduce the heat and cover. Cook for

10 minutes. Add the broad beans; cook for 10 minutes or until tender and the potatoes begin to break up.

3 Meanwhile, make the croûtons. Heat the oil in a frying pan and add the bread. Cook over a medium heat until golden. Drain on kitchen paper.

4 Add the cod to the soup and heat through. Add the spinach and stir for 1–2 minutes, until wilted. Season and stir in the nutmeg and chives. Ladle into bowls and pile the croûtons on top. Serve garnished with fresh chives.

Nutritional information per portion: Energy 603Kcal/2525kJ; Protein 37.9g; Carbohydrate 44.7g, of which sugars 12.2g; Fat 31.6g, of which saturates 12.4g; Cholesterol 96mg; Calcium 398mg; Fibre 7.6g; Sodium 375mg.

Jamaican rice and bean soup with salt cod

Based on the classic Caribbean dish of rice and peas, this recipe is made with black-eyed beans, but kidney beans can be used instead. This hearty soup can be served as a complete meal.

SERVES 6

15ml/1 tbsp sunflower oil

75g/3oz/6 tbsp butter

115g/4oz thick rindless bacon rashers (strips), cut into thick strips

1 onion, chopped

2 garlic cloves, chopped

1 red chilli, seeded and chopped

225g/8oz/generous 1 cup long grain rice

2 fresh thyme sprigs

1 cinnamon stick

400g/14oz can black-eyed beans (peas), drained and rinsed

900ml/1½ pints/3¾ cups water

350g/12oz salt cod, soaked for 24 hours, changing the water several times

plain (all-purpose) flour, for dusting

400g/14oz can coconut milk

175g/6oz baby spinach leaves

30ml/2 tbsp chopped fresh parsley

salt and ground black pepper

1 Heat the oil and 25g/1oz/2 tbsp of the butter in a large, heavy-based pan. Add the bacon strips and cook for 3–4 minutes, until golden. Stir in the onion, garlic and chilli and cook for a further 4–5 minutes.

2 Stir in the rice. Cook for 1–2 minutes, until the grains are translucent. Stir in the thyme, cinnamon stick and black-eyed beans and cook for 1–2 minutes. Pour in the water and bring to the boil. Reduce the heat to low and cook for 25–30 minutes.

3 Meanwhile, wash the soaked salt cod under cold running water. Pat dry with kitchen paper and remove the skin. Cut into large bitesize pieces and toss in the flour until evenly coated. Shake off the excess flour.

4 Melt the remaining butter in a large, heavy-based frying pan. Add the cod, in batches if necessary, and cook for 4–5 minutes until tender and golden. Remove the cod and set aside.

5 Stir the coconut milk into the cooked rice and beans. Remove the cinnamon stick and cook for 2–3 minutes. Stir in the spinach and cook for a further 2–3 minutes. Add the cod and chopped parsley, season and heat through. Ladle the soup into bowls and serve.

Nutritional information per portion: Energy 443Kcal/1852kJ; Protein 30g; Carbohydrate 43.2g, of which sugars 5.1g; Fat 16.8g, of which saturates 8.3g; Cholesterol 71mg; Calcium 105mg; Fibre 3.8g; Sodium 999mg.

Seafood chowder

Chowder takes its name from the French word for cauldron – chaudière – the type of pot traditionally used for soups and stews. This substantial dish can be served with crusty bread.

SERVES 4–6

200g/7oz/generous 1 cup drained, canned corn kernels

600ml/1 pint/2¹/₂ cups milk

15g/¹/₂oz/1 tbsp butter

1 small leek, sliced

1 small garlic clove, crushed

2 rindless smoked streaky (fatty) bacon rashers (strips), chopped

1 small green (bell) pepper, seeded and diced

1 celery stalk, chopped

115g/4oz/generous ¹/₂ cup white long grain rice

5ml/1 tsp plain (all-purpose) flour

about 450ml/³/₄ pint/scant 2 cups hot chicken or vegetable stock

4 large scallops, preferably with corals

115g/4oz white fish fillet, such as monkfish or plaice

15ml/1 tbsp finely chopped fresh parsley

good pinch of cayenne pepper

30–45ml/2–3 tbsp single (light) cream (optional)

salt and freshly ground black pepper

1 Place half the corn in a food processor or blender. Add a little milk and process until thick and creamy. Melt the butter in a large pan and fry the leek, garlic and bacon for 4–5 minutes until the leek has softened but not browned. Add the green pepper and celery and sweat over a gentle heat for 3–4 minutes, stirring.

2 Stir in the rice and cook for a few minutes until the grains begin to swell. Sprinkle over the flour. Cook for 1 minute, then gradually stir in the remaining milk and the stock. Bring to the boil over a medium heat, then lower the heat and stir in the creamed corn mixture, with the whole corn kernels. Season well.

3 Cover and simmer the chowder gently for 20 minutes or until the rice is tender, stirring occasionally, and adding a little more stock or water if the mixture thickens too quickly or the rice begins to stick to the bottom of the pan.

4 Remove the corals and slice the scallops into 5mm/¹/₄in pieces. Cut the fish into bitesize chunks. Stir the scallops and fish into the chowder, cook for 4 minutes, then stir in the corals, parsley and cayenne. Cook for a few minutes to heat through, then stir in the cream, if using. Serve.

Nutritional information per portion: Energy 361Kcal/1520kJ; Protein 21.9g; Carbohydrate 47.1g, of which sugars 13.6g; Fat 10.1g, of which saturates 4.9g; Cholesterol 41mg; Calcium 213mg; Fibre 2.1g; Sodium 437mg.

Thai prawn and squash soup

This squash soup comes from northern Thailand. It is quite hearty, something of a cross between a soup and a stew. The bland flavour of the squash is fired up by the chilli mixture.

SERVES 4

1 butternut squash, about 300g/11oz
1 litre/1³/₄ pints/4 cups vegetable stock
90g/3¹/₂oz/scant 1 cup French beans, sliced
15ml/1 tbsp Thai fish sauce (nam pla)
225g/8oz raw prawns (shrimp)
small bunch fresh basil
cooked rice, to serve

FOR THE CHILLI PASTE

115g/4oz shallots, sliced
10 drained bottled green peppercorns
1 small green chilli, seeded and chopped
2.5ml/¹/₂ tsp shrimp paste

1 Peel the butternut squash and cut it in half. Scoop out the seeds with a teaspoon and discard, then cut the flesh into neat cubes. Set aside.

2 Make the chilli paste by pounding the shallots, peppercorns, chilli and shrimp paste together using a mortar and pestle.

3 Heat the stock in a large pan, then stir in the chilli paste. Add the squash and the beans. Bring to the boil and cook for 15 minutes.

4 Add the fish sauce, prawns and basil. Bring to simmering point, then simmer for 3 minutes. Serve in bowls, accompanied by rice.

Nutritional information per portion: Energy 64Kcal/271kJ; Protein 11.3g; Carbohydrate 3.4g, of which sugars 2.8g; Fat 0.7g, of which saturates 0.2g; Cholesterol 110mg; Calcium 82mg; Fibre 1.7g; Sodium 199mg.

Thai pumpkin, prawn and coconut soup

The natural sweetness of the pumpkin is heightened by the addition of a little sugar in this attractive soup, but this is balanced by the chillies, shrimp paste and dried shrimp.

SERVES 4–6

450g/1lb pumpkin
2 garlic cloves, crushed
4 shallots, finely chopped
2.5ml/½ tsp shrimp paste
1 lemon grass stalk, chopped
2 fresh green chillies, seeded
15ml/1 tbsp dried shrimp, soaked for
   10 minutes in warm water to cover
600ml/1 pint/2½ cups chicken stock
600ml/1 pint/2½ cups coconut milk
30ml/2 tbsp Thai fish sauce (nam pla)
5ml/1 tsp granulated (white) sugar
115g/4oz small cooked shelled prawns
   (shrimp)
salt and ground black pepper
2 red chillies, seeded and sliced, and
   10–12 fresh basil leaves, to garnish

1 Peel the pumpkin and cut it into quarters with a sharp knife. Scoop out the seeds with a teaspoon and discard. Cut the flesh into chunks about 2cm/¾in thick and set aside.

2 Put the garlic, shallots, shrimp paste, lemon grass, green chillies and salt to taste in a mortar. Drain the dried shrimp, discarding the soaking liquid, and add to the mortar, then use a pestle to grind the mixture into a paste. Or, use a food processor or blender and process to a paste.

3 Bring the chicken stock to the boil in a large pan. Add the paste and stir well to dissolve. Add the pumpkin and simmer for 10–15 minutes, or until the pumpkin is tender.

4 Stir in the coconut milk, then bring the soup back to simmering point. Do not let it boil. Add the fish sauce, sugar and pepper to taste.

5 Add the prawns and cook for a further 2–3 minutes, until heated through. Serve in warmed bowls, garnished with chillies and basil.

Nutritional information per portion: Energy 73Kcal/310kJ; Protein 6.5g; Carbohydrate 10.4g, of which sugars 9.8g; Fat 0.9g, of which saturates 0.5g; Cholesterol 56mg; Calcium 102mg; Fibre 1.3g; Sodium 399mg.

Wonton and prawn tail soup

A well-flavoured chicken stock is a must for this Chinese classic, which is popular on fast-food stalls in towns throughout southern China. Serve it as an appetizer or part of a main meal.

SERVES 4

200g/7oz minced (ground) pork
200g/7oz cooked, peeled prawns
    (shrimp), thawed if frozen
10ml/2 tsp rice wine or dry sherry
10ml/2 tsp light soy sauce
5ml/1 tsp sesame oil
24 thin wonton wrappers
1.2 litres/2 pints/5 cups chicken stock

12 tiger prawns (jumbo shrimp), shelled,
    with tails still on
350g/12oz pak choi (bok choy), coarsely
    shredded
salt and ground black pepper
4 spring onions (scallions), sliced, and
    1cm/1/2in piece fresh root ginger,
    finely shredded, to garnish

1 Put the pork, prawns, rice wine or sherry, soy sauce and sesame oil in a large bowl. Add plenty of seasoning and mix the ingredients.

2 Put about 10ml/2 tsp of pork mixture in the centre of each wonton wrapper. Bring up the sides of the wrapper and pinch them together to seal the filling in a small bundle.

3 Bring a large pan of water to the boil. Add the wontons and cook for 3 minutes, then drain well and set aside.

4 Pour the stock into a pan and bring to the boil. Season to taste. Add the tiger prawns and cook for 2–3 minutes, until just tender. Add the wontons and pak choi and cook for 1–2 minutes. Garnish with spring onions and ginger to serve.

COOK'S TIP
Wonton wrappers are sometimes called wonton skins. Available fresh or frozen, they are made from a wheat dough that is similar to filo pastry. Store fresh wonton wrappers in the refrigerator and use within a week.

Nutritional information per portion: Energy 208Kcal/874kJ; Protein 26.8g; Carbohydrate 11.8g, of which sugars 2.2g; Fat 6.2g, of which saturates 2g; Cholesterol 179mg; Calcium 234mg; Fibre 2.4g; Sodium 655mg.

Mediterranean seafood soup
with saffron rouille

Vary the fish content of this soup according to the freshest available, but choose firm varieties that will not flake and fall apart easily during cooking.

SERVES 4

450g/1lb fresh clams, scrubbed
120ml/4fl oz/1/2 cup white wine
15ml/1 tbsp olive oil
4 garlic cloves, crushed
5ml/1 tsp fennel seeds
pinch of dried chilli flakes
1 fennel bulb, cored and sliced
1 red (bell) pepper, seeded and sliced
8 plum tomatoes, halved
1 onion, cut into thin wedges
225g/8oz small waxy potatoes, sliced
1 bay leaf
1 fresh thyme sprig

600ml/1 pint/2½ cups fish stock
1 mini French stick
225g/8oz monkfish fillet, sliced
350g/12oz red mullet or snapper, scaled,
    filleted and cut into strips
45ml/3 tbsp Pernod
salt and ground black pepper
fennel fronds, to garnish

FOR THE ROUILLE

a few saffron threads
150ml/¼ pint/²/₃ cup mayonnaise
dash of Tabasco sauce

1 Discard any open clams that do not shut when tapped sharply. Place the rest in a large pan with the wine. Cover and cook over a high heat for 4 minutes, until the shells have opened.

2 Drain the clams, strain their cooking liquid and set it aside. Discard any unopened shells and reserve eight clams in their shells. Remove the remaining clams from their shells and set aside.

3 Heat the oil in a pan. Add the garlic, fennel seeds and chilli flakes and cook for about 2 minutes, until softened.

4 Add the fennel, pepper, tomatoes, onion and cooking liquid. Cover and cook for 10 minutes, stirring occasionally.

5 Stir in the potatoes, bay leaf and thyme, then pour in the fish stock. Cover and cook for 15–20 minutes, until the vegetables are tender.

6 Meanwhile, make the saffron rouille. Pound the saffron threads to a powder in a mortar, then beat it into the mayonnaise with the Tabasco sauce. Cut the French stick into eight thin slices and toast them on both sides. Set aside.

7 Add the monkfish, red mullet and Pernod to the soup and cook for 3–4 minutes, until tender. Add all the clams (with and without shells) and heat through for 30 seconds. Remove the bay leaf and thyme sprigs, and season the soup well. Spoon the rouille on to the toasts. Ladle the soup into bowls, garnish each bowl with a frond of fennel and serve with the toasts.

Nutritional information per portion: Energy 728Kcal/3048kJ; Protein 50.2g; Carbohydrate 40g, of which sugars 10.9g; Fat 37.1g, of which saturates 5.4g; Cholesterol 111mg; Calcium 238mg; Fibre 4.7g; Sodium 1940mg.

Scallop and jerusalem artichoke soup

The subtle sweetness of scallops combines well with the flavour of Jerusalem artichokes in this attractive and satisfying golden soup.

SERVES 6

1kg/2¼ lb Jerusalem artichokes, scrubbed and peeled
juice of ½ lemon
115g/4oz/½ cup butter
1 onion, finely chopped
600ml/1 pint/2½ cups fish stock
300ml/½ pint/1¼ cups milk
generous pinch of saffron threads
6 large or 12 small scallops, with their corals
150ml/¼ pint/⅔ cup whipping cream
salt and ground white pepper
45ml/3 tbsp flaked almonds and 15ml/1 tbsp finely chopped fresh chervil, to garnish

1 Cut the Jerusalem artichokes into 2cm/¾in chunks and drop into a bowl of cold water which has been acidulated with the lemon juice.

2 Melt half the butter, add the onion and cook until softened. Drain the artichokes and add to the pan. Cook for 5 minutes. Pour in the stock and milk and add the saffron. Bring to the boil and simmer until tender.

3 Separate the scallop corals from the flesh. Prick the corals. Slice each scallop in half horizontally. Heat half the remaining butter in a frying pan. Cook the scallops and corals for about 1 minute on each side. Then dice them, keeping them separate. Set aside.

4 Transfer the cooked artichokes to a food processor or blender. Add half the white scallop meat and purée. Return to the clean pan, season and keep hot.

5 Heat the remaining butter in a frying pan, add the almonds and toss until golden brown. Add the diced corals and cook for 30 seconds. Stir the cream into the soup and add the remaining white scallop meat. Ladle into bowls and garnish with almonds, corals and chervil.

Nutritional information per portion: Energy 408Kcal/1691kJ; Protein 12.8g; Carbohydrate 18.8g, of which sugars 16.4g; Fat 31.9g, of which saturates 17.5g; Cholesterol 86mg; Calcium 150mg; Fibre 4.7g; Sodium 247mg.

Lobster bisque

Bisque is a luxurious, velvety soup which can be made with any crustaceans, such as crab or shrimp. If lobster is your favourite shellfish, this version is for you.

SERVES 6

500g/1¼ lb fresh lobster, cut into pieces
75g/3oz/6 tbsp butter
1 onion, chopped
1 carrot, diced
1 celery stick, diced
45ml/3 tbsp brandy
250ml/8fl oz/1 cup dry white wine
1 litre/1¾ pints/4 cups fish stock
15ml/1 tbsp tomato purée (paste)
75g/3oz/scant ½ cup long grain rice
1 fresh bouquet garni
150ml/¼ pint/⅔ cup double (heavy) cream, plus extra to garnish
salt, ground white pepper and cayenne pepper

1 Melt half the butter in a pan, add the vegetables and cook over a low heat until soft. Put in the lobster and stir gently until the shells turn red.

2 Pour in the brandy and set alight. When the flames die down, add the wine and boil until reduced by half. Pour in the stock and simmer for 2–3 minutes. Remove the lobster.

3 Stir in the tomato purée and rice, add the bouquet garni and cook until the rice is tender. Remove the lobster meat from the shell, dice and set aside. Return the shells to the pan. When the rice is cooked, discard all the larger bits of shell. Transfer the mixture to a food processor or blender and purée.

4 Press the purée through a fine sieve (strainer) over the clean pan. Stir then heat until almost boiling. Season with salt, pepper and cayenne, then lower the heat and stir in the cream. Dice the remaining butter and whisk into the bisque. Add the lobster and extra cream and serve.

Nutritional information per portion: Energy 347Kcal/1438kJ; Protein 8.5g; Carbohydrate 12.9g, of which sugars 2.6g; Fat 24.3g, of which saturates 15g; Cholesterol 94mg; Calcium 48mg; Fibre 0.6g; Sodium 195mg.

Louisiana seafood gumbo

Gumbo is a soup, but is served over rice as a main course. In Louisiana, oysters are cheap and prolific, and would be used there instead of the mussels.

SERVES 6

450g/1lb fresh mussels, cleaned

450g/1lb prawns (shrimp), in the shell

1 cooked crab, about 1kg/2¼lb

small bunch of parsley, leaves chopped
    and stalks reserved

150ml/¼ pint/²⁄₃ cup vegetable oil

115g/4oz/1 cup plain (all-purpose) flour

1 green (bell) pepper, chopped

1 large onion, chopped

2 celery sticks, sliced

3 garlic cloves, finely chopped

75g/3oz smoked spiced sausage, skinned
    and sliced

275g/10oz/1¹⁄₂ cups white long grain
    rice

6 spring onions (scallions), shredded

cayenne pepper, to taste

Tabasco sauce, to taste

salt

1 Bring 250ml/8fl oz/1 cup water to the boil. Add the mussels, cover and cook over a high heat shaking frequently for 3 minutes. As the mussels open, transfer them to a sieve (strainer) set over a bowl. Discard any that fail to open. Shell the mussels, discarding the shells. Return the liquid from the bowl to the pan and make the quantity up to 2 litres/3¹⁄₂ pints/8 cups with water.

2 Peel the prawns and set aside. Put the shells and heads into the pan. Remove the meat from the crab, separating the brown and white meat. Add the shell to the pan with salt. Bring the stock to the boil, skimming it. When there is no more froth, add the parsley stalks and simmer for 15 minutes. Cool, then strain and make up to 2 litres/3¹⁄₂ pints/8 cups with water.

3 Heat the oil and stir in the flour. Stir over a medium heat with a wooden spoon until the roux is golden. Add the pepper, onion, celery and garlic and cook for 3 minutes until the onion is soft. Stir in the sausage. Reheat the stock. Stir the brown crab meat into the roux. Ladle in the hot stock a little at a time, stirring until it has all been incorporated. Bring to a low boil, partially cover, then simmer for 30 minutes.

4 Meanwhile, cook the rice until the grains are tender. Add the prawns, mussels, white crab meat and spring onions to the gumbo. Return to the boil and season with salt, cayenne and a dash of Tabasco. Simmer for 1 minute, then add the chopped parsley. Ladle the soup over the rice in bowls.

Nutritional information per portion: Energy 518Kcal/2161kJ; Protein 23.6g; Carbohydrate 54.8g, of which sugars 2.1g; Fat 22.9g, of which saturates 3.7g; Cholesterol 55mg; Calcium 143mg; Fibre 1.5g; Sodium 728mg.

Crab, coconut and coriander soup

This soup has all the flavours associated with the Bahia region of Brazil: creamy coconut, palm oil, fragrant coriander and chilli.

SERVES 4

30ml/2 tbsp olive oil
1 onion, finely chopped
1 celery stick, finely chopped
2 garlic cloves, crushed
1 fresh red chilli, seeded and chopped
1 large tomato, peeled and chopped
45ml/3 tbsp chopped fresh coriander
  (cilantro)

1 litre/1¾ pints/4 cups fresh
  crab or fish stock
500g/1¼lb crab meat
250ml/8fl oz/1 cup coconut milk
30ml/2 tbsp palm oil or vegetable oil
juice of 1 lime
salt
hot chilli oil and lime wedges, to serve

1 Heat the olive oil in a pan over a low heat. Stir in the onion and celery, and sauté gently for 5 minutes, until softened and translucent. Stir in the garlic and chilli and cook for a further 2 minutes.

2 Add the chopped tomato and half the coriander and increase the heat. Cook, stirring, for 3 minutes, then add the stock. Bring to the boil, then simmer for 5 minutes.

3 Stir the crab, coconut milk and palm oil into the pan and simmer over a very low heat for a further 5 minutes. The consistency should be thick, but not stew-like, so add some water if needed.

4 Stir in the lime juice and remaining coriander, then season with salt to taste. Serve in heated bowls with the chilli oil and lime wedges on the side.

Nutritional information per portion: Energy 228Kcal/951kJ; Protein 23.6g; Carbohydrate 5.4g, of which sugars 5g; Fat 12.6g, of which saturates 3.7g; Cholesterol 90mg; Calcium 199mg; Fibre 1.1g; Sodium 767mg.

Provençal seafood soup

This soup is traditionally made with a selection of seafood such as mussels, scallops and prawns. Select the freshest fish in season for a wonderful result.

SERVES 4-6

450g/1lb fresh mussels
about 250ml/8fl oz/1 cup white wine
675–900g/1½–2lb white fish fillets
6 large scallops
30ml/2 tbsp olive oil
3 leeks, chopped
1 garlic clove, crushed
**1 red and 1 yellow (bell) pepper, seeded
   and chopped**
175g/6oz fennel bulb, chopped
400g/14oz can chopped tomatoes
**150ml/¼ pint/⅔ cup passata (bottled
   strained tomatoes)**
1 litre/1¾ pints/4 cups fish stock
**generous pinch of saffron threads, soaked
   in 15ml/1 tbsp hot water**
175g/6oz/scant 1 cup basmati rice, soaked
**8 large raw prawns (shrimp), peeled and
   deveined**
salt and ground black pepper
30–45ml/2–3 tbsp fresh dill, to garnish

1 Clean the mussels, discarding any that do not close when tapped with a knife. Place them in a heavy pan. Add 90ml/6 tbsp of the wine, cover, bring to the boil and cook for 3 minutes or until the mussels are open.

2 Strain, reserving the liquid. Discard any mussels that have not opened. Set aside half the mussels in their shells; shell the rest.

3 Cut the fish into 2.5cm/1in cubes. Detach the corals from the scallops and slice the white flesh into three or four pieces. Add the scallops to the fish and the corals to the shelled mussels.

4 Heat the oil and fry the leeks and garlic for 3–4 minutes, until soft. Add the pepper and fennel, and fry for 2 minutes. Add the tomatoes, passata, stock, saffron water, mussel liquid and wine. Season and cook for 5 minutes. Drain the rice, stir it in, cover and simmer for 10 minutes.

5 Stir in the white fish. Cook over a low heat for 5 minutes. Add the prawns, cook for 2 minutes, then add the scallop corals and shelled mussels and cook for 2–3 minutes. Add extra wine or stock if needed. Spoon the soup into bowls, top with mussels in their shells and sprinkle with dill.

Nutritional information per portion: Energy 568Kcal/2385kJ; Protein 59.9g; Carbohydrate 50.5g, of which sugars 12.9g; Fat 9.7g, of which saturates 1.6g; Cholesterol 163mg; Calcium 182mg; Fibre 5.9g; Sodium 418mg.

Mussel soup with lemon and pumpkin

Based on the classic French shellfish dish, moules marinière, this mussel soup is thickened with fresh pumpkin and flavoured with dill and lemon. This elegant soup is ideal for a dinner party.

SERVES 4

1kg/2¼lb fresh mussels
300ml/½ pint/1¼ cups dry white wine
1 large lemon
1 bay leaf
15ml/1 tbsp olive oil
1 onion, chopped
1 garlic clove, crushed
675g/1½lb pumpkin or squash, peeled,
    seeds and pith removed and chopped
    into chunks
900ml/1½ pints/3¾ cups vegetable
    stock
30ml/2 tbsp chopped fresh dill
salt and ground black pepper
lemon wedges, to serve

1 Clean the mussels, discarding any that do not close when tapped, and put the rest into a pan with the wine. Pare large pieces of rind from the lemon and squeeze the juice, add both to the mussels with the bay leaf. Cover and bring to the boil, then cook for 4–5 minutes, shaking the pan, until the mussels open.

2 Drain the mussels over a bowl to reserve the cooking liquid. Discard the lemon rind and bay leaf, and any unopened mussels. When they are cool, set aside a few and shell the rest. Strain the cooking liquid.

3 Heat the oil and cook the onion and garlic for 4–5 minutes. Add the pumpkin and the strained cooking liquid to the pan. Simmer, uncovered, for 5–6 minutes. Add the stock and cook for a further 25 minutes, until the pumpkin is tender.

4 Cool the soup slightly, then process in a food processor or blender. Return the soup to the rinsed-out pan and season. Add the dill and the shelled mussels, then bring just to the boil. Serve with the lemon wedges and garnish with the reserved mussels.

Nutritional information per portion: Energy 161Kcal/678kJ; Protein 14.3g; Carbohydrate 4.2g, of which sugars 3.3g; Fat 4.6g, of which saturates 0.8g; Cholesterol 30mg; Calcium 203mg; Fibre 1.7g; Sodium 161mg.

Spanish seafood soup

This hearty soup contains all the colours and flavours of the Mediterranean. It is substantial enough to serve as a main course, but can also be diluted with a little white wine and water to make an elegant appetizer for six.

SERVES 4

675g/1¹/₂lb raw prawns (shrimp), in the shell
900ml/1¹/₂ pints/3³/₄ cups cold water
1 onion, chopped
1 celery stick, chopped
1 bay leaf
45ml/3 tbsp olive oil
2 slices stale bread, crusts removed
1 small onion, finely chopped
1 large garlic clove, chopped
2 large tomatoes, halved
¹/₂ large green (bell) pepper, finely chopped
500g/1¹/₄lb cockles (small clams) or mussels, cleaned
juice of 1 lemon
45ml/3 tbsp chopped fresh parsley
5ml/1 tsp paprika
salt and ground black pepper

1 Pull the heads off the prawns and put them in a pan with the cold water. Add the onion, celery and bay leaf and simmer for 20–25 minutes. Peel the prawns, adding the shells to the stock as you go along.

2 Heat the oil in a flameproof casserole and fry the bread slices quickly, then set aside. Fry the onion until soft, adding the garlic towards the end.

3 Scoop the seeds out of the tomatoes and discard. Chop the flesh and add to the casserole with the green pepper. Fry briefly.

4 Strain the stock into the casserole and bring to the boil. Check over the cockles or mussels, discarding any that are open or damaged. Add half the cockles or mussels to the stock. When open, use a slotted spoon to transfer some of them out on to a plate. Remove the mussels or cockles from the shells and discard the shells. Meanwhile, repeat the process to cook the remaining cockles or mussels.

5 Return the cockles or mussels to the soup and add the prawns. Add the bread, torn into little pieces, and the lemon juice and chopped parsley. Season with paprika, salt and pepper and stir gently to dissolve the bread. Serve at once in soup bowls, providing a plate for the empty shells.

Nutritional information per portion: Energy 234Kcal/978kJ; Protein 23.3g; Carbohydrate 11.3g, of which sugars 4.5g; Fat 10.9g, of which saturates 1.7g; Cholesterol 67mg; Calcium 216mg; Fibre 2g; Sodium 1193mg.

Saffron seafood soup

Filling yet not too rich, this golden soup will make a delicious meal on early summer evenings, served with lots of hot fresh bread and a glass of fruity, dry white wine.

SERVES 4

1 parsnip, quartered

2 carrots, quartered

1 onion, quartered

2 celery sticks, quartered

2 smoked bacon rashers (strips), rinds
    removed

juice of 1 lemon

pinch of saffron threads

450g/1lb fish heads

450g/1lb fresh mussels, scrubbed

1 leek, shredded

2 shallots, finely chopped

30ml/2 tbsp chopped dill, plus extra
    sprigs to garnish

450g/1lb haddock, skinned and boned

3 egg yolks

30ml/2 tbsp double (heavy) cream

salt and ground black pepper

1 Put the parsnip, carrots, onion, celery, bacon, lemon juice, saffron threads and fish heads in a large pan with 900ml/1½ pints/3¾ cups water and boil for about 20 minutes or until reduced by half.

2 Discard any mussels that are open and that do not close when tapped sharply. Add the rest of the mussels to the pan of stock. Cook for about 4 minutes, until they have opened. Strain the soup and return the liquid to the pan. Discard any unopened mussels, then remove the remaining ones from their shells and set aside.

3 Add the leek and shallots to the soup, and simmer for 5 minutes. Add the dill and haddock, and simmer for a further 5 minutes. Remove the haddock and flake it using a fork.

4 In another bowl, whisk together the eggs and double cream. Whisk in a little of the hot soup, then whisk the mixture back into the hot liquid. Whisk as it heats through and thickens, but do not let it boil.

5 Add the haddock and mussels to the soup and check the seasoning. Garnish with dill and serve.

Nutritional information per portion: Energy 278Kcal/1167kJ; Protein 33.2g; Carbohydrate 9.8g, of which sugars 8.5g; Fat 12.1g, of which saturates 4.8g; Cholesterol 222mg; Calcium 147mg; Fibre 3.4g; Sodium 377mg.

Saffron-flavoured mussel soup

There's a fragrant taste of the sea in this delicious, creamy soup. Saffron goes very well with shellfish, and gives the soup a lovely pale yellow colour.

SERVES 4

1.5kg/3–3¹/₂lb fresh mussels
600ml/1 pint /2¹/₂ cups white wine
a few fresh parsley stalks
50g/2oz/¹/₄ cup butter
2 leeks, finely chopped
2 celery sticks, finely chopped
1 carrot, chopped
2 garlic cloves, chopped
large pinch of saffron threads
600ml/1 pint/2¹/₂ cups double (heavy)
   cream
3 tomatoes, peeled, seeded and chopped
salt and ground black pepper
30ml/2 tbsp chopped fresh chives, to
   garnish

1 Clean the mussels and pull away the beards. Put into a large pan with the wine and parsley stalks. Cover, bring to the boil and cook for 4–5 minutes, shaking the pan, until the mussels have opened. Discard the stalks and any unopened mussels.

2 Drain the mussels over a large bowl, reserving the cooking liquid. When cool enough to handle, remove half of the cooked mussels from their shells. Set aside with the remaining mussels in their shells.

3 Melt the butter in a large pan, add the leeks, celery, carrot and garlic, and cook for 5 minutes. Strain the reserved mussel cooking liquid through a fine sieve (strainer). Add to the pan and cook over a high heat for 8–10 minutes to reduce the liquid. Strain into a clean pan, add the saffron and cook for 1 minute.

4 Add the cream and bring back to the boil. Season. Add the mussels and the tomatoes and heat gently. Serve, sprinkled with the chives.

Nutritional information per portion: Energy 1054Kcal/4359kJ; Protein 22.8g; Carbohydrate 7.5g, of which sugars 7.4g; Fat 93.4g, of which saturates 57.1g; Cholesterol 277mg; Calcium 327mg; Fibre 1.4g; Sodium 372mg.

Meat and poultry soups

Hearty meaty soups are just the thing for warming you up on cold winter days and a substantial soup such as Chicken, Leek and Celery Soup can be a meal in itself. Or, try something lighter such as Chinese Chicken and Chilli Soup as an appetizer or lunch, or, for a special occasion, perhaps make Cream of Duck Soup with Blueberry Relish.

Moroccan chicken soup
with **charmoula butter**

This tasty soup, inspired by the ingredients of North Africa, is spiced with chilli and served with a rich and pungent lemon butter creamed with crisp breadcrumbs.

SERVES 6

50g/2oz/¼ cup butter
450g/1lb chicken breasts, cut into strips
1 onion, chopped
2 garlic cloves, crushed
7.5ml/1½ tsp plain (all-purpose) flour
15ml/1 tbsp harissa
1 litre/1¾ pints/4 cups chicken stock
400g/14oz can chopped tomatoes
400g/14oz can chickpeas, drained and
    rinsed
salt and ground black pepper
lemon wedges, to serve

FOR THE CHARMOULA
50g/2oz/¼ cup butter, at room
    temperature
30ml/2 tbsp chopped fresh
    coriander (cilantro)
2 garlic cloves, crushed
5ml/1 tsp ground cumin
1 red chilli, seeded and chopped
pinch of saffron threads
finely grated rind of ½ lemon
5ml/1 tsp paprika
25g/1oz/1 cup dried breadcrumbs

1 Melt the butter in a heavy-based pan. Add the chicken and cook for 5–6 minutes until starting to brown. Remove the chicken from the pan and set aside. Add the onion and garlic and cook for 4–5 minutes, until soft.

2 Stir in the flour and cook for 3–4 minutes, stirring continuously, until beginning to brown. Stir in the harissa and cook for a further 1 minute. Gradually pour in the stock and cook for 2–3 minutes, until slightly thickened. Stir in the tomatoes. Return the chicken to the soup and add the chickpeas. Cover and cook over a low heat for 20 minutes. Season well.

3 To make the charmoula, put the butter into a bowl and beat in the coriander, garlic, cumin, chilli, saffron threads, lemon rind and paprika. When the mixture is well combined, stir in the breadcrumbs.

4 Ladle the soup into six warmed bowls. Spoon a little of the charmoula into the centre of each and leave for a few seconds to allow the butter to melt into the soup before serving with lemon wedges.

Nutritional information per portion: Energy 313Kcal/1312kJ; Protein 25g; Carbohydrate 18.3g, of which sugars 3.3g; Fat 16.1g, of which saturates 9g; Cholesterol 88mg; Calcium 53mg; Fibre 3.6g; Sodium 207mg.

Chicken, leek and celery soup

This makes a substantial main course soup with fresh crusty bread. You will need nothing more than a salad and cheese to accompany this dish, or just fresh fruit to follow.

SERVES 4–6

1.4kg/3lb free-range chicken
1 small head of celery, trimmed
1 onion, coarsely chopped
1 fresh bay leaf
a few fresh parsley stalks
a few fresh tarragon sprigs
2.4 litres/4 pints/10 cups cold water
3 large leeks

65g/2¹/₂oz/5 tbsp butter
2 potatoes, cut into chunks
150ml/¹/₄ pint/²/₃ cup dry white wine
30–45ml/2–3 tbsp single (light) cream
   (optional)
salt and ground black pepper
90g/3¹/₂oz pancetta, grilled until crisp,
   to garnish

1 Cut the breasts off the chicken and set aside. Chop the rest of the chicken carcass into 8–10 pieces and place in a large pan. Chop 4–5 of the outer sticks of the celery and add them to the pan with the onion. Tie the bay leaf, parsley and tarragon together and add to the pan. Pour in the water to cover and bring to the boil. Reduce the heat, cover and simmer for 1¹/₂ hours.

2 Remove the chicken and cut off and reserve the meat. Strain the stock, then return to the pan and boil rapidly until it has reduced to 1.5 litres/ 2¹/₂ pints/6¹/₄ cups.

3 Meanwhile, set 150g/5oz of the leeks aside. Slice the remaining leeks and the remaining celery, reserving any celery leaves. Chop the celery leaves and set aside. Melt half the butter in a large heavy-based pan. Add the sliced leeks and celery, cover and cook for 10 minutes, or until soft but not browned. Add the potatoes, wine and 1.2 litres/2 pints/5 cups of the stock. Season well, bring to the boil and reduce the heat. Part-cover and simmer for 15–20 minutes.

4 Meanwhile, skin the reserved chicken breasts and cut the flesh into small pieces. Melt the remaining butter in a frying pan, add the chicken and fry for 5–7 minutes, until cooked. Thickly slice the remaining leeks, add to the pan and cook for 3–4 minutes, until just cooked.

5 Process the soup with the cooked chicken from the stock in a food processor or blender. Taste and adjust the seasoning, and add more stock if it is thick. Stir in the cream, if using, and the chicken and leek mixture. Reheat and serve in bowls. Crumble the pancetta over and sprinkle with the celery leaves.

Nutritional information per portion: Energy 294Kcal/1246kJ; Protein 40.5g; Carbohydrate 22.1g, of which sugars 5.9g; Fat 2.8g, of which saturates 0.7g; Cholesterol 105mg; Calcium 69mg; Fibre 4.9g; Sodium 124mg.

Pumpkin, rice and chicken soup

This is a warm, comforting soup, which would be ideal for a light lunch. For a more substantial meal, just add extra rice and make sure you use all the chicken.

SERVES 4

1 wedge of pumpkin, about 450g/1lb, peeled
15ml/1 tbsp sunflower oil
25g/1oz/2 tbsp butter
6 green cardamom pods
2 leeks, chopped
115g/4oz/generous ½ cup basmati rice, soaked
350ml/12fl oz/1½ cups milk
salt and freshly ground black pepper
strips of pared orange rind, to garnish

FOR THE CHICKEN STOCK

2 chicken quarters
1 onion, quartered
2 carrots, chopped
1 celery stalk, chopped
6–8 peppercorns
900ml/1½ pints/3¾ cups water

1 Place the stock ingredients in a pan and bring to the boil. Skim, then lower the heat, cover and simmer for 1 hour. Strain the stock into a bowl and discard the vegetables.

2 Skin and bone one or both chicken pieces and cut the flesh into strips. Remove the seeds and pith from the pumpkin. Cut the flesh into small cubes.

3 Heat the oil and butter and fry the cardamom for 2–3 minutes. Add the leeks and pumpkin. Cook for 3–4 minutes, then lower the heat, cover and sweat for 5 minutes. Add 600ml/1 pint/2½ cups of the stock to the mixture.

4 Bring to the boil, then lower the heat, cover and simmer for 15 minutes. Make the remaining stock up to 300ml/½ pint/1¼ cups with water.

5 Drain the rice and put into a pan. Pour in the stock, bring to the boil, then simmer for 10 minutes until tender. Season.

6 Remove the cardamom, then process the soup in a food processor or blender. Pour back into a clean pan and add the milk, chicken and rice. Heat to simmering. Garnish with the orange rind and black pepper.

Nutritional information per portion: Energy 315Kcal/1320kJ; Protein 24.6g; Carbohydrate 29.9g, of which sugars 6.3g; Fat 10.8g, of which saturates 4.9g; Cholesterol 71mg; Calcium 140mg; Fibre 2.1g; Sodium 122mg.

Chicken and leek soup with prunes and barley

This recipe is based on the traditional Scottish soup, cock-a-leekie. The unusual combination of leeks and prunes is surprisingly delicious.

SERVES 6

1 chicken, weighing about 2kg/4¼lb
900g/2lb leeks
1 fresh bay leaf
a few each fresh parsley stalks and
   thyme sprigs
1 large carrot, thickly sliced
2.4 litres/4 pints/10 cups chicken or
   beef stock
115g/4oz/generous ½ cup pearl barley
400g/14oz ready-to-eat prunes
salt and ground black pepper
chopped fresh parsley, to garnish

1 Cut the breasts off the chicken and set aside. Place the carcass in a pan. Cut half the leeks into 5cm/2in lengths and add them to the pan. Tie the bay leaf, parsley and thyme into a bouquet garni and add to the pan with the carrot and stock. Bring to the boil, cover and simmer for 1 hour. Skim off any scum. Add the chicken breasts and cook for 30 minutes, until just cooked.

2 Leave until cool enough to handle, then strain the stock. Reserve the chicken meat and discard the skin, bones, herbs and vegetables. Skim the fat, then return to the pan.

3 Rinse the pearl barley, then cook in a pan of boiling water for 10 minutes. Drain, rinse and drain. Add the barley to the stock. Bring to the boil, then lower the heat and cook for 15–20 minutes, until the barley is just cooked and tender. Season with salt and pepper.

4 Add the prunes. Slice the remaining leeks and add to the pan. Bring to the boil, then simmer for 10 minutes until the leeks are cooked. Slice the chicken and add to the soup. Serve the soup and sprinkle with parsley.

Nutritional information per portion: Energy 359Kcal/1526kJ; Protein 41.7g; Carbohydrate 44g, of which sugars 26.9g; Fat 3g, of which saturates 0.6g; Cholesterol 105mg; Calcium 73mg; Fibre 7.4g; Sodium 104mg.

Chicken and coconut soup

This recipe combines the flavours of Thailand in a smooth European-style soup, and the finished dish is complemented by a topping of crisp shallots.

SERVES 6

40g/1½oz/3 tbsp butter

1 onion, finely chopped

2 garlic cloves, chopped

2.5cm/1in piece fresh root ginger, finely chopped

10ml/2 tsp Thai green curry paste

2.5ml/½ tsp turmeric

400ml/14fl oz can coconut milk

475ml/16fl oz/2 cups chicken stock

2 lime leaves, shredded

1 lemon grass stalk, finely chopped

8 skinless, boneless chicken thighs

350g/12oz spinach, roughly chopped

10ml/2 tsp Thai fish sauce (nam pla)

30ml/2 tbsp lime juice

30ml/2 tbsp vegetable oil

2 shallots, thinly sliced

small handful of Thai purple basil leaves

salt and ground black pepper

1 Melt the butter in a large pan. Add the onion, garlic and ginger. Cook for 4–5 minutes, until soft. Stir in the curry paste and turmeric, and cook for 2–3 minutes, stirring continuously.

2 Pour in two-thirds of the coconut milk and cook for 5 minutes. Add the stock, lime leaves and lemon grass with the chicken. Simmer for 15 minutes until the chicken is tender. Remove the chicken and cool.

3 Add the spinach to the pan and cook for 3–4 minutes. Stir in the

remaining coconut milk and seasoning, then process the soup in a food processor or a blender.

4 Return the soup to the rinsed-out pan. Cut the chicken thighs into bitesize pieces and stir into the soup with the fish sauce and lime juice. Reheat the soup without boiling.

5 Meanwhile, heat the oil in a frying pan and cook the shallots for 6–8 minutes, until golden. Drain. Serve the soup topped with basil leaves and fried shallots.

Nutritional information per portion: Energy 136Kcal/570kJ; Protein 14.1g; Carbohydrate 5.2g, of which sugars 4.9g; Fat 6.7g, of which saturates 3.8g; Cholesterol 49mg; Calcium 125mg; Fibre 1.4g; Sodium 344mg.

Chinese chicken and chilli soup

Ginger and lemon grass add an aromatic note to this tasty, refreshing Chinese-style soup, which can be served as a light lunch or appetizer.

SERVES 4

150g/5oz boneless chicken breast
   portion, cut into thin strips
2.5cm/1in piece fresh root ginger,
   finely chopped
5cm/2in piece lemon grass stalk,
   finely chopped
1 red chilli, seeded and thinly sliced
8 baby corn cobs, halved lengthways
1 large carrot, cut into thin sticks
1 litre/1¾ pints/4 cups hot
   chicken stock
12 small shiitake mushrooms, sliced
4 spring onions (scallions), thinly sliced
115g/4oz/1 cup vermicelli rice noodles
30ml/2 tbsp soy sauce
salt and ground black pepper

1 Place the chicken, ginger, lemon grass and chilli in an ovenproof dish. Add the baby corn and the carrot sticks. Pour over the hot chicken stock and cover the dish.

2 Heat the oven to 200°C/400°F/ Gas 6. Place the dish in the oven and cook for 30–40 minutes, or until the stock is simmering and the chicken and vegetables are tender. Add the mushrooms and spring onions, cover and return to the oven for 10 minutes.

3 Meanwhile place the noodles in a large bowl and cover with boiling water. Soak for the required time, following the packet instructions.

4 Stir the soy sauce into the soup, taste for seasoning and add salt and pepper as required.

5 Drain the noodles and divide them among four warmed serving bowls.

6 Divide the soup between the bowls and serve immediately.

Nutritional information per portion: Energy 165Kcal/693kJ; Protein 13.3g; Carbohydrate 26g, of which sugars 3.1g; Fat 0.9g, of which saturates 0.2g; Cholesterol 26mg; Calcium 23mg; Fibre 1.4g; Sodium 852mg.

Cream of duck soup with blueberry relish

This delicious, rich soup is ideal for smart occasions. You can use a whole duck if you wish, but cooking with pieces such as breasts and legs is easier.

SERVES 4

2 duck breasts
4 streaky (fatty) bacon rashers (strips)
1 onion, chopped
1 garlic clove, chopped
2 carrots, diced
2 celery sticks, chopped
4 large open mushrooms, chopped
15ml/1 tbsp tomato purée (paste)
2 duck legs
15ml/1 tbsp plain (all-purpose) flour
45ml/3 tbsp brandy
150ml/^{1}/$_4$ pint/^{2}/$_3$ cup port
300ml/^{1}/$_2$ pint/1^1/$_4$ cups red wine
900ml/1^1/$_2$ pints/ 3^3/$_4$ cups chicken stock

1 bay leaf
2 sprigs fresh thyme
15ml/1 tbsp redcurrant jelly
150ml/^{1}/$_4$ pint/^{2}/$_3$ cup double (heavy)
   cream
salt and ground black pepper

FOR THE BLUEBERRY RELISH
150g/5oz/1^1/$_4$ cups blueberries
15ml/1 tbsp caster (superfine) sugar
grated rind and juice of 2 limes
15ml/1 tbsp chopped fresh parsley
15ml/1 tbsp balsamic vinegar

1 Score the skin and fat on the duck breasts. Preheat a heavy pan. Place the duck breasts in the pan, skin-side down, and cook for 8–10 minutes, until golden. Turn and cook for a further 5–6 minutes. Remove the duck from the pan and set aside. Drain off some of the fat, leaving 45ml/3 tbsp in the pan.

2 Chop the bacon and add to the pan along with the onion, garlic, carrots, celery and mushrooms, and cook for 10 minutes. Stir in the tomato purée and cook for 2 minutes. Remove the skin and bones from the duck legs and chop the flesh. Add to the pan and cook for 5 minutes.

3 Stir in the flour and cook for 1 minute. Gradually stir in the brandy, port, wine and stock and bring to the boil, stirring. Add the bay leaf, thyme and redcurrant jelly, then stir until the jelly melts. Simmer for 1 hour.

4 Meanwhile, make the relish. Put the blueberries, caster sugar, lime rind and juice, parsley and vinegar in a small bowl. Very lightly bruise the blueberries with a fork, leaving some of the berries whole. Set aside.

5 Strain the soup into a clean pan. Bring to the boil, reduce the heat and simmer for 10 minutes. Meanwhile, remove and discard the skin and fat from the duck breasts and cut the meat into strips. Add the meat strips to the soup with the double cream and season well. Bring just to boiling point. Ladle the soup into warmed bowls and top each serving with a dollop of the blueberry relish. Serve piping hot.

Nutritional information per portion: Energy 642Kcal/2673kJ; Protein 39.2g; Carbohydrate 14.2g, of which sugars 13.6g; Fat 35g, of which saturates 17.2g; Cholesterol 252mg; Calcium 83mg; Fibre 2.8g; Sodium 384mg.

Celeriac soup with cabbage, bacon and herbs

Versatile, yet often overlooked, celeriac is a winter vegetable that makes excellent soup. It tastes wonderful topped with a complementary seasonal version of a salsa.

SERVES 4

50g/2oz butter
2 onions, chopped
675g/1¹/₂lb celeriac, roughly diced
450g/1lb potatoes, roughly diced
1.2 litres/2 pints/5 cups vegetable stock
150ml/¹/₄ pint/²/₃ cup single (light) cream
salt and ground black pepper
sprigs of fresh thyme, to garnish

FOR THE CABBAGE AND BACON TOPPING
1 small Savoy cabbage
50g/2oz/¹/₄ cup butter
175g/6oz rindless streaky (fatty) bacon, roughly chopped
15ml/1 tbsp chopped fresh thyme
15ml/1 tbsp chopped fresh rosemary

1 Melt the butter in a pan. Add the onions and cook for 4–5 minutes, until softened. Add the celeriac. Cover the vegetables with a wetted piece of baking parchment, then put a lid on the pan and cook gently for 10 minutes.

2 Remove the paper. Stir in the potatoes and stock, bring to the boil. Simmer for 20 minutes. Cool slightly. Using a slotted spoon, remove half the celeriac and potatoes and set aside. Purée the soup in a food processor or blender. Return the soup to the pan with the reserved celeriac and potatoes.

3 Prepare the cabbage and bacon mixture. Discard the outer leaves from the cabbage. Roughly tear the remaining leaves, discarding any hard stalks, and blanch them for 2–3 minutes. Refresh under cold running water and drain.

4 Melt the butter in a large frying pan and cook the bacon for 3–4 minutes. Add the cabbage, thyme and rosemary, and stir-fry for 5–6 minutes, until tender. Season well.

5 Add the cream to the soup and season it well, then reheat gently until piping hot. Ladle the soup into warmed bowls and pile the cabbage mixture in the centre of each portion. Garnish with sprigs of fresh thyme.

Nutritional information per portion: Energy 462Kcal/1919kJ; Protein 12.3g; Carbohydrate 24.3g, of which sugars 7.3g; Fat 35.7g, of which saturates 20.4g; Cholesterol 97mg; Calcium 144mg; Fibre 4.3g; Sodium 954mg.

Irish bacon broth

A hearty meal in a soup bowl. The bacon hock contributes flavour and some meat to this dish, but it may be salty so remember to taste and add extra salt only if required.

SERVES 6–8

1 bacon hock, about 900g/2lb
75g/3oz/¹/₃ cup pearl barley
75g/3oz/¹/₃ cup lentils
2 leeks, sliced, or onions, diced
4 carrots, diced
200g/7oz swede (rutabaga), diced
3 potatoes, diced
small bunch of herbs (thyme, parsley,
   bay leaf)
1 small cabbage, trimmed and quartered
   or sliced
salt and ground black pepper
chopped fresh parsley, to garnish
brown bread, to serve

1 Soak the bacon in cold water overnight. Next morning, drain, put into a large pan and cover with cold water. Bring to the boil and skim off any scum. Add the barley and lentils. Bring back to the boil and simmer for 15 minutes.

2 Add the vegetables, some black pepper and the bunch of herbs to the pan. Bring back to the boil, reduce the heat and simmer gently for 1¹/₂ hours, or until the meat is tender.

3 Lift the bacon hock from the pan with a slotted spoon. Remove the skin, then take the meat off the bones and break it into bitesize pieces. Return the bacon to the pan with the cabbage. Discard the herbs and cook for a little longer until the cabbage is cooked to your liking.

4 Adjust the seasoning and ladle into serving bowls, garnish with parsley and serve with freshly baked brown bread.

Nutritional information per portion: Energy 276Kcal/1166kJ; Protein 26.6g; Carbohydrate 33.6g, of which sugars 8.4g; Fat 4.8g, of which saturates 1.6g; Cholesterol 13mg; Calcium 87mg; Fibre 4.8g; Sodium 765mg.

Cock-a-leekie with Puy lentils and thyme

This traditional Scottish soup is made with chicken cooked in a home-made beef stock. Puy lentils add an earthy flavour to this version.

SERVES 4

2 leeks, cut into 5cm/2in julienne strips
115g/4oz/½ cup Puy lentils
1 bay leaf
a few sprigs of fresh thyme
115g/4oz minced (ground) beef
2 skinless, boneless chicken breasts
900ml/1½ pints/3¾ cups good home-
    made beef stock
8 ready-to-eat prunes, cut into strips
salt and ground black pepper
fresh thyme sprigs, to garnish

1 Bring a pan of salted water to the boil and cook the leeks for 1–2 minutes. Drain and refresh under cold running water. Drain again and set aside.

2 Put the lentils into a pan with the bay leaf and thyme and cover with cold water. Bring to the boil and cook for 25–30 minutes until tender. Drain and refresh under cold water.

3 Put the beef and chicken in a pan and pour over enough stock to cover. Bring to the boil and cook for 15–20 minutes, or until tender. Using a slotted spoon, remove the chicken from the stock and leave to cool. When the chicken is cool enough to handle, cut into strips. Return to the pan and add the lentils and the remaining stock. Bring just to the boil and season to taste.

4 Divide the leeks and prunes among four bowls. Ladle over the chicken and lentil broth. Garnish with a few fresh thyme sprigs and serve immediately.

Nutritional information per portion: Energy 275Kcal/1160kJ; Protein 32.3g; Carbohydrate 23.5g, of which sugars 7.4g; Fat 6.4g, of which saturates 2.4g; Cholesterol 70mg; Calcium 47mg; Fibre 4.1g; Sodium 82mg.

Bacon and chickpea soup with tortilla chips

This soup is enhanced by the addition of paprika and cumin butter. The spiced tortilla chips add a contrasting chunky texture when eaten with the smooth creamy soup.

SERVES 4–6

400g/14oz/2 cups dried chickpeas,
soaked overnight in cold water

115g/4oz/1/2 cup butter

150g/5oz pancetta or streaky (fatty)
bacon, roughly chopped

2 onions, finely chopped

1 carrot, chopped

1 celery stick, chopped

15ml/1 tbsp chopped fresh rosemary

2 fresh bay leaves

2 garlic cloves, halved

FOR THE TORTILLA CHIPS

75g/3oz/6 tbsp butter

2.5ml/1/2 tsp sweet paprika

1.5ml/1/4 tsp ground cumin

175g/6oz plain tortilla chips

salt and ground black pepper

1 Drain the chickpeas, put in a large pan and cover with plenty of cold water. Bring to the boil and simmer for 20 minutes. Strain and set aside.

2 Melt the butter in a pan and add the pancetta. Fry until just turning golden. Add the vegetables and cook for 5–10 minutes until soft.

3 Add the chickpeas to the pan with the rosemary, bay leaves, garlic cloves and enough water to cover completely. Bring to the boil, half cover, turn down the heat and simmer for 45–60 minutes, stirring the soup occasionally.

4 Let the soup cool slightly, then process in a food processor or blender until smooth. Return to the rinsed-out pan and season. Reheat gently.

5 Preheat the oven to 180°C/ 350°F/Gas 4. Melt the butter with the paprika and cumin in a pan, then brush over the tortilla chips. Reserve any leftover spiced butter. Spread the chips out on a baking sheet and warm in the oven for 5 minutes.

6 Ladle the soup into bowls, pour some of the reserved spiced butter over each and sprinkle with paprika. Serve with the warm tortilla chips.

Nutritional information per portion: Energy 996Kcal/4154kJ; Protein 31.4g; Carbohydrate 80.1g, of which sugars 6.6g; Fat 63.3g, of which saturates 30.1g; Cholesterol 126mg; Calcium 252mg; Fibre 14.3g; Sodium 1186mg.

Miso soup with pork and vegetables

This is quite a rich and filling soup. Its Japanese name, Tanuki Jiru, *means raccoon soup for hunters, but, as raccoons are not eaten nowadays, pork is used instead.*

SERVES 4

200g/7oz lean boneless pork

15cm/6in piece gobo or 1 parsnip, peeled

50g/2oz mooli (daikon), peeled

4 fresh shiitake mushrooms

1/2 konnyaku or 125g/41/2oz tofu

a little sesame oil, for stir-frying

600ml/1 pint/21/2 cups second dashi
stock, or the same amount of water
and 10ml/2 tsp dashi-no-moto
(freeze-dried stock granules)

70ml/41/2 tbsp miso

2 spring onions (scallions), chopped

5ml/1 tsp sesame seeds

1 Press the meat down on a board and slice horizontally into thin long strips, then cut the strips crossways into stamp-size pieces. Set aside.

2 Cut the gobo diagonally into 1cm/1/2in thick slices. Plunge into water to stop discolouring. If using parsnip, cut in half lengthways, then cut into 1cm/1/2in thick slices.

3 Cut the mooli into 1.5cm/2/3in thick slices, then cut into 1.5cm/2/3in cubes. Remove the shiitake stalks and cut the caps into quarters.

4 Place the konnyaku, if using, in a pan of boiling water and cook for 1 minute. Drain and cool. Cut in quarters lengthways, then into 3mm/1/8in thick pieces.

5 Heat a little oil until purple smoke rises. Stir-fry the pork, then add the konnyaku and the vegetables except the spring onions. When the meat has browned, add the stock. Bring to the boil and skim off the foam. Cover and simmer for 15 minutes.

6 Put the miso in a bowl and mix with 60ml/4 tbsp hot stock until smooth. Stir one-third of the miso into the soup; taste and add more if required. Add the spring onion. Serve hot, sprinkled with sesame seeds.

Nutritional information per portion: Energy 110Kcal/459kJ; Protein 16g; Carbohydrate 1.3g, of which sugars 0.9g; Fat 4.5g, of which saturates 1g; Cholesterol 32mg; Calcium 295mg; Fibre 0.4g; Sodium 573mg.

Russian pea, bacon and barley soup

This thick and warming soup, Grochowka, is a Russian version of pea and ham soup. It makes a substantial appetizer, or it may be served as a meal in its own right.

SERVES 6

225g/8oz/1¼ cups yellow split peas, rinsed in cold water

25g/1oz/¼ cup pearl barley, rinsed in cold water

1.75 litres/3 pints/7½ cups vegetable or ham stock

50g/2oz smoked streaky (fatty) bacon, cubed

25g/1oz/2 tbsp butter

1 onion, finely chopped

2 garlic cloves, crushed

225g/8oz celeriac, cubed

15ml/1 tbsp roughly chopped fresh marjoram

salt and freshly ground black pepper

sprigs of marjoram, to garnish

bread, to serve

1 Put the peas and barley in a bowl, cover with plenty of water and leave to soak overnight.

2 The next day, drain and rinse the peas and barley. Put them in a pan, pour in the stock and bring to the boil, then simmer gently for 40 minutes.

3 Dry-fry the bacon cubes in a frying pan for 5 minutes, or until browned and crispy. Remove from the pan, leaving the fat behind, and set aside. Add the butter to the frying pan, add the onion and garlic and cook for 5 minutes. Add the celeriac and cook for a further 5 minutes, or until the onion is just starting to colour.

4 Add the vegetables and bacon to the pan of stock, peas and barley. Season with salt and pepper, then cover and simmer for 20 minutes, or until the soup is thick. Stir in the marjoram and add extra pepper to taste. Garnish with marjoram sprigs and serve with hot crusty bread.

Nutritional information per portion: Energy 189Kcal/799kJ; Protein 11g; Carbohydrate 25.8g, of which sugars 1.8g; Fat 5.5g, of which saturates 2.8g; Cholesterol 13mg; Calcium 39mg; Fibre 2.4g; Sodium 190mg.

Sweet and sour pork soup

This very quick, sharp and tangy soup is perfect for an informal supper. It can also be made with shredded chicken breast instead of pork.

SERVES 6–8

900g/2lb pork fillet, trimmed
1 unripe papaya, halved, seeded, peeled
   and shredded
3 shallots, chopped
5 garlic cloves, chopped
5ml/1 tsp black peppercorns, crushed
15ml/1 tbsp shrimp paste
30ml/2 tbsp vegetable oil
1.5 litres/2$\frac{1}{2}$ pints/6$\frac{1}{4}$ cups chicken
   stock
2.5cm/1in piece fresh root ginger, grated
120ml/4fl oz/$\frac{1}{2}$ cup tamarind water
15ml/1 tbsp honey
juice of 1 lime
2 small red chillies, seeded and sliced
4 spring onions (scallions), sliced
salt and ground black pepper

1 Cut the pork into very fine strips, 5cm/2in long. Mix with the papaya and set aside. Process the shallots, garlic, peppercorns and shrimp paste in a food processor or blender to form a paste.

2 Heat the oil in a heavy-based pan and fry the paste for 1–2 minutes. Add the stock and bring to the boil. Reduce the heat. Add the pork and papaya, ginger and tamarind water.

3 Simmer the soup for 7–8 minutes, until the pork is tender.

4 Stir in the honey, lime juice, and most of the sliced chillies and spring onions. Season to taste with salt and ground black pepper.

5 Ladle the soup into bowls and serve immediately, garnished with the remaining chillies and onions.

Nutritional information per portion: Energy 229Kcal/963kJ; Protein 32.8g; Carbohydrate 11.1g, of which sugars 10.9g; Fat 6.2g, of which saturates 2.1g; Cholesterol 95mg; Calcium 37mg; Fibre 2.3g; Sodium 111mg.

Pork and rice soup

Originating in China, this dish has now spread throughout the whole of South-east Asia and is a favourite comfort food. It is served with a few strongly flavoured accompaniments.

SERVES 2

900ml/1½ pints/3¾ cups vegetable
   stock
200g/7oz/1¾ cups cooked rice
225g/8oz minced (ground) pork
15ml/1 tbsp Thai fish sauce (nam pla)
2 heads pickled garlic, finely chopped
1 celery stick, finely diced
salt and ground black pepper

TO GARNISH
30ml/2 tbsp groundnut (peanut) oil
4 garlic cloves, thinly sliced
4 small red shallots, finely sliced

1 Make the garnish by heating the groundnut oil in a frying pan and cooking the garlic and shallots over a low heat until brown. Drain on kitchen paper and reserve.

2 Pour the stock into a large pan. Bring to the boil and add the rice.

3 Season the pork. Add the pork by taking teaspoons of it and tapping the spoon on the side of the pan so that the meat falls into the soup in small lumps.

4 Stir in the fish sauce and pickled garlic and simmer gently for 10 minutes, until the pork is cooked. Stir in the celery.

5 Serve the rice soup in individual warmed bowls. Sprinkle the prepared garlic and shallots on top and season with pepper.

Nutritional information per portion: Energy 375Kcal/1574kJ; Protein 26.8g; Carbohydrate 31.1g, of which sugars 0.2g; Fat 16.8g, of which saturates 4g; Cholesterol 71mg; Calcium 32mg; Fibre 0.3g; Sodium 89mg.

Golden chorizo and chickpea soup

This hearty Spanish soup is substantial enough to make a complete meal. Small uncooked chorizo sausages are available from Spanish delicatessens, but ready-to-eat chorizo can be used instead.

SERVES 4

115g/4oz/²⁄₃ cup dried chickpeas
45ml/3 tbsp olive oil
450g/1lb uncooked mini chorizo sausages
pinch of saffron threads
5ml/1 tsp dried chilli flakes
6 garlic cloves, finely chopped
450g/1lb tomatoes, roughly chopped
350g/12oz new potatoes, quartered
2 bay leaves
450ml/¾ pint/scant 2 cups water
60ml/4 tbsp chopped fresh parsley
salt and ground black pepper
30ml/2 tbsp extra virgin olive oil, to garnish
crusty bread, to serve

1 Put the chickpeas in a large bowl, cover with plenty of cold water and leave to soak overnight.

2 Next day, drain and place in a pan. Cover with plenty of fresh water and bring to the boil. Skim off the scum. Cover and simmer for 2–3 hours, until tender. Add more boiling water, if necessary, to keep the chickpeas covered. Drain, reserving the liquid.

3 Heat the oil in a frying pan. Add the chorizo and fry for 5 minutes, until they are pale golden brown. Drain and set aside.

4 Soak the saffron threads in a little warm water. Add the chilli flakes and garlic to the fat in the frying pan and cook briefly. Stir in the saffron with its water, the tomatoes, chickpeas, potatoes, chorizo and bay leaves. Pour in 450ml/¾ pint/ 2 cups of the cooking liquor and the water and season.

5 Bring to the boil, then simmer for 45–50 minutes until the potatoes are tender. Add the parsley and adjust the seasoning. Ladle the soup into soup plates and drizzle olive oil over each portion. Serve with bread.

Nutritional information per portion: Energy 642Kcal/2674kJ; Protein 21.7g; Carbohydrate 42.3g, of which sugars 8.1g; Fat 44g, of which saturates 12.5g; Cholesterol 68mg; Calcium 174mg; Fibre 6.1g; Sodium 997mg.

Toulouse sausage with borlotti beans

The recipe for this satisfying soup is based loosely on cassoulet. French sausages and Italian beans contribute flavour and substance, and the soup is topped with golden breadcrumbs.

SERVES 6

250g/9oz/generous 1¼ cups borlotti
    beans
115g/4oz piece pancetta, finely chopped
6 Toulouse sausages, thickly sliced
1 large onion, finely chopped
2 garlic cloves, chopped
2 carrots, finely diced
2 leeks, finely chopped
6 tomatoes, peeled, seeded and chopped
30ml/2 tbsp tomato purée (paste)
1.27 litres/2¼ pints/5⅔ cups vegetable
    stock
175g/6oz spring greens (collards),
    roughly shredded
25g/1oz/2 tbsp butter
115g/4oz/2 cups fresh white
    breadcrumbs
50g/2oz/⅔ cup grated Parmesan cheese
salt and ground black pepper

1 Put the borlotti beans in a large bowl, cover with plenty of cold water and leave to soak overnight.

2 Next day, place the beans in a pan and cover with plenty of cold water. Bring to the boil, then boil for 10 minutes. Drain well. Heat a large pan and dry-fry the pancetta until browned and the fat runs. Add the sausages and cook for 4–5 minutes until beginning to brown.

3 Add the onion and garlic and cook for 3–4 minutes until softened. Add the beans, carrots, leeks, tomatoes and tomato purée, then add the stock. Stir, bring to the boil and cover. Simmer for 1¼ hours or until the beans are tender, then stir in the spring greens and cook for 12–15 minutes. Season.

4 Meanwhile, melt the butter in a frying pan and fry the breadcrumbs, stirring, for 4–5 minutes, until golden, then stir in the Parmesan. Ladle the soup into bowls. Sprinkle over the breadcrumb mix. Serve with crusty bread.

Nutritional information per portion: Energy 574Kcal/2405kJ; Protein 29g; Carbohydrate 47.7g, of which sugars 10.2g; Fat 31g, of which saturates 12.5g; Cholesterol 75mg; Calcium 284mg; Fibre 10.7g; Sodium 1179mg.

Beef and barley soup

This traditional farmhouse soup makes a wonderfully restorative dish on a cold day. The flavours develop particularly well if it is made in advance and reheated.

SERVES 6–8

450–675g/1–1¹/₂lb rib steak, or other
   stewing beef on the bone
2 large onions
50g/2oz/¹/₄ cup pearl barley
50g/2oz/¹/₄ cup green split peas
3 large carrots, chopped
2 white turnips, peeled and chopped
   into dice
3 celery stalks, chopped
1 large or 2 medium leeks, thinly sliced
   and thoroughly washed in cold water
sea salt and ground black pepper
chopped fresh parsley, to serve

1 Bone the meat and put the bones and half an onion, roughly sliced, into a large pan. Cover with cold water, season and bring to the boil. Skim if necessary, then simmer until needed.

2 Meanwhile, trim any fat or gristle from the meat and cut into small pieces. Chop the remaining onions finely. Drain the stock from the bones, make it up with water to 2 litres/3¹/₂ pints/9 cups, and return to the rinsed-out pan with the meat, onions, barley and split peas.

3 Season, bring to the boil, and skim if necessary. Reduce the heat, cover and simmer for about 30 minutes.

4 Add the rest of the vegetables and simmer for 1 hour, or until the meat is tender. Check the seasoning.

5 Serve in large warmed bowls, generously sprinkled with parsley.

Nutritional information per portion: Energy 167Kcal/705kJ; Protein 16g; Carbohydrate 21.4g, of which sugars 7.8g; Fat 2.6g, of which saturates 0.8g; Cholesterol 34mg; Calcium 54mg; Fibre 3.6g; Sodium 58mg.

Mexican beef chilli soup with Monterey Jack nachos

Steaming bowls of beef chilli soup, packed with beans, are delicious topped with crushed tortillas and cheese. Pop the bowls under the grill to melt the cheese, if you wish.

SERVES 4

45ml/3 tbsp olive oil

350g/12oz rump steak, cut into small pieces

2 onions, chopped

2 garlic cloves, crushed

2 green chillies, seeded and finely chopped

30ml/2 tbsp mild chilli powder

5ml/1 tsp ground cumin

2 bay leaves

30ml/2 tbsp tomato purée (paste)

900ml/1½ pints/3¾ cups beef stock

2 x 400g/14oz cans mixed beans, drained and rinsed

45ml/3 tbsp chopped fresh coriander (cilantro) leaves

salt and ground black pepper

FOR THE TOPPING

bag of plain tortilla chips, lightly crushed

225g/8oz/2 cups Monterey Jack (Cheddar) cheese, grated

1 Heat the oil in a large pan over a high heat and cook the meat all over until golden. Use a slotted spoon to remove it from the pan.

2 Reduce the heat and add the onions, garlic and chillies, then cook for 4–5 minutes, until softened.

3 Add the chilli powder and ground cumin, and cook for a further 2 minutes. Return the meat to the pan, then stir in the bay leaves, tomato purée and beef stock. Bring to the boil.

4 Reduce the heat, cover the pan and simmer for about 45 minutes, or until the meat is tender.

5 Put a quarter of the beans into a bowl and mash with a potato masher. Stir these into the soup to thicken it slightly. Add the remaining beans and simmer for about 5 minutes. Season and stir in the chopped coriander. Ladle the soup into warmed bowls and spoon tortilla chips on top. Pile grated cheese over the tortilla chips and serve.

Nutritional information per portion: Energy 749Kcal/3135kJ; Protein 50g; Carbohydrate 54.1g, of which sugars 10.3g; Fat 37.2g, of which saturates 16.1g; Cholesterol 106mg; Calcium 609mg; Fibre 14.5g; Sodium 1473mg.

Beef soup with cabbage and horseradish cream

This brilliant winter soup has a spicy topping and really is a complete main course in a bowl. The joint of beef can be cooked as rare or as well done as you like.

SERVES 6

900g/2lb red cabbage, shredded

2 onions, finely sliced

1 large cooking apple, peeled, cored and chopped

45ml/3 tbsp soft light brown sugar

2 garlic cloves, crushed

1.5ml/¼ tsp grated nutmeg

2.5ml/½ tsp caraway seeds

45ml/3 tbsp red wine vinegar

1 litre/1¾ pints/4 cups beef stock

675kg/1½lb sirloin joint

30ml/2 tbsp olive oil

salt and ground black pepper

watercress, to garnish

FOR THE HORSERADISH CREAM

15–30ml/1–2 tbsp fresh horseradish

10ml/2 tsp wine vinegar

2.5ml/½ tsp Dijon mustard

150ml/¼ pint/⅔ cup double (heavy) cream

1 Preheat the oven to 150°C/300°F/Gas 2. Mix together the first eight ingredients and 45ml/3 tbsp of the stock. Season, then put into a buttered casserole and cover.

2 Bake for 2½ hours, adding more stock if necessary to avoid drying. Remove from the oven and set aside. Increase the oven temperature to 230°C/450°F/Gas 8.

3 Trim off most of the fat from the sirloin, leaving a thin layer. Tie the joint with string. Heat the oil in a frying pan until smoking. Add the beef and cook until well browned. Transfer to a roasting tin. Roast for 15–20 minutes for medium-rare or 25–30 minutes for well-done beef.

4 For the horseradish cream, grate the horseradish and mix with the vinegar, mustard and seasoning into 45ml/3 tbsp of the cream. Lightly whip the remaining cream and fold in the horseradish mixture. Chill.

5 Spoon the cabbage into a pan and pour in the remaining stock. Bring to boiling point. Let the beef rest for 5 minutes, then remove the string and carve into slices. Ladle the soup into bowls and divide the beef among them. Spoon a little horseradish on top, and garnish with watercress.

Nutritional information per portion: Energy 395Kcal/1645kJ; Protein 29.4g; Carbohydrate 19.4g, of which sugars 18.5g; Fat 22.5g, of which saturates 11.1g; Cholesterol 92mg; Calcium 104mg; Fibre 3.8g; Sodium 97mg.

Lamb country soup

Traditionally, buttered chunks of brown bread, or Irish soda bread, would be served with this hearty one-pot meal which is based on the classic Irish stew.

SERVES 4

15ml/1 tbsp vegetable oil

675g/1¹/₂lb boneless lamb chump chops, trimmed and cut into small cubes

2 small onions, quartered

2 leeks, thickly sliced

1 litre/1³/₄ pints/4 cups water

2 large potatoes, cut into chunks

2 carrots, thickly sliced

sprig of fresh thyme, plus extra to garnish

15g/¹/₂oz/1 tbsp butter

30ml/2 tbsp chopped fresh parsley

salt and ground black pepper

brown or Irish soda bread, to serve

1 Heat the oil in a large pan, add the lamb in batches and fry, turning occasionally, until browned all over. Use a slotted spoon to remove the lamb from the pan and set aside.

2 When all the lamb has been browned, add the onions to the pan and cook for 4–5 minutes, until the onions are browned. Return the meat to the pan and add the leeks. Pour in the water, then bring to the boil. Reduce the heat, then cover and simmer for about 1 hour.

3 Add the potatoes, carrots and thyme, and cook for 40 minutes, until the lamb is tender. Remove from the heat and leave to stand for 5 minutes, then skim off the fat.

4 Pour off the stock into a clean pan and whisk the butter into it. Stir in the chopped parsley and season well, then pour the liquid back over the soup ingredients.

5 Ladle into warmed bowls, garnish with thyme and serve with bread.

Nutritional information per portion: Energy 453Kcal/1893kJ; Protein 36.5g; Carbohydrate 20.5g, of which sugars 6.2g; Fat 25.6g, of which saturates 11.3g; Cholesterol 136mg; Calcium 53mg; Fibre 3.7g; Sodium 185mg.

Beef and lamb soup

This substantial soup, full of savoury meats, vegetables and chickpeas is baked in a very low oven for several hours. A parcel of rice can be added to the broth part-way through cooking, which produces a lightly pressed rice with a slightly chewy texture.

SERVES 8

250g/9oz/1 cup chickpeas, soaked
   overnight
45ml/3 tbsp olive oil
1 onion, chopped
10 garlic cloves, chopped
1 parsnip, sliced
3 carrots, sliced
5–10ml/1–2 tsp ground cumin
2.5ml/¹/₂ tsp ground turmeric
15ml/1 tbsp chopped fresh root ginger
2 litres/3¹/₂ pints/8 cups beef stock
1 potato, peeled and cut into chunks

¹/₂ marrow (large zucchini), sliced
400g/14oz canned tomatoes, diced
45–60ml/3–4 tbsp brown or green lentils
2 bay leaves
250g/9oz salted meat such as salt beef
250g/9oz piece of lamb
¹/₂ large bunch fresh coriander (cilantro),
   chopped
200g/7oz/1 cup long grain rice
1 lemon, cut into wedges, and a spicy
   garnish such as fresh chillies, finely
   chopped, to serve

1 Preheat the oven to 120°C/250°F/Gas ¹/₂. Drain the chickpeas.

2 Heat the oil in a large flameproof casserole, add the onion, garlic, parsnip, carrots, cumin, turmeric and ginger and cook for 2–3 minutes. Add the chickpeas, stock, potato, marrow, tomatoes, lentils, bay leaves, salted meat, lamb and coriander. Cover and cook in the oven for 3 hours.

3 Put the rice on a double thickness of muslin (cheesecloth) and tie together at the corners, allowing enough room for the rice to expand while it is cooking.

4 Two hours before the end of cooking, remove the casserole from the oven. Place the rice parcel in the casserole, anchoring the edge of the muslin parcel under the lid so that the parcel is held above the soup and allowed to steam. Return the casserole to the oven and continue cooking for a further 2 hours.

5 Carefully remove the lid and the rice. Skim any fat off the top of the soup and ladle the soup into bowls with a scoop of the rice and one or two pieces of meat. Serve with lemon wedges and a spoonful of hot sauce or chopped fresh chillies.

Nutritional information per portion: Energy 385Kcal/1621kJ; Protein 25.6g; Carbohydrate 48.6g, of which sugars 5.3g; Fat 10.8g, of which saturates 2.7g; Cholesterol 24mg; Calcium 116mg; Fibre 5.4g; Sodium 54mg.

Fragrant beetroot and vegetable soup with spiced lamb kubbeh

The Jewish community from Cochin in India is famous for its cuisine. This soup is served with dumplings made of bright yellow pasta wrapped around a spicy lamb filling.

SERVES 6–8

15ml/1 tbsp vegetable oil

$^{1}/_{2}$ onion, finely chopped

6 garlic cloves

1 carrot, diced

1 courgette (zucchini), diced

$^{1}/_{2}$ celery stick, diced (optional)

4–5 cardamom pods

2.5ml/$^{1}/_{2}$ tsp curry powder

4 vacuum-packed beetroot (beets) (cooked not pickled), finely diced and juice reserved

1 litre/1$^{3}/_{4}$ pints/4 cups vegetable stock

400g/14oz can chopped tomatoes

45–60ml/3–4 tbsp chopped fresh coriander (cilantro) leaves

2 bay leaves

15ml/1 tbsp sugar

salt and ground black pepper

15–30ml/1–2 tbsp white wine vinegar, to serve

FOR THE KUBBEH (DUMPLINGS)

2 large pinches of saffron threads

15ml/1 tbsp hot water

15ml/1 tbsp vegetable oil

1 large onion, chopped

250g/9oz lean minced (ground) lamb

5ml/1 tsp vinegar

$^{1}/_{2}$ bunch fresh mint, chopped

115g/4oz/1 cup plain (all-purpose) flour

2–3 pinches of salt

2.5–5ml/$^{1}/_{2}$–1 tsp ground turmeric

45–60ml/3–4 tbsp cold water

FOR THE GINGER AND CORIANDER PASTE

4 garlic cloves, chopped

15–25ml/1–1$^{1}/_{2}$ tbsp chopped fresh root ginger

$^{1}/_{2}$–4 fresh mild chillies

$^{1}/_{2}$ large bunch fresh coriander (cilantro)

30ml/2 tbsp white wine vinegar

extra virgin olive oil

1 For the paste, process the garlic, ginger and chillies in a food processor. Add the coriander, vinegar, oil and salt and process to a purée. Set aside.

2 To make the kubbeh filling, place the saffron and hot water in a small bowl and leave to infuse (steep). Meanwhile, heat the oil in a pan and fry the onion until softened. Put the onion and saffron water in a food processor and blend. Add the lamb, season and blend. Add the vinegar and mint, then chill.

3 To make the kubbeh dough, put the flour, salt and ground turmeric in a food processor, then gradually add the water as you work, processing until it

forms a sticky dough. Knead the dough on a floured surface for approximately 5 minutes, then wrap it in a plastic bag and leave to stand on its own for 30 minutes.

4 Divide the dough into 10–15 pieces. Roll each into a ball. Using a pasta machine or a rolling pin, roll into very thin rounds. Lay the rounds on a well-floured surface. Place a spoonful of filling in the middle of each. Dampen the edges of the dough, bring together and seal. Set aside on a floured surface.

5 To make the soup, heat the oil, add the onion and fry until softened. Add half the garlic, the carrot, courgette, celery, cardamom and curry powder, and cook for 2–3 minutes. Add three of the diced beetroot, the stock, tomatoes, coriander, bay leaves and sugar to the pan. Simmer for 20 minutes. Add the other beetroot, the juice and garlic. Season and set aside until ready to serve.

6 To serve, reheat the soup and poach the dumplings in a large pan of salted boiling water for about 4 minutes. Using a slotted spoon, remove the dumplings from the water as they are cooked and place on a plate to keep warm. Ladle the soup into bowls, adding a dash of vinegar to each bowl, then add a few dumplings and a spoonful of the ginger paste to each. Serve immediately.

Nutritional information per portion: Energy 351Kcal/1462kJ; Protein 24g; Carbohydrate 7.6g, of which sugars 1.9g; Fat 23.9g, of which saturates 6.9g; Cholesterol 78mg; Calcium 619mg; Fibre 1.5g; Sodium 624mg.

Lamb shanks in barley broth

Succulent roasted lamb shanks studded with garlic and rosemary make a fabulous meal when served in a hearty vegetable, barley and tomato broth.

SERVES 4

4 small lamb shanks
4 garlic cloves, cut into slivers
handful of fresh rosemary sprigs
30ml/2 tbsp olive oil
2 carrots, diced
2 celery sticks, diced
1 large onion, chopped
1 bay leaf

few sprigs of fresh thyme
1.2 litres/2 pints/5 cups lamb stock
50g/2oz pearl barley
450g/1lb tomatoes, peeled and roughly
   chopped
grated rind of 1 large lemon
30ml/2 tbsp chopped fresh parsley
salt and ground black pepper

1 Preheat the oven to 150°C/300°F/Gas 2. Make small cuts all over the lamb and insert slivers of garlic and sprigs of rosemary into them.

2 Heat the oil in a flameproof casserole and brown the shanks two at a time. Remove and set aside. Add the carrots, celery and onion in batches and cook until browned. Put all the vegetables in the casserole with the bay leaf and thyme. Pour in stock to cover, place the shanks on top and roast for 2 hours.

3 Meanwhile, pour the remaining stock into a pan. Add the pearl barley, then bring to the boil, cover and simmer for 1 hour, or until the barley is tender.

4 Remove the lamb shanks from the casserole using a slotted spoon. Skim the fat from the surface of the roasted vegetables, then add them to the broth. Stir in the tomatoes, lemon rind and parsley. Bring the soup back to the boil, then simmer for 5 minutes. Add the shanks and heat through, then season. Put a shank into each bowl, then ladle the broth over the meat and serve at once.

Nutritional information per portion: Energy 287Kcal/1199kJ; Protein 22.5g; Carbohydrate 19.5g, of which sugars 7.6g; Fat 13.7g, of which saturates 0.9g; Cholesterol 0mg; Calcium 35mg; Fibre 2.3g; Sodium 24mg.

Indian lamb soup with rice and coconut

This meaty soup thickened with long grain rice and flavoured with cumin and coriander seeds is based on the classic Indian mulligatawny soup.

SERVES 6

2 onions, chopped
6 garlic cloves, crushed
5cm/2in piece fresh root ginger, grated
90ml/6 tbsp olive oil
30ml/2 tbsp black poppy seeds
5ml/1 tsp cumin seeds
5ml/1 tsp coriander seeds
2.5ml/½ tsp ground turmeric
450g/1lb boneless lamb chump chops,
    trimmed and cut into bitesize pieces
1.5ml/¼ tsp cayenne pepper
1.2 litres/2 pints/5 cups lamb stock
50g/2oz/generous ⅓ cup long grain rice
30ml/2 tbsp lemon juice
60ml/4 tbsp coconut milk
salt and ground black pepper
fresh coriander (cilantro) sprigs and
    toasted flaked coconut, to garnish

1 Process the onions, garlic, ginger and 15ml/1 tbsp of the oil in a food processor or blender to form a paste. Set aside.

2 Heat a frying pan. Add the poppy, cumin and coriander seeds and toast for a few seconds. Grind the seeds to a powder. Stir in the turmeric. Set aside.

3 Heat the rest of the oil in a pan. Fry the lamb in batches over a high heat for 4–5 minutes until browned all over. Remove the lamb and set aside.

4 Add the onion, garlic and ginger paste and cook for 1–2 minutes. Stir in the ground spices and cook for 1 minute. Return the meat to the pan. Add the cayenne, stock and seasoning. Bring to the boil, cover and simmer for 30–35 minutes until the lamb is tender.

5 Stir in the rice, then cover and cook for a further 15 minutes. Add the lemon juice and coconut milk and simmer for a further 2 minutes. Ladle the soup into bowls and garnish with coriander and lightly toasted flaked coconut. Serve hot.

Nutritional information per portion: Energy 249Kcal/1036kJ; Protein 15.8g; Carbohydrate 7.5g, of which sugars 0.8g; Fat 17.3g, of which saturates 4.5g; Cholesterol 56mg; Calcium 14mg; Fibre 0.2g; Sodium 64mg.

Moroccan harira

There are many versions of this traditional Moroccan hearty main-course meat and vegetable soup. As well as lemon slices, some people also add lemon juice to their soup.

SERVES 4

450g/1lb well-flavoured tomatoes
225g/8oz lamb, cut into pieces
2.5ml/$\frac{1}{2}$ tsp ground turmeric
2.5ml/$\frac{1}{2}$ tsp ground cinnamon
25g/1oz/2 tbsp butter
60ml/4 tbsp chopped fresh coriander
   (cilantro)
30ml/2 tbsp chopped fresh parsley
1 onion, chopped
50g/2oz/$\frac{1}{4}$ cup split red lentils
75g/3oz/$\frac{1}{2}$ cup dried chickpeas, soaked
   overnight in cold water
600ml/1 pint/2$\frac{1}{2}$ cups water
4 baby (pearl) onions or shallots
25g/1oz/$\frac{1}{4}$ cup fine noodles
salt and ground black pepper
fresh coriander, chopped, lemon slices
   and ground cinnamon, to garnish

1 Plunge the tomatoes into boiling water for 30 seconds, then refresh in cold water. Peel off the skins. Cut into quarters and remove the seeds. Chop the flesh roughly.

2 Put the pieces of lamb, ground turmeric, cinnamon, butter, fresh coriander, parsley and onion into a large pan, and cook over a medium heat, stirring, for 5 minutes. Add the chopped tomatoes and continue to cook for 10 minutes, stirring the mixture frequently.

3 Rinse the lentils under running water and drain them well. Stir them into the contents of the pan, with the drained chickpeas and the measured water. Season with salt and pepper. Bring to the boil, lower the heat, cover, and simmer gently for 1$\frac{1}{2}$ hours.

4 Add the onions or shallots. Cook for 25 minutes. Add the noodles and cook for 5 minutes more. Spoon into bowls and garnish with the fresh coriander, lemon slices and cinnamon.

Nutritional information per portion: Energy 294Kcal/1234kJ; Protein 19.7g; Carbohydrate 25.2g, of which sugars 4.9g; Fat 13.5g, of which saturates 6.6g; Cholesterol 58mg; Calcium 55mg; Fibre 4g; Sodium 119mg.

Soup basics

This section explains how to select the best

ingredients to use for soup and shows you

how to prepare them. In addition, you'll

find helpful tips on how to make stocks,

descriptions of the equipment you will need

and ideas for garnishes to provide the

perfect finishing touch.

Vegetables

Vegetables come in a wide range of shapes, sizes, colours and flavours and lend themselves to making delicious tasty soups. Vegetables contain essential minerals and vitamins and are important for a healthy balanced diet. If they are freshly picked they are at their most nutritious and make good stocks and soups. Pesticide-free vegetables are also now much more available in supermarkets.

Carrots

The best carrots are not restricted to the cold winter months – summer welcomes the slender, sweet new crop, often sold with their feathery tops. Look for firm, smooth carrots – the smaller they are, the sweeter they taste. Carrots should be prepared just before use to preserve their valuable nutrients.

Beetroot

The key ingredient in the classic Russian Borscht, beetroot (beet) also combines well with other flavours, for example in Fragrant Beetroot and Vegetable Soup with Spiced Lamb Kubbeh. If cooking beetroot whole, wash carefully in order not to damage the skin or the

ABOVE: *Celeriac is a bumpy vegetable with a patchy brown/white skin.*

nutrients and colour will leach out. Trim the stalks to about 2.5cm (1in) above the root. Small beetroots are sweeter and more tender than the larger ones.

Celeriac

Strictly speaking, celeriac is a root vegetable, as it is the root of certain kinds of celery. It has a similar but less pronounced flavour than celery, but when cooked it is more akin to potatoes.

Swedes

The globe-shaped swede (rutabaga) has pale orange-coloured flesh with a delicate sweet flavour. Trim off the thick peel, then treat in the same way as other root vegetables. For soups, swede is usually peeled and diced, then cooked with other vegetables and stock until tender. It may be finely chopped and used in chunky vegetable soups, or cooked with stock and other ingredients, then puréed to create a smooth soup.

ABOVE: *Beetroot adds a unique earthy flavour to soups, and its deep ruby-red colour provides a vibrant hue.*

ABOVE: *Carrots give soup a sweet flavour and add colour, too. Choose smooth carrots with a good shape.*

ABOVE: *Cauliflower can be used either raw or cooked.*

Parsnips

These winter root vegetables have a sweet, creamy flavour and are a delicious element in many soups. Parsnips are best purchased after the first frost of the year, as the cold converts their starches into sugar, enhancing their sweetness. Scrub well before use and peel only if the skin is tough. Avoid large roots, which can be rather woody.

ABOVE: *Parsnips are best used in the winter months and make good, hearty, warming soups.*

Turnips

These vegetables have many health-giving qualities, and small turnips with their green tops intact are especially nutritious. Their crisp, ivory flesh, which is enclosed in white, green and pink-tinged skin, has a pleasant, slightly peppery flavour, the intensity of which depends on their size and the time of harvesting. Turnips add a lovely flavour and substance to vegetable-based soups.

Jerusalem artichokes

This small, knobbly tuber has a sweet, nutty flavour. Peeling can be fiddly, although scrubbing and trimming is usually sufficient. Store in the refrigerator for up to one week. Use in the same way as potatoes – they make good, creamy soups.

Cauliflower

The cream-coloured compact florets, or curds, should be encased in large, bright green leaves. There are also varieties with purple or green florets. Raw or cooked cauliflower has a mild flavour and is delicious when combined with other ingredients to make tasty soups such as Curried Cauliflower Soup or Cream of Cauliflower.

Cabbage

There are several varieties of cabbage, and one of the best to use in soups is Savoy, which has substantial, crinkly leaves with a strong flavour. Firm red and white cabbages are also good for soups as they retain their texture.

Potatoes

There are thousands of potato varieties, and many lend themselves to particular cooking methods. Main crop potatoes, such as Estima and Maris Piper, and sweet potatoes (preferably the orange-fleshed variety, which have a better flavour than the cream-fleshed type) are ideal for using in soups. Potatoes are also good as a thickener. Discard any potatoes with green patches. Vitamins and minerals are stored in the skin, so it is best to use potatoes unpeeled.

Broccoli

This nutritious vegetable should be part of everyone's diet. Two types are available: purple-sprouting, which has fine, leafy stems and a delicate head, and calabrese, the more substantial green variety with a tightly budded top and thick stalk. Choose broccoli with bright, compact florets. Yellowing florets, a limp stalk and a pungent smell indicate overmaturity. Broccoli adds flavour, texture and colour to soups.

To prepare broccoli, trim the stalks from the head of broccoli and divide it into florets. The stems of young broccoli can be sliced and used in soups, too. Once cooked, it is often puréed to create an attractive green-coloured soup. It is a versatile vegetable and combines well in soups with other ingredients.

Spinach

This dark green leaf is a superb source of cancer-fighting antioxidants. It contains about four times more beta carotene than broccoli. It is also rich in fibre, which can help to lower harmful levels of LDL cholesterol in the body, reducing the risk of heart disease and stroke. Spinach does contain iron but not in such a rich supply as was once thought. It also contains oxalic acid, which inhibits the absorption of iron and calcium in the body. However, eating spinach with a vitamin C-rich food will increase absorption. Spinach and other leafy green vegetables are ideal shredded and added to soups or cooked in them and then puréed to create nutritious dishes with a lovely deep green colour, ideal for swirling cream into just before serving.

Courgettes

The most widely available summer squash, courgettes (zucchini) have most flavour when they are young. Standard courgettes, as well as baby courgettes, may be used on their own or with other ingredients, such as mint, to create delicious soups.

Cucumbers

These are juicy and have a crisp texture and refreshing, cool taste. Varieties include English cucumbers, ridged cucumbers, gherkins and kirbys. Although they are used most often in salads, cucumbers can be cooked and are ideal for chilled soups such as Chilled Cucumber and Prawn Soup.

RIGHT: *Corn works well in fish-based soups such as chowders.*

Corn

There are several varieties of corn – but when bought still in the husk it is called corn on the cob . Baby corn cobs are picked when immature and are cooked and eaten whole. Corn and baby corn, as well as canned or frozen corn kernels, are all used in creative soup recipes such as Corn and Red Chilli Chowder.

Pumpkins and squashes

These are native to America, where they are traditionally eaten at Thanksgiving. Small pumpkins have sweeter, less fibrous flesh than the larger ones. Pumpkin can be used in smooth soups such as Spicy Roasted Pumpkin Soup. Squash, such as the butternut variety, makes a good alternative to pumpkin.

RIGHT: *Making soup is a good way of using up a glut of courgettes in the autumn.*

BELOW: *Fresh, crisp cucumbers are excellent in chilled soups.*

Fennel

Florence fennel is closely related to the herb and spice of the same name. The short, fat bulbs have a similar texture to celery and are topped with edible feathery fronds. Fennel has a mild aniseed flavour, which is most potent when eaten raw. Cooking tempers the flavour, giving it a delicious sweetness.

Tomatoes

There are dozens of varieties to choose from, which vary in colour, shape and size. The egg-shaped plum tomato is perfect for many types of cooking, including soups, as it has a rich flavour and a high proportion of

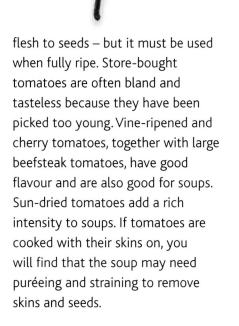

ABOVE: *Chillies add a spicy note to soups, but some are very hot.*

flesh to seeds – but it must be used when fully ripe. Store-bought tomatoes are often bland and tasteless because they have been picked too young. Vine-ripened and cherry tomatoes, together with large beefsteak tomatoes, have good flavour and are also good for soups. Sun-dried tomatoes add a rich intensity to soups. If tomatoes are cooked with their skins on, you will find that the soup may need puréeing and straining to remove skins and seeds.

Peppers

In spite of their name, (bell) peppers have nothing to do with the spice named pepper that is used as a seasoning. They are actually members of the capsicum family and are called sweet peppers, bell peppers and even bull-nose peppers. Peppers add a lovely flavour and colour to soups.

Chillies

Native to America, this member of the capsicum family is extensively used in many cuisines, including Mexican, Indian, Thai, South American and African. There are more than 200 different varieties, and they add a fiery spiciness to soups.

Avocados

Strictly a fruit rather than a vegetable, the avocado has been known by many names – butter pear and alligator pear to name but two. There are four main varieties: Hass, the purple-black small bumpy avocado, the Ettinger and Fuerte, which are pear-shaped and have smooth green skin, and the Nabal, which is rounder in shape. The black-coloured Hass has golden-yellow flesh, while green avocados have pale green to yellow flesh. Avocados can be used to make tempting soups such as Chilled Avocado Soup with Cumin.

LEFT: *Red, green, orange and yellow peppers add wonderful colour to soups.*

Peeling and seeding tomatoes

Tomato seeds can give soups a bitter flavour. Removing the seeds and the tomato skins will also give a smoother result, which is preferable for many soups.

1 Immerse the tomato in boiling water and leave for about 30 seconds – the base of each tomato can be slashed to make peeling easier.

2 Lift out the tomato with a slotted spoon, rinse in cold water to cool slightly, and then peel off the skin.

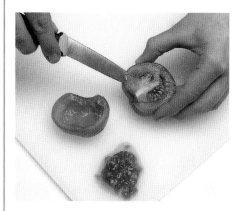

3 Cut the tomato in half, then scoop out the seeds with a knife and remove any hard core. Dice or coarsely chop the flesh according to the recipe.

Aubergines

The dark-purple, glossy-skinned aubergine (eggplant) is the most familiar variety to cooks in the West, although it is the small, ivory-white egg-shaped variety that has inspired its American name. There is also the bright-green pea aubergine that is used in Asian cooking, and a pale purple Chinese aubergine.

Celery

This vegetable has a sharp and savoury flavour, which makes it excellent for soups and stocks. The tangy, astringent taste and crunchy texture of celery contrasts well with the other ingredients. Look for celery with fresh-looking leaves, and avoid any that have outer stalks missing.

ABOVE: *Aubergines, red onions, shallots, white onion and spring onions are all good ingredients for soups.*

Onions

Every cuisine in the world includes onions in one form or another. They are an essential flavouring, offering a range of taste sensations, from the sweet and juicy red onion and powerfully pungent white onion to the light and fresh spring onion (scallion). Pearl onions and shallots are the babies of the family. Shallots and leeks can be used in place of onions in many recipes, while spring onions may be used as a flavouring or garnish. Onions will keep for 1–2 months in a cool, dark place.

Cleaning leeks

Leeks need meticulous cleaning to remove any grit, sand and earth that may hide between the layers of leaves, especially if you grow your own or buy them from organic farmers' markets. The method shown below will ensure that the very last tiny piece of grit and sand will be washed away.

1 Trim off the root, them trim the top of the green part and discard. Remove any tough or damaged outer leaves.

2 Slash the green part of the leek into quarters and rinse the entire leek well under cold running water, separating the layers to remove any hidden dirt or grit. Slice or leave whole, depending on the recipe.

ABOVE: *Garlic is used in Mediterranean soups and in rouille, a garlicky mayonnaise.*

ABOVE: *Shiitake mushrooms are popular in many Japanese soups.*

Mushrooms

The most common cultivated variety of mushroom is actually one type in various stages of maturity. The button (white) mushroom is the youngest and has, as its name suggests, a tight, white, button-like cap. It has a mild flavour. Cap mushrooms are slightly more mature and larger in size, while the flat field (portabello) mushroom is the largest and has dark, open gills. Flat mushrooms have the most prominent flavour. Mushrooms are a useful ingredient in many soups, and add flavour and texture, as well as colour (especially brown cap/chestnut [cremini] or field mushrooms). Several varieties of wild mushroom are now available in supermarkets, for example oyster and shiitake. Fresh and dried wild mushrooms also add delicious taste to some soup recipes.

BELOW: *Fresh sorrel adds a sharp, astringent flavour to soups.*

Garlic

An ingredient that everyone who does any cooking at all will need, garlic is a bulb that is available in many varieties. Their papery skins can be white, pink or purple. Colour makes no difference to taste, but the attraction of the large purple bulbs is that they make a beautiful display in the kitchen. If stored in a cool, dry place and not in the refrigerator, garlic will keep for up to eight weeks.

Leeks

Like onions and garlic, leeks have a long history and are extremely versatile, having their own distinct, subtle flavour. Excellent in soups, leeks add delicious flavour and texture to many recipes. A classic combination of leeks and potatoes produces the popular soup Vichyssoise, which can be served hot or cold as a light starter. Commercial leeks are usually about 25cm (10in) long, but you may occasionally see baby leeks, which are very mild and tender and can also be used in soups.

Rocket

Although usually thought of as a salad vegetable, rocket (arugula) is a herb with a strong peppery taste that adds flavour and colour to soups.

Sorrel

Another salad vegetable that is a herb, sorrel has a refreshing, sharp flavour. In soups it is good mixed with other herbs and green leaves. Salad leaves are best when they are very fresh, and do not keep well. Avoid leaves that are wilted or discoloured. Store in the refrigerator for 3–4 days.

BELOW: *Rocket gives soups a peppery flavour.*

Legumes

Pulses, lentils and peas provide the cook with a diverse range of flavours and textures, and they are a great addition to soups. Low in fat and high in complex carbohydrates, vitamins and minerals, legumes are also a very important source of protein for vegetarians.

PULSES

The edible seeds from plants belonging to the legume family, pulses are packed with protein, vitamins, minerals and fibre, and are low in fat. For the cook, their ability to absorb the flavours of other foods means that pulses can be used as the base for an infinite number of dishes, and many are ideal in soups.

Although legumes can be kept for up to a year, they toughen with time. Buy from stores with a fast turnover of stock store in airtight containers in a cool, dark and dry place.

Broad beans

Usually eaten in their fresh form, broad (fava) beans change in colour from green to brown when dried, making them difficult to recognize. The outer skin can be very tough and chewy, and some people prefer to remove it after cooking. Broad beans add delicious flavour to soups – try Catalan Potato and Broad Bean Soup.

Cannellini beans

These small, white, kidney-shaped beans – sometimes called white kidney beans – have a soft, creamy texture when cooked and are popular in Italian cooking. They can be used in place of haricot (navy) beans and make a tasty addition to soups.

Red kidney beans

These are dark red-brown kidney-shaped beans that keep their shape and colour when cooked. They are excellent in soups as well as many other dishes. Raw kidney beans contain a substance that cannot be digested and which may cause food poisoning if the toxins are not extracted. It is therefore essential that you fast-boil red kidney beans for 15 minutes before use.

Soya beans

These small, oval beans contain all the nutritional properties of animal products but without the disadvantages. Soya beans are extremely dense and need to be soaked for up to 12 hours before cooking. They combine well with robust ingredients such as garlic, herbs and spices, and they make a healthy addition to soups. Soya beans are also used to make tofu, tempeh, textured vegetable protein (TVP), flour, soya milk (an alternative to dairy milk) and the different versions of soy sauce. Tofu is widely used in Asian soups.

Chickpeas

Also known as garbanzo beans, robust and hearty chickpeas have a delicious nutty flavour and creamy texture. They need lengthy cooking and are much used in Middle Eastern cooking, including soups such as North African Spiced Soup.

BELOW: *From left to right: Dried broad beans (fava), can be used in soup recipes when the fresh beans are not in season. Soya beans vary in colour from creamy-yellow through brown to black. All dried beans need to be soaked before cooking. The soaking time varies with different beans.*

Cooking kidney beans

Most types of beans, with the exception of aduki beans and mung beans, require soaking for 5–6 hours or overnight and then boiling rapidly for 10–15 minutes to remove any harmful toxins. This is particularly important for kidney beans, which can cause serious food poisoning if not treated in this way.

1 Spread out beans on a light-coloured cooking surface to check for and remove stones and damaged beans. Put the beans in a sieve (strainer) or colander and wash them well under cold running water.

2 Place the washed beans in a large bowl that allows plenty of room for expansion. Cover with cold water and leave to soak overnight or for 8–12 hours, then drain and rinse.

3 Place the beans in a large pan and cover with fresh cold water. Bring to the boil and boil rapidly for 10–15 minutes, then reduce the heat and simmer for 1–1½ hours until tender. Drain and use as required.

LENTILS AND PEAS

These are among our oldest foods. Lentils are hard even when fresh, so they are always sold dried. Unlike other pulses such as peas, they do not need soaking before being cooked. Do not mix newly bought lentils with ones you have been storing because the older ones will be drier and will take longer to cook.

Red lentils

Orange-coloured lentils are called red split lentils. Sometimes known as Egyptian lentils, are the most familiar variety. They cook in just 20 minutes, disintegrating into a thick purée. Red split lentils are ideal for thickening soups. Try creative recipes such as Red Lentil Soup with Onion or Potage of Lentils, a traditional Jewish soup.

Puy lentils

Originally grown in the Le Puy region of France, these tiny, dark blue-green lentils are considered superior to other varieties of lentils because of their unique peppery flavour. Puy lentils hold their shape during cooking and are great added to soups.

ABOVE: *Red lentils and Puy lentils make excellent thickeners for soup.*

Green and brown lentils

Sometimes referred to as continental lentils, these pulses retain their disc shape when cooked. They take longer to cook than split lentils – about 40–45 minutes – and are ideal for adding to warming soups.

Peas

Dried peas come from the field pea, not the garden pea, which is eaten fresh. Unlike lentils, peas are soft when young and require drying. They are available whole or split; the latter have a sweeter flavour and cook more quickly. Like split lentils, split peas do not hold their shape when cooked, making them perfect for adding to soups. They take about 45 minutes to cook. Dried peas require soaking overnight before use.

Meat and poultry

Packed with high-quality protein, meat is an excellent food and is used in a variety of soup recipes. Most butchers and many supermarkets with fresh meat counters are happy to advise on the best cuts of meat to use for all your recipes, including soups.

Chicken

The stock from cooking chicken makes an ideal basis for many delicious and nutritious soups. If you can, choose corn-fed, free-range or organic birds for the best flavour. Cuts used in soups include breasts, legs and thighs. Boneless thighs or breasts are a good buy.

Duck

There isn't much meat on a duck, especially not on the legs, so buy big

BELOW: *From left to right: corn-fed, free-range and organic chickens give the best flavour to chicken stocks.*

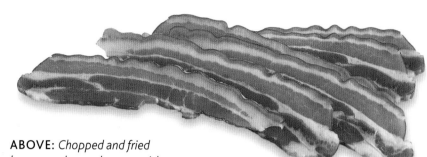

ABOVE: *Chopped and fried bacon can be used as a garnish.*

rather than small birds or choose duck breasts. Although leaner than it used to be, duck is still a fatty meat, so remove as much of the fat as possible before cooking. Duck and most tart fruits such as oranges or cherries are a good combination, and Cream of Duck Soup with Blueberry Relish is another winning recipe. Lean duck can be used instead of chicken in some soup recipes.

Turkey

A turkey isn't just for Christmas – today's smaller birds are perfect for soups. Substitute turkey in recipes such as Chicken, Leek and Celery Soup or Cock-a-Leekie with Puy Lentils and Thyme.

Bacon

Used in soups to add flavour, bacon can be bought sliced, in lardons (thin strips or dice), or in a piece. It is available smoked or unsmoked (green), and in different cuts – lean back or streaky (fatty). Bacon is a key ingredient in Irish Bacon Broth.

Pancetta

This is belly of pork that is cured with salt and spices, and it is either eaten raw in very thin slices, or cut more thickly and used in cooking. It can be substituted for bacon in soup recipes. Try it in the delicious Bacon and Chickpea Soup with Tortilla Chips.

Beef, lamb and pork

Some soup recipes call for the addition of beef, lamb or pork. These not only bring flavour to a dish, but also make a valuable contribution in terms of nutrition, since they are a source of high-quality protein. When making soup, the best cuts of beef, lamb and pork to choose are steak, chops or fillet, although cuts such as pork belly, neck of lamb and minced (ground) beef, lamb or pork are also used, so be guided by the recipe or ask your butcher for advice. Meat bones are also used for making stocks.

Fish

Fish is one of the quickest and easiest foods to cook, and makes an ideal ingredient for soups. As well as being delicious to eat, it is also very nutritious and a great source of easily digestible protein as well as other important nutrients such as B vitamins.

WHAT TO BUY

Both white fish, such as haddock, cod, monkfish and mullet, and oily fish, such as mackerel, halibut and salmon, are used as an ingredient in creative soup recipes. Smoked fish such as smoked haddock or smoked cod are also used to create flavourful soups. The texture of fish soups varies from a thin, aromatic broth to a thick, filling bouillabaisse, and recipes can be adapted according to what type of fish is available. It is always best to buy fresh fish with a firm flesh.

There is a wide range of fresh sea fish generally available, as well as river and lake fish, some caught from our local shores and others imported from farther afield. Although some fish is seasonal, many varieties are available all year round from good fishmongers, supermarkets and town markets.

Round sea fish

This is a large group of fish that includes cod, haddock, whiting, mackerel, ling, coley and pollack as well as more exotic varieties such as John Dory (or porgy), red mullet or snapper and parrot fish. These fish are

ABOVE: *Cod blends well with cream or milk to make delicious fish chowders.*

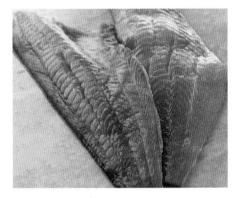

ABOVE: *Smoked haddock is sold whole, as fillets (shown here) or thinly sliced.*

sold whole or in fillets, cutlets or steaks, and can be cut into sizeable chunks and used in heartier soups. They can withstand robust flavours such as spices, herbs, bacon, olives and capers.

Flat sea fish

Plaice, dabs, turbot, sole and skate are common examples of flat sea fish. Flat fish are usually sold whole or filleted and must be very fresh or they lose flavour. They are quick to cook and good in lighter soups.

Freshwater fish

These fish may live in freshwater rivers or lakes and include varieties

ABOVE: *Trout makes a tasty alternative in any soup that uses salmon.*

such as salmon, trout and pike. They are usually sold whole or in fillets, steaks or cutlets. Salmon is rich and only small amounts are required in a soup. Although the flesh is oily, salmon should not be overcooked or the texture and flavour will be spoiled.

Smoked fish

Fish is usually smoked by one of two methods: hot smoke or cold smoke. Examples include haddock, cod, salmon, mackerel, trout and kippers (smoked herrings). Smoked fish is used in soups such as chowders when a stronger flavour is required.

Why fish is so good for you

White fish such as skinless cod, haddock and monkfish are naturally low in fat. Oily fish such as salmon, trout and mackerel are rich in omega-3 fats, which are beneficial to health, and we are actively encouraged to eat oily fish at least once a week. Oily fish are also a good source of all the B vitamins as well as vitamins A and D.

Seafood

Almost all seafood is considered edible, from clams to razor-shells, sea snails and small scallops. Seafood is at its best when eaten fresh and in season, but frozen seafood is a good substitute. All kinds of shellfish, crustaceans and molluscs can be used to make wonderful soups.

Shrimps and prawns
There are many varieties of shrimps and prawns, which are known collectively as shrimp in the United States. The smallest are tiny pink or brown shrimp. Next in size come the pink prawns with a delicate flavour. Then there are the larger variety of prawn, which turn bright red when they are cooked. Best, and most expensive of all, are large succulent king prawns (jumbo shrimp) which have a superb flavour and texture. Similar to these is the cicala, which resembles a small, flat lobster.

CRUSTACEANS AND MOLLUSCS
Crabs and lobsters and bright orange crawfish are all crustaceans. Squid and cuttlefish are molluscs – their shells are located inside their body.

Crab
There are dozens of varieties of crab, ranging from the large common crab to tiny shore crabs that are good only for making soup. All kinds of crab meat, both fresh and canned, can be used in creative soup recipes.

BELOW: *Queen scallops are smaller and cheaper than the larger king scallops, but have the same flavour.*

Deveining raw prawns
Raw prawns and large shrimps are often peeled before cooking. Raw prawns must have their intestinal tracts removed before cooking, a process called "deveining". It is not necessary to devein small shrimps.

1 Pull off the head and legs from each prawn or shrimp, then carefully peel off the body shell. Leave on the tail "fan" if you wish.

2 To remove the intestinal vein from a prawn, carefully make a shallow incision down the centre of the curved back of the prawn using a small sharp knife, cutting all the way from the tail to the head.

3 Pick out the thin black vein that runs the length of the prawn with the tip of the knife and discard.

ABOVE: *The common or brown crab contains plenty of tasty meat, which can be used in delicious soup recipes.*

Scallops

These are available almost all year round, but are best in winter when the roes are full and firm. Always try to buy scallops that have their coral attached. You can buy them shelled, which saves the effort of cleaning them. But, if you clean scallops yourself, the beard and all dark coloured parts must be removed before they are cooked and eaten. Scallops are an ingredient in exotic soups such as Provençal Seafood Soup, Seafood Chowder and Scallop and Jerusalem Artichoke Soup.

Lobster

These are the ultimate luxury seafood. Their flesh has a delicious flavour and makes wonderful soups. Lobsters must be bought live or freshly boiled. Try the luxurious, velvety Lobster Bisque topped with double (heavy) cream to really appreciate this superior seafood.

Squid and cuttlefish

These molluscs are indistinguishable in taste, but cuttlefish have a larger head and a wider body with stubbier tentacles. Once the bone has been removed, cuttlefish are very tender. The shell of a squid is nothing more than a long, thin, transparent quill. Both squid and cuttlefish have ten tentacles. Squid is more commonly used in soup recipes.

Small squid and cuttlefish should be cooked briefly, just until they turn opaque, or they will become rubbery and tough. Larger specimens need long, slow cooking to make them tender, making them ideal for use in some soups.

Mussels

These shellfish have a smooth texture and sweet flavour. Both whole and shelled mussels may be used in soups, and they also make an attractive garnish, cooked and served in their open shells. Try flavourful soups such as Saffron-flavoured Mussel Soup. Farmed mussels are meatier, tastier and less gritty than wild ones.

Clams

There are many different types of clam, ranging from the tiny smooth-shelled variety to long, thin razor shells and the large Venus clams with beautiful ridged shells. All have a sweet flavour and a slightly chewy texture. Because they vary so much in size, it is best to ask the fishmonger exactly how many clams you will need for a particular soup or be guided by the recipe itself.

Preparing squid

Before you start, rinse the squid under cold running water.

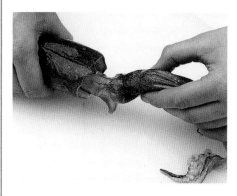

1 Holding the body firmly in one hand, grasp the tentacles at the base with the other, and gently but firmly pull the head away from the body. As you do this the soft yellowish entrails will come away.

2 Use a sharp knife to cut off the tentacles from the head of the squid. Reserve the tentacles but discard the hard beak in the middle. Remove the ink sac and reserve it, then discard the head.

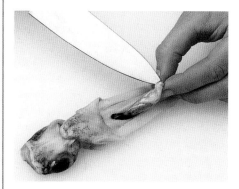

3 Peel the membrane from the body. Pull out the "quill". Wash the body under cold running water. Cut the body, flaps and tentacles to the required size.

Pasta and noodles

The wide range of fresh and dried pasta available ensures that there is plenty of choice when it comes to selecting which pasta to cook. Pasta, especially small shapes, is ideal for use in soups. Noodles, like pasta, provide a good source of carbohydrate and can be used in many delicious soup recipes.

SOUP PASTA

These tiny shapes, of which there are hundreds of different varieties, are mostly made from plain durum wheat pasta, although you may find them made with egg and even flavoured with carrot or spinach.

Buying and storing pasta

The quality of pasta varies – choose good quality Italian brands made from 100 per cent durum wheat, and buy fresh pasta from an Italian delicatessen rather than from the supermarket. If fresh pasta is made from 100 per cent durum wheat, its nutritional content is as good as that of dried pasta. Dried pasta keeps almost indefinitely but if kept in a storage jar, it is best to use it all up before adding any from a new packet.

Types of soup pasta

Teeny-weeny pasta shapes are called pastina in Italian, and there are literally hundreds of different ones to choose from. In Italy they are always served in broths and clear soups. Shapes of pastina vary enormously, and seem to get more and more fanciful as the market demands. The smallest and plainest *pasta per minestre* (pasta for soups) is like tiny grains. Some look like rice and are called *risi* or *risoni*, while others are more like barley and are called *orzi*.

Fregola, from Sardinia, looks like couscous, and has a similar nutty texture and flavour. *Semi di melone* is like melon seeds, while acini de pepe or peperini is named after peppercorns, which it resembles in shape and size if not in colour. Coralline, grattini and occhi are three more very popular tiny pasta shapes.

The next size up are the types of pasta that are most popular with children. These include alfabeti and alfabetini (alphabet shapes), stelline and stellette (stars), rotellini (tiny wagon wheels) and anellini, which can be tiny rings, sometimes with ridges that make them look very pretty, or larger hoops. Ditali are similar to anellini but slightly thicker, while tubettini are thicker still.

Another category of *pasta per minestre* consists of slightly larger shapes, which are more like miniature versions of familiar types of short pasta. Their names end in "ine", "ette" or "etti", denoting that they are the diminutive forms. These include conchigliette (little shells), farfalline and farfallette (little bows), orecchiettini (little ears), renette (like baby penne) and tubetti (little tubes). The size of these types of pasta varies: small ones are used in clear broths; larger ones are often used to make thicker soups.

LEFT: *Tiny soup pasta is available in many different shapes and varieties.*

ABOVE: *Egg noodles add flavour and texture to Chinese soups.*

ABOVE RIGHT: *Rice noodles form the basis of many Asian recipes.*

RIGHT: *Cellophane noodles do not need to be boiled.*

NOODLES

The fast food of the East, noodles can be made from wheat flour, rice, mung bean flour or buckwheat flour. Dried noodles are readily available and will keep for many months in an airtight container. Fresh noodles are also widely found. Noodles can be used in a variety of flavourful soup recipes.

Wheat noodles

These are available in two types: plain and egg. Plain noodles are made from strong flour and water; they can be flat or round and come in various thicknesses. Egg noodles are more common than the wheat variety, and are sold both fresh and dried. The Chinese types are available in various thicknesses. Very fine egg noodles, which resemble vermicelli, are usually sold packaged in individual coils. More substantial wholewheat egg noodles are now widely available from larger supermarkets.

Udon and ramen are types of Japanese noodles. Udon noodles are thick and can be round or flat. They are available fresh, pre-cooked or dried. Wholewheat udon noodles have a more robust flavour. Ramen egg noodles are sold in coils and in Japan are often cooked and served with an accompanying broth.

Rice noodles

These very fine, delicate noodles are made from rice and are opaque-white in colour. Like wheat noodles, they come in various widths, from the very thin strands known as rice vermicelli, which are popular in Thailand and southern China, to the thicker rice sticks, which are used more in Vietnam and Malaysia.

Cellophane noodles

Made from mung beans, cellophane noodles are translucent and do not need to be boiled. They are simply soaked in boiling water for 10–15 minutes. They have a fantastic texture, which they retain when cooked, never becoming soggy.

Buckwheat noodles

Soba are the best-known type of buckwheat noodles. Athough they can vary in colour, generally they are much darker than wheat noodles – almost brownish-grey. In Japan they are traditionally used in soups such as Soba Noodles in Hot Soup with Tempura.

Herbs and spices

Herbs, the aromatic and fragrant plants that we use to add flavour, texture and colour to our dishes, have been cultivated all over the world for centuries. Both fresh and dried herbs add delicious flavours and aromas to many hot and chilled soups.

HERBS

Herbs can make a significant difference to the flavour and aroma of a soup, and they can enliven the simplest of dishes.

Basil

This aromatic herb comes in green and purple. It is widely used in Italian and Thai cooking, generally added at

BELOW: *Basil is an important herb in Italian cooking.*

ABOVE: *Indian-style soups use spicy coriander.*

the last minute so it retains its flavour. The leaves bruise easily, so they are best used whole or torn, rather than cut with a knife.

Bay

These dark-green, glossy leaves are left to dry for a few days before use. They add a robust, spicy flavour to stocks and bouquet garni.

Coriander

Warm and spicy, coriander (cilantro) looks similar to flat leaf parsley but its taste is completely different.

Dill

The mild yet distinctive, aniseed flavour of dill makes a good addition to soups, for example in Sorrel, Spinach and Dill Soup.

Kaffir lime leaves

These glossy green leaves are often used in Asian cuisines, lending a citrus flavour to soups. They are available fresh from Asian stores, or dried from large supermarkets.

ABOVE: *Tarragon goes well with chicken and shellfish.*

Mint

A popular herb, mint has deep green leaves with an unmistakable strong and tangy scent and flavour.

Oregano

This is a wild variety of marjoram with a robust flavour. It goes well with tomato-based soups.

Parsley

There are two types of parsley: flat leaf and curly and both taste relatively similar. Parsley is a good source of vitamin C, iron and calcium.

Tarragon

This small, perennial plant bears slim green leaves, and its distinctive taste is said to be a cross between aniseed and mint. It goes well with chicken and shellfish in soups.

Thyme

This robustly flavoured aromatic herb is good in tomato-based soups. It is also an essential ingredient in a classic bouquet garni.

SPICES

Highly revered for thousands of years, spices – the seeds, fruit, pods, bark and buds of plants – add flavour, colour and interest to the most unassuming of ingredients, while the evocative aroma of spices stimulates the appetite. Spices add delicious flavours to many soup recipes. Always buy spices in small quantities and store in airtight jars.

Chillies

There are many varieties of chillies, which are available fresh as well as in dried, powdered and flaked form. Dried chillies tend to be hotter than fresh, and this is true of chilli flakes, which contain the seeds and the flesh. The best chilli powders do not contain added ingredients such as onion and garlic. All types of chilli may be used in a variety of soup recipes.

Coriander

Alongside cumin, ground coriander is a key ingredient in Indian curry powders and garam masala, and in northern Europe the ivory-coloured seeds are used as a pickling spice. Coriander seeds have a sweet, earthy, burnt-orange flavour that is more pronounced than the fresh leaves. The ready-ground powder rapidly loses its flavour and aroma, so it is best to buy whole seeds, which are easily ground in a mortar using a pestle, or in a coffee grinder. Before grinding them, lightly dry-roast the seeds in a frying pan to enhance their flavour.

Cumin

A familiar component of Indian, Mexican, North African and Middle Eastern cooking, cumin is added to soups to give a delicious flavour and aroma. The seeds have a robust aroma and slightly bitter taste, which is tempered by dry-roasting. Black cumin seeds are milder and sweeter. Ground cumin can be harsh, so it is best to buy the whole seeds and grind them just before use to be sure of a fresh flavour.

Ginger

Fresh root ginger is spicy, peppery and fragrant. When buying fresh ginger, look for firm, thin-skinned and unblemished roots and avoid withered, woody-looking roots as these are likely to be dry and fibrous.

Lemon grass

This long fibrous stalk has a fragrant citrus aroma and flavour when cut. It is familiar in South-east Asian cooking and may be used as an ingredient in soups from this region.

Pepper

Undoubtedly the oldest, most widely used spice in the world, pepper is a versatile seasoning for soups because it can bring out the flavour of the other ingredients.

Saffron

The world's most expensive spice is made from the dried stigmas of *Crocus sativus*. Only a tiny amount of this bright orange spice is needed to add a wonderful colour and delicate flavour to fish and shellfish soups.

Salt

It is usually best to leave the seasoning of soups until the last minute, just before serving. Add salt a little bit at a time, until you have the seasoned flavour you require.

LEFT: *Clockwise from top: black and white peppercorns, cumin, lemon grass stalks, pink peppercorns.*

Equipment

One advantage of making your own soups is that you only need basic equipment such as good knives and a chopping board, as well as a good quality heavy-based pan. A food processor or blender for puréeing is very useful, but if you don't have one many soups can be hand-pressed to make them smooth.

ABOVE: *Using a balloon whisk.*

Heavy-based pan

For making soups you should choose a good quality heavy pan. A good pan that conducts and holds heat well allows the vegetables to cook for longer before browning, so that they can be softened without changing colour. If you are health-conscious, choose a good-quality non-stick pan, and you may be able to slightly reduce the amount of butter or oil that is used to sauté the vegetables.

Vegetable peeler

The quickest way to peel vegetables is to use a swivel peeler. For example, trim off the top and end of a carrot, then hold the carrot in one hand and run the peeler away from you down its length, turning the carrot as you work. Use a julienne peeler to cut vegetables such as carrots and courgettes into

ABOVE: *Two types of vegetable peelers.*

thin julienne strips. Use julienne strips of vegetables in recipes or to make an attractive restaurant-style garnish for chilled or cooked hot soups.

Wooden spoon

Use a wooden spoon to stir soups. This will not damage the base of the pan (important if the pan is non-stick). However, wood absorbs flavours, so always wash and dry the spoon well after use, and don't leave the spoon in the soup while it is cooking.

Whisk

Whisks are available in different sizes, but a balloon whisk is the most useful when making some soups, such as Fish Soup with Rouille and Saffron Seafood Soup. It is also handy for quickly incorporating ingredients such as eggs and cream, which could curdle, or flour mixtures that can form lumps.

Steady the pan or bowl with one hand and, holding the whisk in the other hand, make quick flicking movements.

When using a whisk make sure it is comfortable in your hand and ensure that all the wires are well anchored.

Chopping fresh herbs

Rinse the herbs and dry carefully using kitchen towels. If using herbs with a woody or thick stem, such as rosemary or basil, strip the leaves from the stems with your fingers. Remove the lower stems from herbs such as parsley or coriander (cilantro) – you can chop the upper stems.

Pile the herbs on a chopping board and, using a knife or other sharp tool, chop the herbs roughly, drawing the herbs into a pile as you re-chop. Cut the herbs into smaller pieces (as finely or as coarsely as you wish), holding the tip of the blade against the chopping board and rocking the blade back and forth.

Alternatively, you can use a mezzaluna ("half-moon" in Italian). This is a curved blade attached to two handles, which you rock back and forth over the herbs to chop them. Use the herbs as soon as you have finished chopping them.

ABOVE: *Using a mouli-legume (food mill).*

ABOVE: *Using a hand-held blender.*

ABOVE: *Using a food processor.*

Mouli-legume

A more traditional method is to use a mouli-legume, a cooking instrument from France that is a cross between a sieve (strainer) and a food mill. It sits over a bowl and has a blade to press the food through two fine sieves. The blade is turned by hand to push the soup through the sieves, leaving all the solids behind. It can also grind food into a coarse or fine texture.

Blender

A hand-held blender is brilliant, as it allows you to blend the soup directly in the saucepan. Controlling the speed is extremely easy, to give the required consistency. However, be careful when using a hand-held blender in a non-stick pan, and do not let the blender touch the base or sides of the pan because it will cause damage to the surface.

Electric food processor and blender

The most common items of equipment for puréeing cooked soups, if you wish, are electric food processors and free-standing blenders. Both types of machine are quick and efficient, but the food processor does not produce as smooth a result as a conventional blender, and for some recipes the soup will need to be strained through a sieve (strainer) afterwards. Some food processors will have a blender or liquidizer option, which is fitted alongside the main bowl. Many of the soups that require puréeing can simply be hand-pressed to make them smooth (see left).

Food processors and other free-standing electric mixers can also be used for finely chopping and slicing vegetables to be used in salsas and garnishes. Most models come with extra shredding and grating attachments and blades.

Pressing food through a sieve

A wooden mushroom (or champignon), which looks like a large, flat toadstool, is useful for pressing ingredients through a fine-mesh sieve (strainer) to give a smooth purée if you don't have a food processor or blender. The back of a large spoon or ladle makes a good replacement. It is also a useful method for removing the seeds from cooked tomatoes.

Basic techniques: making stocks

Fresh stocks are indispensable for creating nutritious and home-made soups. They add a depth of flavour that cannot be achieved with plain water and are a good way of using leftovers.

Although many supermarkets now sell tubs of fresh stock, these can be expensive, especially if you need large quantities. Making your own is very easy and much more economical, and because it is made with fresh, natural ingredients it is also tastier and more nutritious. You can, of course, use stock (bouillon) cubes, granules or bouillon powder, but be sure to check the seasoning as these tend to be particularly high in salt. Look for cubes or powder that have a reduced salt content.

Use an appropriate stock for the soup you are making. Onion soup, for example, is improved with a good beef stock. Always use a vegetable stock, though, if you are catering for vegetarians. Recipes are given here for vegetable stock, fish stock, chicken stock, meat stock and basic stocks for Chinese and Japanese cooking.

Freezing stock

Portions of stock can be frozen in ice-cube trays, so you have a constant supply. Frozen stock can be stored for up to 3 months.

Meat stock

The most delicious meat soups rely on a good home-made stock for success. A stock (bouillon) cube will do if you have no time to make your own, but fresh home-made stock will give a much better flavour and basis for soups, so it's well worth spending a little time making your own. Once it is made, meat stock can be kept in the refrigerator for up to 4 days, or frozen for up to 3 months.

MAKES ABOUT 2 LITRES/ 3½ PINTS/8 CUPS

1.8kg/4lb beef bones, such as shin, leg, neck and shank, or veal or lamb bones, cut into 6cm/2½in pieces
2 onions, unpeeled, quartered
2 carrots, roughly chopped
2 celery sticks, with leaves if possible, roughly chopped
2 tomatoes, coarsely chopped
4.5 litres/7½ pints/18¾ cups cold water
a handful of parsley stalks
few sprigs of fresh thyme or 5ml/1 tsp dried
2 bay leaves
10 black peppercorns, lightly crushed

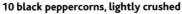

1 Preheat the oven to 230°C/450°F/ Gas 8. Roast the bones, turning occasionally, for 30 minutes, until they start to brown.

2 Add the onions, carrots, celery and tomatoes and baste with the fat in the pan. Roast for a further 20–30 minutes until the bones are well browned. Stir and baste occasionally.

3 Transfer the bones and roasted vegetables to a stockpot or pan. Spoon off the fat from the roasting pan. Add a little of the water to the roasting pan and bring to the boil on top of the stove, stirring to scrape up any browned bits. Pour this liquid into the stockpot.

4 Add the remaining water to the pot. Bring to the boil, skimming frequently. Add the parsley, thyme, bay leaves and peppercorns.

5 Partly cover and simmer the beef stock for 4–6 hours. The bones and vegetables should be covered with enough liquid, so top up with a little boiling water if necessary.

6 Strain the stock through a colander, then skim as much fat as possible from the surface. Cool the stock and then refrigerate. The fat will rise to the top and set in a layer that can be removed easily.

Chicken stock

A good home-made poultry stock is invaluable. Add poultry giblets if available (except the livers) with the wings. Once made, chicken stock can be kept in an airtight container in the refrigerator for 3–4 days, or frozen for up to 3 months.

**MAKES ABOUT 2.5 LITRES/
4¹⁄₂ PINTS/10 CUPS**

1.2–1.3kg/2¹⁄₂–3lb chicken or turkey
   (wings, backs and necks)
2 onions, unpeeled, quartered
1 tbsp olive oil
4 litres/7 pints/16 cups cold water
2 carrots, roughly chopped
2 celery sticks, with leaves if possible,
   roughly chopped
a small handful of parsley stalks
a few sprigs of fresh thyme or 5ml/
   1 tsp dried
1 or 2 bay leaves
10 black peppercorns, lightly crushed

1 Put the poultry wings, backs and necks into a stockpot or large pan together with the onion quarters and the oil.

2 Cook over a moderate heat, stirring occasionally, until the poultry pieces and onions are evenly browned.

3 Add the water and stir well to mix in the sediment on the bottom of the pan. Bring to the boil and skim off any impurities as they rise to the surface of the stock.

4 Add the carrots, celery, fresh parsley, thyme, bay leaf and peppercorns. Partly cover the stockpot and simmer the stock for 3 hours.

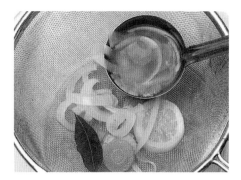

5 Strain the stock through a sieve (strainer) into a bowl. Discard the chicken bones and the vegetables. Leave the stock to cool, then chill in the refrigerator for an hour.

6 When cold, carefully remove the fat that will have set on the surface. The stock is now ready to use. Bring to the boil before use.

Fish stock

Making fish stock is quicker than poultry or meat stock. Ask your fishmonger for heads, bones and trimmings from white fish. Lobster or crab shell pieces (taken after boiling lobster or crab and scooping out the meat) can also be used in place of fish trimmings to make a very tasty fish stock, together with onions, celery sticks, carrots, lemons, dry white wine or white wine vinegar and herbs, such as parsley, bay leaves and black peppercorns.

MAKES 1 LITRE/1³/4 PINTS/4 CUPS

675g/1¹/2lb heads, bones and trimmings from white fish

1 onion, sliced

2 celery sticks with leaves, chopped

1 carrot, sliced

¹/2 lemon, sliced (optional)

1 bay leaf

a few sprigs of fresh parsley

6 black peppercorns

1.35 litres/2¹/4 pints/6 cups cold water

150ml/¹/4 pint/²/3 cup dry white wine

1 Rinse the white fish heads, bones and trimmings well under cold running water. Put in a stockpot or large pan with the vegetables and lemon, if using, the herbs, peppercorns, water and wine. Bring to the boil, skimming the surface frequently, then reduce the heat and simmer for 25 minutes.

2 Strain the stock without pressing down on the ingredients in the sieve (strainer). If not using immediately, leave to cool and then refrigerate. Use within 2 days.

Stock for Chinese cooking

A good well-flavoured stock is an excellent basis for soup-making, and is ideal for using in Asian soups or for any savoury recipe that requires liquid. Meat and poultry are usually added to stocks for Chinese recipes. Refrigerate the stock when it has cooled – it will keep for up to 4 days. Alternatively, it can be frozen in small containers, plastic freezer bags or even ice-cube trays for up to 3 months and defrosted when required. Ensure that you label the stock carefully for easy identification later.

MAKES 2.5 LITRES/4¹/2 PINTS/ 11 CUPS

675g/1¹/2lb chicken portions

675g/1¹/2lb pork spare ribs

3.75 litres/6¹/2 pints/15 cups cold water

3–4 pieces fresh root ginger, unpeeled, crushed

3–4 spring onions (scallions), each tied into a knot

45–60ml/3–4 tbsp Chinese rice wine or dry sherry

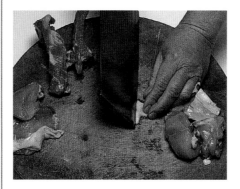

1 Use a sharp knife or a meat cleaver to trim off any excess fat from the chicken portions and spare ribs, then chop the meat into small pieces.

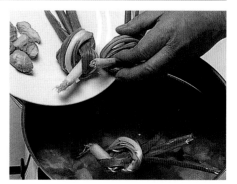

2 Place the chicken and spare rib pieces into large pan with the cold water. Add the ginger and the spring onions tied in knots.

3 Bring the stock to the boil and skim off the froth. Reduce the heat and simmer over a gentle heat, uncovered, for 2–3 hours.

4 Strain the stock, discarding the pork, chicken, ginger and spring onion knots. Add the Chinese rice wine or dry sherry and simmer for 2–3 minutes.

Vegetable stock

Use this versatile stock as the basis for all vegetarian soups. It may also be used for meat, poultry or fish soups. Once the stock is strained, ensure that it is cooled quickly (over a bowl of water) then chilled. Always bring the stock to the boil before use.

MAKES 2.5 LITRES/4½ PINTS/ 10 CUPS

2 leeks, roughly chopped
3 celery sticks, roughly chopped
1 large onion, unpeeled, roughly chopped
2 pieces fresh root ginger, chopped
1 yellow (bell) pepper, chopped
1 parsnip, chopped
mushroom stalks
tomato peelings
45ml/3 tbsp light soy sauce
3 bay leaves
a bunch of parsley stalks
3 sprigs of fresh thyme
1 sprig of fresh rosemary
10ml/2 tsp salt
freshly ground black pepper
3.5 litres/6 pints/15 cups cold water

1 Put all the ingredients into a stockpot or large pan. Bring slowly to the boil, then lower the heat and simmer for 30 minutes, stirring from time to time.

2 Allow to cool, strain, then discard all the vegetables. The stock is now ready to use.

Stock for Japanese cooking

Dashi is the basic stock that gives the characteristically Japanese flavour to many dishes. Known as *Ichiban-dashi*, it is used for delicately flavoured dishes. If time is short you can buy instant stock, which is available in all Japanese supermarkets, either in granule form, in concentrate or even in a tea-bag style. Follow the instructions on the packet.

MAKES ABOUT 800ML/ 1⅓ PINTS/3½ CUPS
10g/¼oz dried kombu seaweed
10–15g/¼–½oz dried bonito flakes

1 Wipe the kombu seaweed with a damp cloth and cut two slits in it with scissors, so that it flavours the stock effectively.

2 Soak the kombu in 900ml/1½ pints/3¾ cups cold water for about 30–60 minutes.

3 Heat the kombu in its soaking water in a pan over a moderate heat. Just before the water boils, remove the seaweed. Add the bonito flakes and bring to the boil over a high heat, then remove the pan from the heat.

4 Leave the stock until all the bonito flakes have sunk to the bottom of the pan. Line a sieve (strainer) with kitchen paper and place it over a large bowl, then strain. Use as required or cool and chill for up to 2 days.

Thickening soups

Many soups do not need any thickening ingredients added, as the puréed soup is thick enough. Vegetables such as potatoes, onions and carrots, once they are cooked and puréed in a soup, will help to thicken the soup. If your soup does need thickening, try one of the methods below.

Beurre manié

This smooth flour and butter paste is used to thicken soups at the end of the cooking time. Equal quantities of plain flour and butter are kneaded together, then a small knob of the paste is added to the soup. The butter melts, releasing the flour particles but without creating lumps, and it is whisked until it is fully incorporated before adding the next. The soup is brought to the boil and simmered for about 1 minute, until thickened and to avoid a raw flour flavour.

Cream

Double (heavy) cream can be used to thicken a fine soup, such as Simple Cream of Onion Soup or Asparagus and Pea Soup. It is always added towards the end of cooking, then the soup is gently reheated until the soup is slightly reduced, thickened and also piping hot. If the soup is allowed to boil the cream may curdle.

Ground almonds

Used as a thickener in soups, ground almonds also add extra flavour as well as texture to the soup. However, ground almonds do not thicken soup in the same way that ingredients such as flour and cornflour (cornstarch) do, to make a thick, smooth soup. Instead they add body, texture, flavour and richness.

Cornflour or arrowroot

These fine flours are mixed with a little cold water (about double the volume of the dry ingredient) to make a smooth, thick, but runny paste. Stir the paste into the hot soup and simmer, stirring, until thickened.

Cornflour (cornstarch) takes about 3 minutes to thicken completely and lose its raw flavour. Arrowroot achieves maximum thickness on boiling and tends to become slightly thinner if it is allowed to simmer for any length of time, so this is usually avoided. Cornflour gives an opaque result, but arrowroot becomes clear when it boils, so it is useful for thickening clear liquids and soups.

Breadcrumbs

The more rustic approach is to use fresh white breadcrumbs to thicken a soup. Breadcrumbs can be toasted in oil before being stirred into a simmering soup, or added directly to a finished dish.

Eggs

Beaten eggs, egg yolks, or a mixture of eggs and a little cream can be used to enrich and slightly thicken a smooth soup. Whisk into the hot soup, but do not allow it to boil once they are added or it will curdle and the soup will be spoiled.

ABOVE: *Making beurre manié.*

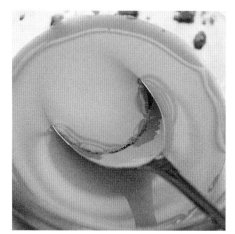

ABOVE: *Mixing cornflour with water.*

ABOVE: *Adding breadcrumbs.*

Garnishes

Ideally, garnishes should look attractive, be edible, complement the flavour of the soup and add that finishing touch. Some typical ones include sprinkling the soup with chopped herbs or stirring them in just before serving. Below are some typical garnishes, as well as a few more unusual ones.

Herbs
Adding a handful of chopped fresh herbs to a bowl of soup just before serving can make a good soup look great. A bundle of chives makes a dainty garnish. Cut 5–6 chives to about 6cm/2½in long and carefully tie them in a bundle using another length of chive.

Fried croûtons
This classic garnish, made from either plain or flavoured bread, adds texture as well as flavour to soups. To make croûtons, cut some bread into small cubes and fry in a little oil. Toss the bread continuously so that the cubes are golden all over, then drain on kitchen paper.

Grilled croûtes
Topped with grilled cheese, croûtes not only look good, but taste great in all sorts of soups. To make them, toast small slices of baguette on both sides. If you like, you can rub the toast with a cut clove of garlic, then sprinkle it with grated Cheddar or Parmesan, a crumbled blue cheese, such as Stilton, or a slice of goat's (chèvre) cheese. Grill (broil) briefly until the cheese is beginning to melt.

Crisp-fried shallots
Finely sliced shallots make a quick garnish for smooth lentil and vegetable soups. Cut them crossways into rings, then fry until crisp.

Crisps
These make a crunchy garnish – try shop-bought thick-cut crisps (potato chips) or tortilla chips; alternatively, you can make your own. Wafer-thin slices of beetroot (beet), pumpkin and parsnip can all be deep-fried in hot oil for a few moments to produce delicious and unusual crisps.

Vegetable julienne
An effective way of preparing ingredients for adding a splash of colour to soup is to cut them into julienne strips or matchsticks. Shreds of vegetables such as spring onions (scallions) or red and green chillies make great garnishes.

Swirled cream
A swirl of single or soured cream is the classic professional finish for many soups. The technique is simplicity itself.

1 Transfer the cream into a jug (pitcher) with a good pouring lip. Pour a swirl on to the surface of each bowl of soup.

ABOVE: *Frying croûtes in oil.*

ABOVE: *Making vegetable julienne.*

2 Draw the tip of a fine skewer quickly backwards and forwards through the cream to create a delicate pattern on the surface. Serve the soup immediately.

Index

SOUTH AFRICAN
ANIMALS
IN THE WILD

SOUTH AFRICAN
ANIMALS
IN THE WILD

Photography: Anthony Bannister

Text: Professor John Skinner,
Director, Mammal Research Institute,
University of Pretoria

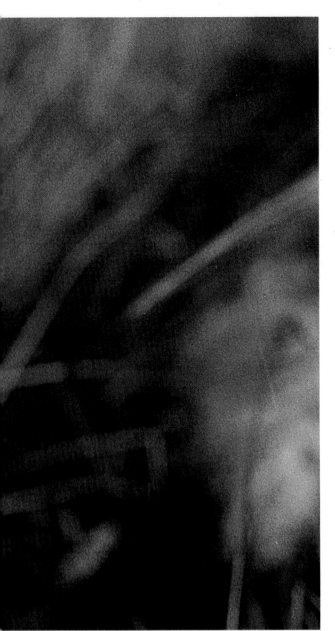

Photographer's acknowledgements

The photographs in this book reflect the generous assistance
I have received from many individuals and organizations.
Unfortunately the list is too long to include in full, but some of
those to whom I owe special thanks are: Mercedes-Benz South
Africa for their assistance with my incredible Galändewagen
four-wheel drive vehicle; Frank and Hirsch Limited for expertly
maintaining my 'armoury' of Nikon cameras and lenses; the
Director and Staff of the National Parks Board, the four provincial
Departments of Nature Conservation and the National Zoological
Gardens for their assistance and for kind permission to photograph in areas under their control; Ann van Dyk of the De Wildt
Cheetah Breeding Station; and Professor John Skinner and Dr
Rudi van Aarde for their utmost co-operation. My gratitude also
goes to the girls in my office and photographic library: Lesley
Hay, Joy Trollope, Lyn Lapham, Lyn Wood and Trish Brownlow,
for their hard work and the happy atmosphere they create; to my
son Andrew and daughter Sue for their valued assistance on
field trips; and finally, to my wife Barbara for keeping our busy
home together, and for caring for David and Patrick.

ANTHONY BANNISTER

Page 1: Suricate keeping guard at a burrow entrance.
Pages 2 and 3: Red hartebeest herd.
Left: Cape clawless otter pup.
Overleaf: Springbok on the move.

Central News Agency (Pty) Ltd
CNA Building, Laub Street,
New Centre, Johannesburg 2001

This book has been designed and produced for CNA by
C. Struik Publishers, Struik House, Oswald Pirow Street, Foreshore, Cape Town 8001

First published 1985

Copyright (text) © John Skinner
Copyright (photographs) © Anthony Bannister,
except for the following which have been reproduced with the kind permission of
Peter Best (p. 109); Anthony Hall-Martin (pp. 40, 49 top, 88 top, 94/95);
Peter Johnson (pp. 28/29 bottom, 46, 47, 48, 75 bottom, 90, 91);
C. J. McCartney (p. 108); Gus Mills (pp. 84 top, 89 top); National Parks Board
(pp. 96, 97 top); Oceanographic Research Institute (p. 107);
Rudi van Aarde (p. 78 middle). Copyright remains with the owners.

Designer: Martin Field
Setting and reproduction by Unifoto (Pty) Ltd, Cape Town
Printed and bound by National Book Printers, Goodwood

All rights reserved. No part of this publication may be reproduced, stored in a retrieval
system or transmitted in any form or by any means, electronic, mechanical, photocopying,
recording or otherwise, without the permission of the copyright owners.

ISBN 0 620 07448 5

Introduction

When one thinks of South Africa's wild animals it is the large mammals that spring immediately to mind, especially the so-called 'big five' – lion, elephant, hippo, rhino and the buffalo. This book is about these mammals and the many others with which South Africa is so richly endowed – the tiny elephant-shrew and hedgehog, the graceful cheetah and stealthy leopard, and antelope from the minute blue duiker to the massive eland and kudu, to name but a few.

There are in the world today about 4 500 species of mammals compared with 8 600 species of birds and 23 000 species of fishes. Of these, 338 species of mammals inhabit southern Africa and the coastal seas surrounding it. A representative selection has been chosen for this book, with photographs and text presenting interesting details about each. While Africa is famous for its diversity of large mammalian species, the small mammals are even more diverse and unique but these are unfortunately seldom seen as most of them move around in the twilight or early morning, or under cover of darkness.

All the species in this book can be viewed in our national parks but, as will become apparent from the text, many occur only in specific regions. National parks in South Africa cover an area of 2 971 541 hectares. To this we can add the more than 70 provincial nature reserves, covering an area of 400 000 hectares, and the 300 000 hectares under the control of the Department of Environment Affairs. Many of these areas have been selected specifically to include certain habitats so that species of mammals peculiar to such areas can be conserved. It is not widely known that the South African Defence Force, which regards conservation as an important priority, controls some 450 000 hectares. This gives a total area of 5,7 million hectares, or 5,2 per cent of the surface area of the Republic of South Africa, which is devoted to conservation. Farmers, who control by far the largest area of South Africa, are also becoming increasingly conservation conscious.

Mammals have adapted structurally, physiologically and behaviourally to enable them to flourish in a wide variety of habitats. The way in which different mammals have evolved to exploit different environmental conditions makes a fascinating study. For the past two decades, scientists of the Mammal Research Institute at the University of Pretoria have played a leading role in studying the mammals of southern Africa. Much of their research has been published recently under the authorship of Dr Reay Smithers in the book *The Mammals of the Southern African Subregion.* Mammalian populations fluctuate within the limits imposed by the environment. For example, while some species will migrate, escaping to areas with more favourable conditions, yet others hibernate to achieve the same objective. The different species have developed in different ecosystems to utilize a unique niche in that system: for example carnivores eat meat, herbivores eat grass and other plants; some mammals live in burrows, others live in trees; some are diurnal, others nocturnal, and so on. There are few characteristics absolutely diagnostic of mammals but one of these is the possession of mammary glands in the female. Typical mammals have four limbs, maintain a constant body temperature, are covered with hair and give birth to live young. There are, however, exceptions to these rules – for example, the echidna and platypus, both monotremes (primitive egg-laying mammals which do not occur in South Africa), and the whales which lack hind limbs and are naked.

The mammalian body is supported by an internal skeleton consisting of a vertebral column, the skull, the ribs and the limb bones. A major characteristic of mammals is that they are endothermic. This means they can maintain their body temperature at a standard level (usually 36-38 °C) by producing heat within their bodies. This ability allows them to exploit a wide range of climatic conditions, from the polar regions to the tropics and from sandy deserts to rain forests.

The skin of mammals is also important as, in addition to hair, it contains many glands. The mammary glands are vital in that they provide nourishment for the young after birth. These glands open via nipples from which the young suckle.

The skin glands of some mammals are specialized, such as the sweat glands or scent glands which are used for advertising, either as attractants or deterrents. Some mammals have very highly developed scent glands: the hyaenas have anal glands as large as tennis balls, and the mongooses and many of their relatives have anal glands which exude

quantities of fluid. Many antelope have preorbital glands (just under the eye) from which they spread a sticky substance on to grass stalks to mark their territories.

Mammal skin is usually covered by hairs. The hairs grow from living cells but are not themselves alive. The hairs serve to insulate the body, and mammals living in temperate regions tend to shed their hair in summer when it is hot, growing an undercoat for winter as the days begin to shorten. Some marine mammals, like fur seals, have thick coats but others such as whales, which have very few hairs, are insulated against the cold water by a thick layer of blubber under the skin.

Just as hairs are dead products of the skin, so too are nails, claws, hooves and horns. Horns are supported by cores of bone emanating from the skull and forming part of the skeleton. Rhinoceros horn is the exception in that it has no core of bone and is entirely a product of the skin.

Hair colours are very important for camouflage and do not necessarily represent the colour of the skin. Consider, for example, the hair pattern in the giraffe (patches) or zebra (stripes), while in both species skin pigmentation is a dark grey. Light colours help reflect the sun's rays, particularly shortwave radiation, whereas dark colours tend to absorb most of the radiation.

Endothermic animals such as mammals also control heat exchange by behavioural mechanisms. They seek shade, or lie on cold or warm surfaces. Many desert mammals are nocturnal, escaping from the high day temperatures by living in burrows. In cold conditions mammals reduce heat loss by seeking protection from the wind or by huddling together. Many species of small mammals build nests to escape from the rigours of climatic changes. Large mammals frequently change their position. For example, it has been found by researchers in Namibia that zebras and wildebeest graze with their bodies at right angles to the sun in the early morning; later in the day, when they want to lose heat, they graze with their long-axis to the sun's direct rays and thus reduce absorption.

In summary, therefore, mammals are unique when compared with other animals in that they can regulate their own body temperature, their eggs are fertilized within the female reproductive tract, and their young (except for marsupials which do not occur in South Africa) are born at an advanced stage of development. Following birth they are dependent on their mothers for a supply of milk, after which they are weaned.

Giraffe

Giraffes are by far the tallest of all living animals – most males grow to about five metres and females to about four and a half metres. Their great height makes them superbly suited to feed off the tops of trees, thereby exploiting a food source available to no other browser. Because of their specialized feeding habits, giraffes can only live where there are tallish trees and bushes. So, although they may sometimes be seen on grassy plains, they are usually just crossing from one wooded area to another. They are extremely well adapted to hot, arid conditions and are, therefore, also found along the dry watercourses of the Kaokoveld in Namibia wherever there is adequate bush.

Giraffes were once widespread throughout South Africa, but at one stage were virtually exterminated except for those in national parks and private game reserves in the eastern Transvaal lowveld. Today they are once again becoming more widely distributed. One major reason for this is that the species is regarded as a prime candidate for game farming because it fills a feeding niche not occupied by any other mammal.

Giraffes have fascinated man since ancient times; Set, the Egyptian god of evil, was depicted as having the head of a giraffe and the body of a man and, like the giraffe, was thought to live in desert regions. The first giraffe imported into Europe was brought by Julius Caesar in 46 BC to the zoo at Alexandria. With the decline of the Roman Empire, however, giraffes vanished from Europe and they were only reintroduced in 1215 when the Sultan of Egypt gave a giraffe to Frederick II, the Holy Roman Emperor, in exchange for a polar bear.

There seems to have been a co-evolution between giraffes and their favourite forage trees, the acacias *(below),* and to a lesser extent the combretums. Although the acacias are very thorny this does not bother giraffes because they use their mobile lips and tongues to strip the plant parts they want from between the thorns. Such reliance on the acacias has its drawbacks, however, as the trees are deciduous, losing their leaves in August. For a time, despite the fact that other tree species in their habitat are well foliaged, the giraffes are vulnerable and during droughts, when the acacias are also affected,

they have been known to die in large numbers. Giraffes are a truly remarkable example of natural selection, as their long necks involve morphological adaptations such as changes in blood vessels, nerves and muscles. A frequently asked question is 'How many neck vertebrae does a giraffe have?' The answer is seven, the same as all mammals, they are just far larger. The head is so far above the heart and lungs that giraffes require a very high blood pressure and deep breathing to supply sufficient oxygen to the brain. Despite the high blood pressure in the body, however, in the brain it remains the same as that for man. This is made possible by a fine network of blood vessels, known as a rete mirabile, below the brain, which 'buffers' the blood being pumped under pressure to the head. When giraffes bend down to drink, they reduce the rush of blood to the head by spreading their legs, and the rete does the rest.

Giraffes are often seen in groups but they do not usually gather in large herds. Groups are generally made up of cows with their offspring, although bachelor and mixed herds are also found. Bull giraffes tend to move from group to group rather than form any fixed associations.

Nyala

The **nyala** belongs to a group of mainly browsing antelopes which includes the kudu *(overleaf)* and eland *(page 18)*. Males and females differ greatly in appearance, with the nyala bull *(right and below)* weighing almost twice as much as the cow. Only males carry horns and they are more spectacularly marked, having a dark brown or even black appearance.

Nyala are found only in the extreme eastern parts of South Africa, occurring in a wide variety of habitats wherever there are sufficient bushy thickets for food and cover, as well as nearby water. Although rarely seen in the Kruger National Park, except in the Pafuri area, their numbers have increased there in recent times. In most of the Natal parks, on the other hand, they are extremely plentiful and during a recent investigation into declining waterbuck numbers it was discovered that one of the reasons for this was that waterbuck were being pushed out of their prime habitat by the expanding nyala population.

Males are most commonly seen alone, but occasionally in twos or threes, invariably displaying to one another when they meet *(below)*. The sight is rather comical as each male raises his spinal crest to make himself look as impressive as possible and then slowly circles his opponent in a stiff-legged gait. Female groups *(right)* may be larger and are sometimes joined by males. Large groups of nyala have been recorded, but all these have been in open habitats where their increased numbers provide greater safety from predators.

Kudu

The **kudu** bull *(opposite)*, with its handsome spiral horns, is surely the most magnificent of the African antelopes and when groups of a dozen or more gather prior to the mid-winter breeding season they provide a spectacular sight. Unfortunately mid-winter also marks the peak of the hunting season, when this stately animal becomes a much sought-after trophy. As with nyala, kudu cows *(left and below)* differ markedly from the bulls – they are noticeably smaller and do not have horns.

Kudu are almost exclusively browsers and will eat grass only in exceptional circumstances. They are ruminants, that is they chew the cud, and they have a specially adapted stomach, divided into four sections, which enables them to digest plants. The enzymes necessary to break down the vegetable matter are not produced by the animals but are provided by micro-organisms living in the large stomach, or rumen.

Like the giraffe, kudu are vulnerable during droughts when acacias shed their leaves in response to the arid conditions, and during the ensuing food shortage kudu die in large numbers. Although starvation is the obvious reason for these deaths, other theories have been recently advanced.

Disease is often the cause of large-scale deaths among kudu and in Namibia recently many thousands died as a result of a rabies epidemic within the species. It seems likely that the rabies was transmitted from one kudu to the next via their saliva during grooming. Although in the 1950s the species was regarded as a carrier of tuberculosis and thought to infect cattle, today it is known that the kudu itself is particularly susceptible to the disease. With careful management, therefore, game farming with kudu can be very rewarding and the species is highly regarded for this purpose. As with the giraffe, the kudu's browsing habits make it ideal for farming in combination with cattle, which are primarily grazers, and provide many bushveld farmers with the opportunity to increase the productivity of their land.

Cape Eland

The **Cape eland** is the largest of the African antelope; it is even bigger than the somewhat misnamed giant eland which only occurs north of the equator. Unlike its relatives, the nyala and kudu, the eland flourishes in the more arid regions of southern Africa, where it will either browse or graze depending on the food available. It often has to travel considerable distances from one water point to the next and during these migrations it obtains enough liquid for its needs from juicy plants.

Eland are prominently depicted in Bushman rock art in southern Africa and they were prized by these people for their flesh and the fat stored in the dewlap. Because of their excellent meat and milk, eland were long thought to be ideal for domestication as they are also very resistant to disease. Many decades ago a number were even exported to Russia, where a dairy herd still exists today – eland milk is believed to have outstanding medicinal properties, but there is no proof to justify these claims.

Studies by the Mammal Research Institute in South Africa have, however, shown that the eland is not as well suited to game farming as was originally thought. It is a nomadic species and does not thrive in captivity. When confined it tends to damage trees by breaking off branches, adeptly twisting the limbs between its horns. Although the eland tames easily, the bulls are unpredictable and not to be trusted, and there are many reports of their attacking people. They are also very difficult to confine as in spite of their size eland are great jumpers and can clear a 2,5 metre fence from a standing start.

Gemsbok

The striking **gemsbok** is a gregarious oryx and may gather in herds of up to 12 individuals. Smaller groups of two or three are also common, however, and occasionally a lone male may be seen. Males and females are very similar but the females' horns are longer and more slender. The gemsbok inhabits the arid western parts of southern Africa and even thrives in the inhospitable wastelands of the central Namib Desert. To do so it has adapted superbly to dry conditions; it is able to travel great distances in search of food and can go for long periods without drinking, as succulent desert plants and early morning dew on leaves provide enough moisture for its needs.

The gemsbok's ability to conserve body fluids is remarkable. For example, its urine is very concentrated and only a small quantity is excreted at a time, while the faecal pellets are very dry. A further water-saving mechanism is the ability, during the heat of the day, to tolerate a body temperature increase of some five or six degrees above the 37 °C regarded as normal for most mammals. The gemsbok reduces the rate of heat absorption as much as possible, however, by keeping its cylindrical body angled away from the sun. Then at night, when the desert air cools sharply, this 'stored' body heat is lost through radiation and the animal's temperature returns to normal without water loss. Throughout this process, however, the gemsbok's brain has to be maintained at normal body temperature. To achieve this, blood passes through a network of capillaries in the nose where it is cooled by the evaporation of moisture as air is drawn through the nostrils. This cooled blood then moves to and surrounds the arterial network below the brain. In this way heat is exchanged with warmer blood on its way to the brain, thus cooling it.

Adult gemsbok have formidable horns and fights at water holes are common, even between females at times, when rival herds meet. It seems that the horns are little defence against predators, however, as research has shown this antelope to fall prey to spotted hyaenas in the Kalahari and the Namib, where particularly the very young and the old are this carnivore's major food source.

Roan and Sable

The **roan** *(left)* is the second largest antelope in southern Africa, only the Cape eland being bigger. Its very wide distribution notwithstanding, the roan is considered endangered in many parts, and the Kruger National Park with its population of some 340 has long been regarded as the most important conservation area for the species in southern Africa.

One of the main reasons for the plight of the roan is its particular habitat needs, for it prefers woodland in which there are open areas through which it can move, grazing taller stands of grass. It does not tolerate woodland where trees form close canopies or thickets and, for this reason, bush encroachment and over-use of grasslands by

other species has in many areas limited its recovery.
Another factor is the roan's susceptibility to disease. In the Kruger
National Park, where it is particularly vulnerable to anthrax, the
Park's biologists have done a superb job in developing a vaccine
and inoculating the herds. During darting the antelope are marked
with a dye so that the biologists can identify inoculated individuals.
In 1968 sixteen roan were translocated from the Waterberg to the
Percy Fyfe Nature Reserve, where they now flourish to such an
extent as a breeding herd that 12 were returned recently to their
original home in the Lapalala Game Reserve in the Waterberg.
The stately **sable** *(above and top left)* can use its great scythe-like
horns to good effect. Bulls are fiercely territorial and will set about
trespassers in no uncertain terms. Under confined conditions, such

as in game parks, they are especially aggressive and evict young
males from the herd when they reach 15 to 18 months. If these
youngsters are unable to escape they are invariably killed.
In the mating season bulls can be seen testing cows to see whether
they are on heat. They can tell this by sampling the cow's urine and
then demonstrating flehmen *(above)* in which the male wrinkles up
his nose following stimulation of sensory receptors in the nostrils.
Sable are able to adapt better to habitat changes than roan and are
less vulnerable to disease, but they are nevertheless regarded as
rare animals. While a nucleus population in the Hans Merensky
Nature Reserve has been used to establish new breeding herds in
other Transvaal reserves, the Kruger National Park remains South
Africa's major area of conservation for the sable.

Waterbuck

Waterbuck are easily identified as both the male and the female have a distinctive target-like white ring around the rump. The purpose of this marking is not clear, but could be a device to help their young follow them through thick vegetation. Only the males have horns.

Waterbuck lack the water-conserving ability of antelope inhabiting arid regions and, as their name implies, they are never found far from reedbeds, vleis, rivers and dams, or wherever else there is permanent water. Although their dependence on water limits their distribution they do thrive outside of reserves, and on many farms in the northern Transvaal waterbuck have migrated up water courses to colonize suitable areas.

These predominantly grazing antelope are gregarious, forming small herds of six to twelve led by a territorial bull. Breeding takes place throughout the year and when a calf is born it is hidden in the thick undergrowth where it will remain for the first four weeks, until it is strong enough to follow its mother.

Tsessebe and Red Hartebeest

Like roan and sable, **tsessebe** *(above and left)* were once relatively widespread in the Transvaal but were later almost exterminated through hunting and destruction of their habitat. Bush encroachment continues to threaten the species as tsessebe are very dependent on open savanna where there is a permanent water supply. Until recently they remained only in the Kruger National Park, near Klaserie in the Transvaal lowveld, and in a few scattered groups in inaccessible areas in the Waterberg. Today the outlook for tsessebe is much brighter as the Transvaal Division of Nature Conservation has had considerable success in translocating these antelope to other reserves for breeding and redistribution.

Although tsessebe usually live in small family parties – a territorial bull, his harem and their offspring – large herds do occur *(above)*, often in association with other plains animals such as Burchell's zebra. Confusion in distinguishing between tsessebe and the **red hartebeest** *(right)* is unlikely as the latter is found usually in the more arid parts of southern Africa. Red hartebeest are particularly plentiful in the Kalahari Gemsbok National Park where herds of up to 20 members are common. Hartebeest and tsessebe have an awkward rocking gait when they run, but this belies their speed and stamina for they are among the fastest of the plains antelope and can keep going at full tilt for many kilometres to escape predators.

Bontebok and Blesbok

Bontebok *(left and far left)* and **blesbok** *(below)* were long thought to be separate species, but in recent times they have been classified as subspecies of the same animal. Even this is in some doubt and a growing number of scientists regard them simply as colour variations of the same species. Certainly there is little to distinguish them physically, apart from slight differences in colour and facial markings. Both animals occur only in South Africa, but their ranges do not overlap as the bontebok is confined to a small area within the south-western Cape, while the blesbok has a wider distribution across the Cape midlands and into the Orange Free State.

In the mid-1800s, the bontebok was poised at the brink of extinction and, had it not been for the far-sightedness and timely action of a group of Bredasdorp farmers, the species would have been wiped out as was the blue antelope which once inhabited the same region. These farmers protected 27 bontebok to form a breeding population on the farm Nacht Wacht where they thrived. In 1931 the first Bontebok National Park was proclaimed and 22 antelope from the original stock were relocated there. The project was not a success, however, as the area was unsuitable – bontebok are exclusively grazing animals and short grass and adequate drinking water are essential habitat requirements. In 1960, the problem was solved when 84 bontebok were moved to the larger, better area which is the present National Park. The future of the bontebok now seems assured – numbers have increased and since 1969 surplus stock has been made available to farmers for game farming and breeding.

Blesbok, too, were hunted extensively, to the point where they were seldom seen. As with the bontebok it was the farmer who came to the rescue, conserving small herds for game farming. Blesbok are highly regarded for this purpose as they are easily confined by farm fences, and their meat is excellent.

As with bontebok rams, male blesbok are very territorial and before the autumn mating season they are a common sight as they display themselves at regular intervals across the veld to attract females. They are very reluctant to leave their posts and this contributed to their previous vulnerability as they made easy targets for hunters. Also, displaying bulls were once regarded as rejects from the herd and farmers were often unwittingly guilty of shooting their prime rams. This had serious repercussions as it created a 'vacuum' of a few weeks before they were replaced by other rams – a male blesbok needs to establish a territory before breeding. Such a shortage of breeding males, even though temporary, can be disastrous for the birth rate for once the breeding season has passed the females do not come on heat again for a full year.

Blesbok ewes lamb in November, after the first rains. This strategy is typical of antelope which have evolved in the highveld with its summer rainfall, for it ensures that lambs are born when there is plenty of green grass to nourish nursing mothers.

Some 80 per cent of breeding ewes drop their lambs within a fortnight of each other. This phenomenon occurs with many plains antelope and is an interesting survival mechanism as, at a time when lambs are very vulnerable, predators are so swamped with prey that most of the young blesbok survive.

Wildebeest

Wildebeest are often referred to as the clowns of the veld. Certainly their appearance is most comical and their head- and tail-tossing antics draw many a smile. There are two species, the **blue wildebeest** *(left and above)* which is widely distributed throughout savanna woodland habitats and the **black wildebeest** *(top)* which is far less abundant and is only found in the grasslands of the central plateau. Black wildebeest bulls, like the moulting specimen above, establish well-defined territories and make a great display when approached, snorting, threshing their blond tails and foot-stamping. Black wildebeest are predominantly grazers and tend to remain in the same area for long periods, thus maintaining grazing pressure on the land. In times past this presented no real problem, for once grazing had been exhausted and/or the water supply depleted, they would move on in search of better conditions, leaving the veld to recover. Such migrations are no longer possible because of the fenced boundaries of game reserves and farms.

Blue wildebeest are also grazers, needing frequent access to water and fresh grazing to which they will migrate over great distances. This is the antelope one associates most with vast herds trekking across the African plains. Although now far more restricted in their movements, migrating herds are still well known in East Africa and to a lesser extent in the Kalahari in Botswana.

As with blesbok and many other plains antelope, wildebeest females form into 'calving herds' and give birth within a few days of each other. In the main photograph, the female on the right has just given birth, note the afterbirth. The female on the left is typically inquisitive about a new arrival to the herd. Within a few minutes the calves are able to stand and suckle and though they are vulnerable to predation at this stage, within a day they can run fast enough to keep up with the herd.

Cape Buffalo

The large, heavily built **Cape buffalo** is regarded as one of the 'big five' by trophy hunters and photographers alike. It is a formidable, well-respected adversary and a wounded buffalo is especially danger-ous. The low-slung horns, particularly those of males, are massive and develop heavy central bosses. They are not only obvious weapons of attack and defence, but probably also help the animal to main-tain normal body temperature, as within the bosses there is a network of capillaries where blood can be cooled.

Buffalo usually live in very large herds *(see overleaf)* and even today these can number several thousand animals. These herds, however, are fairly loosely organ-

ized, being made up of smaller units which disperse and come together depending on the supply of food and water. Bulls often group together in bachelor herds.

Herds usually drink twice a day, in the morning and evening – the buffalo often walk into the water up to their bellies when drinking and also wallow in the muddy shallows and banks. In addition to a permanent supply of water they also need areas of veld where the grass is tall and there is plenty of shade as they spend the greater part of the day resting and do most of their grazing at night. Their mouth parts are well suited to feeding on long grass; using their tongues to pull the grass into their mouths, they bite off the stalks by moving the lower incisors against the dental pad in the upper jaw.

These large grazers can have a profound effect on grass cover if herd numbers build up excessively. For this reason the Kruger National Park authorities need to cull several thousand each year to prevent overgrazing in the fertile environment of the Park.

During the recent wet cycle in the lowveld, buffalo numbers increased considerably in all game reserves, but in the subsequent drought they suffered badly as they cannot adapt to dry conditions and find it difficult to find enough food when the grass is short. Adequate fodder is particularly important to ensure good milk pro-duction in nursing cows and the majority of births take place in January and February, following the major growth period of grass.

Like so many wild animals buffalo are troubled by skin parasites and, while wallowing helps to keep these in check, many persist, especially ticks which burrow through the buffalo's thick hide. The red-billed oxpecker (*left*) is a welcome visitor, therefore, as it scours the buffalo, pecking out the ticks which are its staple food. As many as a dozen of the birds may be seen on a beast at any one time and they serve another useful function as they will fly up calling raucously to alert the herd to any possible danger.

Impala

Impala have evolved along the moist, eastern side of Africa and are never far from permanent drinking water *(below)*. They favour acacia-mopane woodland habitats which provide them with a good supply of high-protein browse.

Male and female impala look very much alike, but the rams are easily identified by their stately lyre-shaped horns *(bottom left)* and during the rutting season are a common sight in the game parks as, with much clashing of horns *(left)*, they do battle to establish and protect their territories.

Like wildebeest, impala lambs are born within a very short period and when the ewe is ready to give birth she withdraws from the herd to find a sheltered spot *(right)*. After a few days mother and offspring return to the herd.

Impala are prolific breeders and their large numbers make them a major food source for all the big predators.

Springbok

With ears pricked, alert to any sign of danger, the **springbok** ewe *(left)* is a lovely sight and it is appropriate that as one of South Africa's most plentiful antelope it is our national animal and the coveted emblem of our sportsmen. Springbok have evolved in the arid, western half of Africa – although they are also found on the highveld – and, like other antelope which have adapted to a drier climate, they need little drinking water. They obtain most of their liquid requirements from young succulent grasses and Karoo scrub and by grazing at night when the moisture content of vegetation is higher.

In the past century springbok were renowned for their great treks when herds of thousands upon thousands would migrate over considerable distances, moving instinctively towards areas where rain had fallen and grazing was good. Such 'tidal waves' of springbok are not known today but herds can still be impressively large as the photographs show. Normally slow moving, springbok are nevertheless extremely fleet-footed and can achieve speeds approaching 90 kilometres an hour, often leaving the ground in great leaps of up to 15 metres in length. When agitated, springbok will perform spectacular, vertical jumps known as stotting ('pronking'), when, with arched back and all fours leaving the ground at the same time, they leap as high as two metres into the air.

Springbok venison is highly regarded and is in great demand both locally and abroad. The antelope are ideally suited to game farming as they can be contained by ordinary fencing and have a high reproductive rate.

Reedbuck and Bushbuck

As their name suggests, **reedbuck** *(top right)* are found near vleis or in reedbeds where there are stands of tall grass. Because of their particular habitat needs reedbuck have a very patchy distribution in South Africa. They have also been exterminated throughout much of their range and are regarded as an endangered species in the Transvaal outside of the Kruger National Park.

Reedbuck are almost exclusively grazers and are strongly attracted to fresh sprouting grass following burning. Water is essential – reedbuck cannot survive without it and will move to new areas if pools near their feeding grounds dry up. They are shy, secretive animals which tend to feed during the evening or early morning when it is cooler, and spend much of the day resting up in some shaded spot. During dry periods, however, when food is hard to come by, they are seen more frequently during the day. When surprised they make a characteristic whistle produced by expelling air through the nostrils. They breed throughout the year, but most young are born in the summer months.

Bushbuck, like their cousins the nyala, are handsome, well-dressed creatures, but they are seldom seen for they are secretive, predominantly nocturnal animals and confine themselves to thick bush and riverine forest. Often the only hint of their presence is a characteristic warning 'bark'. Even if they are within sight they are difficult to spot, for – as the photographs *(left and bottom right)* show – bushbuck have distinctive white markings on a dark brown body which blend with the dappled light of their environment. Lambs are born throughout the year but are seen even less frequently than adults as their mothers hide them away in the dense undergrowth. Bushbuck are generally solitary but sometimes occur in pairs or in small groups.

Only the rams have horns and these they use to great effect against rival rams, often in a fight to the death, as well as against predators. If cornered, wounded rams are dangerous and fight courageously. Many stories tell of encounters where man and his dogs have been bested and sometimes even killed.

African Elephant

By any standard the **African elephant** is massive and is by far the largest and heaviest of the world's land mammals. Mature males such as the specimen opposite may reach a mass of five tons and cows not much less.

All males have tusks as do most females – the cows of the Addo National Park being the exception. Even at birth calves have a tiny pair, but these are like milk teeth in humans and when the baby elephant is about a year old they are replaced by a permanent pair which grows throughout the animal's life. The tusks are in fact large, continuously growing upper incisors, covered at an early stage of development by a cap of smooth enamel which is quickly lost. Wear of the tusks is uneven and consequently right and left tusks may differ in size.

The elephant's bulk makes heat loss difficult, especially as it lacks sweat glands. But it has evolved a unique way to cope with the problem. The elephant's ears are enormous and although they weigh only some 20 kilograms apiece, they form roughly 20 per cent of the animal's surface area. And it is these huge organs that provide the major avenue for heat loss as they are richly supplied with blood vessels and as blood passes through them at a rate of 5-12 litres a minute, it is cooled in much the same way as water passing through the radiator of a motor car. The elephant also flaps its ears to move air over them and to produce a cooling breeze over the body. Although the ears are responsible for as much as three quarters of the heat loss necessary to maintain normal body temperature, water is needed to complete the job and some 30 litres are required daily, not for drinking but solely for the elephant to spray over its body to keep cool. Elephants will drink as much as 150 litres a day if they

can. Wallowing in mudholes *(overleaf)* is a favourite pastime, not only helping to cool their bodies but ridding them of parasites as well. Elephants also consume vast quantities of food – about 200 kilograms a day each – and this they get from trees and grass using their versatile trunks to pluck the vegetation and transfer it to their mouths. They are very destructive feeders, especially the bulls which will push down whole trees to reach a few juicy leaves and will strip the bark from certain species, particularly acacias, causing them to die.

A characteristic of elephants is their matriarchal society, females and their young associating in very closely knit groups. These in turn combine with other family groups to form the breeding herds. Calves may be born at any time of the year following a gestation period of 22 months.

Bulls tend to congregate in bachelor herds but these are loose associations with members tending to come and go. Very old males are usually solitary. Serious fighting can break out between males over a female on heat but usually some head pushing and tusking *(below)* is enough to settle the issue.

Elephants in southern Africa are also famous because of the last survivors of a once-viable herd occurring in the Knysna Forest. Only three elephants are left in the forest and, alas, this is not a habitat of their choice but one which they have sought as a result of persecution by man. The same fate nearly overtook the Addo elephants, but fortunately a national park was declared and a heavy-duty perimeter fence was erected to restrain them from marauding forays into neighbouring farms and suffering the same fate as the Knysna elephants which resorted to this practice.

Duiker

The minute **blue duiker** *(above and above right)* is the smallest of the South African antelope with the male and the female each weighing only about four kilograms. It occurs in Natal from the Umfolozi down the coast and in the Cape between East London and George. The somewhat limited distribution range is further restricted by the species' specialized habitat needs as it is confined to forest, thickets and dense coastal bush. The blue duiker is seldom seen as at the slightest hint of danger it darts away into the forest growth, following its regularly used paths. As a result it is frequently caught by poachers exploiting this habit. It feeds on leaves and shoots as well as fruit. Both sexes are horned. The blue duiker breeds throughout the year, giving birth to a single young at the end of each gestation period.

Though also small, the **common duiker** *(left)* is five times larger than its blue cousin. Its colour is extremely variable and although it is often referred to as the grey duiker it is in some regions distinctly reddish. Unlike the blue duiker, only the male carries horns. This species also frequents wooded areas, but the duikers' ranges do not overlap as the common species is widely distributed throughout the montane forest regions of South Africa while the blue duiker is found only along the coast.

The common duiker feeds in the early evening and at dawn, but its main period of activity can extend well after sunset. It is principally a browsing animal and rarely eats grass, but fruits and seeds of trees are included in the diet. Studies by the Mammal Research Institute have shown the antelope to be something of a problem in the pine plantations of the eastern Transvaal, as the young trees can be seriously damaged during their first year of growth as a result of duiker browsing. The common duiker has also been known to eat young birds.

Oribi and Klipspringer

The **oribi** *(above and right)* and the **klipspringer** *(opposite)* inhabit two different extremes of habitat: the former, the open grassy plains of the highveld, and the latter, stony koppies wherever these occur.

Oribi are yellowish with a rusty tinge and have a fine, silky coat which is much shorter in summer than in winter. Only male oribi have horns. Although oribi once had a wide distribution in South Africa, in many areas their existence is being threatened for two major reasons. First, large areas of their former habitat are now being used for crops or plantations of wattle, pine and eucalyptus trees. And secondly, their preference for an open habitat has made the oribi vulnerable to poachers, particularly to those using dogs. As a result their numbers have been substantially reduced in the eastern Transvaal and the eastern Cape. Their survival is presently dependent on the goodwill of farmers setting aside land for them and making sure they are protected. Oribi are most frequently seen alone, although they do occur in family groups. They are territorial, using the secretions produced by a gland below each eye to demarcate their home ranges. The size of territories varies from 30 to 60 hectares depending on the suitability of the habitat. Oribi are predominantly grazers and studies have shown that they seldom, if ever, drink water, obtaining all their moisture requirements from succulent plant parts.

They breed during the summer months and females hide their newly born offspring for up to four weeks. Lambs only join the family party after about three months.

The **klipspringer** is much the same size as the oribi and is superbly adapted to life in its rocky habitats. The coat is golden-yellow to brown, the upper parts being grizzled with black. The hairs of the klipspringer's coat are unique, being hollow, flattened and spiny, and are thought to play an important part in protecting the antelope from intense radiation both directly from the sun and indirectly from its rocky surroundings through reflection of the sun's rays. The hair is also long (in the region of 20 millimetres), and insulates the klipspringer's body from extreme temperatures. It is easily shed, possibly affording the animal some protection from predators such as the leopard. The species' most special adaptation, however, is its hooves, which are oval in shape and have long, narrow soles and blunt tips which enable the klipspringer to bounce sure-footedly from rock to rock.

In addition to secretions from glands just in front of the eyes, the klipspringer uses dung heaps to mark its territory which varies in size from 15 to 50 hectares. The male klipspringer will also make his presence known by visual displays and sometimes uses such bold behaviour to challenge predators.

Researchers have discovered that a tick which parasitizes the red rock rabbit completes its cycle on the klipspringer. To get on to its host the tick is attracted to twigs marked with secretions from the antelope's facial glands and crawls up the stems. As and when the klipspringer reaffirms its territory the tick is ready to climb on to the beast.

Klipspringers are predominantly browsers but they also eat berries, fruit, seeds and flowers. Following a gestation period of about five months, a single lamb weighing about a kilogram is born. These lambs remain hidden for the first three months of their lives.

Steenbok and Grysbok

Steenbok *(right and below)* are widely spread throughout South Africa and are second only to impala as the most numerous game species in the Kruger National Park. They are small, graceful antelope, rufous brown in colour. Only the male *(below)* has horns. Because they inhabit open country and are daytime feeders they are often seen. Steenbok are territorial and both sexes will defend their territories against intruders, a habit shared with the klip-springer. They obtain their moisture requirements from their food and are known to dig for bulbs and roots as well as for selecting succulent plant parts. A characteristic of steenbok is that before they defecate or urinate, they first clear a spot with their front hooves and then, afterwards, carefully cover the contents by scraping soil over the spot. They are particularly well adapted to a hot, arid climate and because of their small size can make use of tall grass and small shrubs to escape the heat of the day. They breed throughout the year giving birth to a single lamb.

Grysbok *(opposite)* are confined to the fynbos region of the southern Cape. Hardly anything is known about these small antelope, particularly as they are nocturnal. Although they are predominantly grazers, they also eat fruits. They also pose something of a problem for wine farmers as they are particularly fond of vine shoots.

50

Hippopotamus

The **hippopotamus,** among the largest of the land mammals, once occurred in rivers throughout South Africa, but the species has been hunted to the point where it now only occurs in nature reserves. It is very susceptible to heat and sunburn and in summer spends much of the day in the water, often with only its eyes, nostrils and ears above the surface, and sometimes submerging completely, staying underwater for as long as six minutes if alarmed.

Hippos do not feed in the water and at night they leave their daytime habitat to forage on land. They are grazers and, as one would assume from their size, they consume vast quantities of grass, cropping it very closely. Usually their feeding grounds are within a few kilometres of their water territories, but during droughts when they are very vulnerable to starvation they frequently have to wander great distances and have been known to trek 30 kilometres to find enough food. They are notorious for foraging crops, which provide them with a highly nutritious source of food, and are the bane of agriculturists who use the rich alluvial soils near rivers and waterways to plant their crops.

Mating takes place in water and the gestation period is about eight months. Females can conceive from the age of four years, but males develop later and only reach puberty when they are about seven years old. This enables them to remain with the family group for longer as once they start taking an interest in the females they are expelled by the herd bull.

The hippo yawn is often a sign of aggression and even a young animal *(above right)* displays a formidable array of teeth. The huge canines in the lower jaw are the largest and heaviest of their teeth, and during the last century hippos were often shot for this ivory. The canines and the incisors are useless for feeding and are used only as weapons of attack or defence. To crop grass they use the hard edges of their lips. The cheek teeth are used to grind the food which is then broken down in the multi-chambered stomach with the aid of microbes. In common with the elephant, but unlike antelopes, the hippopotamus does not chew the cud.

Zebra

Mountain zebra are restricted to mountainous areas and are divided into two subspecies, the one living in the highlands of Namibia and Angola and the other, known as the **Cape mountain zebra** *(left)*, being endemic to high altitude regions of the Cape. On the other hand, **Burchell's zebra** *(below, below left and overleaf)*, also known as plains zebra, flourish on the eastern side of Africa from Kenya to Natal. Mountain zebra are remarkably nimble and their hooves are able to grip on almost sheer rock faces. They are also better adapted to an arid environment.

In early times Cape mountain zebra occurred as far north as the Suurberg and Stormberg but by 1936 the species was almost extinct. In 1937 the Mountain Zebra National Park was proclaimed and held five stallions and one mare. By 1950 only two stallions remained and their numbers were bolstered by five stallions and six mares from an adjoining farm. This number proved sufficient to form a breeding herd and the population currently stands at 235. A further 35 Cape mountain zebra have been relocated in other sanctuaries in the province. Zebras are not territorial animals and usually form family groups comprising a stallion, his harem of mares and their offspring. Bachelor herds also form and sometimes associate with family groups where they are tolerated by the herd stallion provided the bachelor males remain submissive.

Rhinoceros

The name **rhinoceros** derives from the Greek words *rhis,* meaning nose and *keras,* meaning horn, and relates to this mammal's most obvious characteristic. The horns have no bony core such as those of antelopes, but instead consist of compacted fibres placed on the skull. The horns grow continuously but wear and tear restricts growth of the front horn to about 60 centimetres, the second horn to about 24 centimetres.

Both species, the **black** or **hook-lipped rhinoceros** *(left and opposite)* and its larger relative, the **white** or **square-lipped rhinoceros** *(above and overleaf),* were formerly widespread throughout southern Africa, but with hunting, and the increase in human settlement and resultant pressure on land, they were in danger of becoming extinct. In the Kruger National Park the last naturally occurring hook-lipped rhino was seen in 1936. Hook-lipped rhino were saved from extinction in South Africa by the proclamation of the Natal game reserves and through this protection, numbers have increased steadily to the point where they have been relocated to other sanctuaries.

59

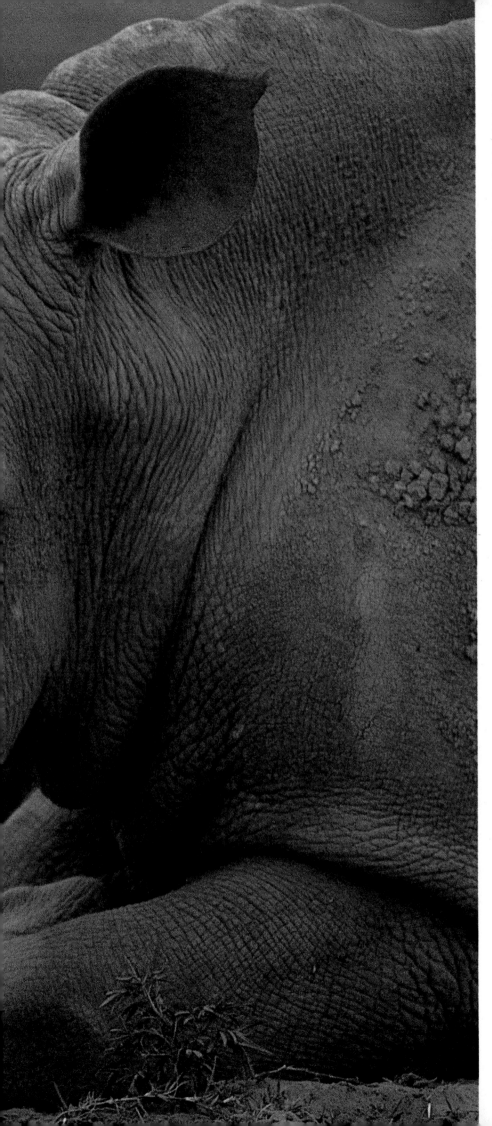

An interesting translocation was that of seven hook-lipped rhinos from Kenya to the Addo Elephant National Park in 1961.

These represent the subspecies *Diceros bicornis michaele* which are now endangered in Kenya, so the twelve existing in Addo have become very important. The hook-lipped rhinoceros is a browser and needs a good supply of fodder trees and shrubs. Climatic cycles are therefore very important in population growth. During wet cycles when the bush flourishes and there is plenty of food, rhino populations increase, but during dry cycles less food is available and populations tend to decrease. They are dependent on surface water for drinking and wallowing which helps them to keep cool and to rid themselves of parasites. Hook-lipped rhinos are solitary creatures and are well known for their aggressive attitude towards intruders and will charge at the least provocation. They have poor vision and rely mostly on sense of smell to locate an adversary. Extremely agile for their size, they can quickly change direction, even when charging at about 50 kilometres an hour.

During courtship the bulls, although not territorial, are extremely intolerant of others. Calves weigh about 40 kilograms at birth, following a gestation period of 15 months. Females with young calves are notoriously ill-tempered and should be avoided.

The case for conservation is epitomized by the saga of saving the **square-lipped rhino** *(left)* from extinction in South Africa. The species came close to being wiped out in the early years of this century, but thanks to timely action taken by the Natal Parks Board and other authorities, the saving of this rhino has become one of the most successful conservation projects in South Africa. At the turn of the century there were only about ten square-lipped rhinos in Natal and, by 1916, these had increased to about 40. By 1930 estimates were put at about 140 and by 1960 at just over 700. Since 1960 numbers in the Natal game reserves have more than doubled and nearly 300 have been relocated in other sanctuaries.

While the future of the square-lipped rhino has been ensured in South Africa, in north-eastern Africa west of the Nile River, it has suffered severely from poaching and only a few survive. The alarming decline is a result of the rapid increase in the value of rhino horns. Although thought to be popular as an aphrodisiac and for medicinal purposes, it is the use of rhino horns for making dagger handles in north Yemen which is largely responsible for the demand.

In contrast to black rhinos, the white rhinos are grazers, having a marked preference for short grass. They lack incisor teeth, using instead their sensitive movable upper lips to crop grass to within a centimetre of the ground. Surface water is important for drinking and wallowing.

Rhinos are long-lived, with hook-lipped rhinos reaching 40 years and square-lipped rhinos 45 years of age. Females first begin to breed at the age of four to five years. Males may breed at seven to eight years but social factors, such as certain bulls dominating the females in the herd, usually preclude this.

Chacma Baboon

All baboons in South Africa are **chacma baboons,** but within the species there is a confusingly wide range in colour variation, both between individual troop members and between troops. Some of these colour differences are due to sex and age; for example, old males tend to be much darker.

Troops may comprise 100 or more individuals and display a high degree of social organization. The number of dominant males in a troop varies, each has a different role to play and they are in the forefront of encounters with other troops. Certain males are responsible for activities such as sentry duty and while the rest of the troop is feeding, they will take up a vantage point so that they can warn of approaching predators. Other males will keep the young from straying while the troop is on the move. Although there are many stories of vicious inter-troop battles, this is not the norm. In three-quarters of encounters between troops recorded by scientists from the Mammal Research Institute, it was found that no fighting occurred, but that when it did, it was indeed very fierce, with even immature members participating.

Chacma baboons are frequently seen in the company of antelope or other foraging animals. Their companions benefit from the association for the baboons dislodge wild fruits which would otherwise be out of the antelopes' reach, and at the same time help to promote the safety of the grazing species by acting as look-outs.

Baboons have an extremely wide-ranging diet, including insects and a variety of vegetable matter: there are many records of their raids on mealie fields and fruit orchards, making them highly unpopular with farmers. They are also known to prey on the young of antelope such as klipspringer and steenbok, as well as farm livestock.

In keeping with the strong social behaviour of baboons, there is a close bond between the newly born and its mother. She will carry her baby about and groom it constantly for two to three months, not permitting other females to pick it up until it can walk. Young are suckled for about six months.

Vervet Monkey
and Lesser Bushbaby

The **vervet monkey** *(left)* inhabits savanna woodland and is widespread throughout southern Africa. It is very gregarious, occurring in troops of up to 20. There is a 'pecking order' within troops, and during squabbles subordinate monkeys are often bitten, particularly on the base of the tail – a convenient method of recognizing low-ranking monkeys. Vervet monkeys are very vocal and will give vent to feelings of hunger, pain or alarm. The presence of young seems to strengthen bonds within a troop for females are very maternal and protective towards infants, and will even accept strange juveniles into the troop. Vervet monkeys spend much time in trees searching for food but they are equally at home foraging on the ground, if food is to be found there. Predominantly herbivorous, they include fruit, seeds, flowers, buds, leaves, bark, gum, roots and bulbs in their diet, but they also take small animals. Scientists from the Mammal Research Institute have found that young vervet monkeys learn about food from adults, whereas with chacma baboons it is often the other way around, for the young baboons are inquisitive and willing to experiment and the adults often learn from them.

The **lesser bushbaby** *(right)* is one of our most appealing small mammals. Found throughout the Transvaal, it usually occurs in some numbers in acacia woodlands as the gum exuded by acacias forms the bulk of its diet. It also feeds on insects, deftly catching them in both hands.

As its huge eyes suggest, the lesser bushbaby is a nocturnal animal and during the day families of up to seven individuals hide in disused birds' nests or in dense clumps of foliage. Research shows that the lesser bushbaby is most active in the first few hours after sunset, when it emerges from its resting place.

After mating and a gestation period of 123 days, two young are usually born, each weighing some nine grams. When setting out to forage the mother will carry her young from the nest, leave them 'parked' on a branch, and then return them to the nest before dawn. The lesser bushbaby's hands and feet are specially adapted to grip the branches along which they move, and their palms and the tip of each digit are cushioned by an enlarged, soft pad.

Warthog and Bushpig

Warthogs *(above and left)* occur in the western parts of north-eastern Transvaal, in the Cape Province along the southern border of Botswana, and in the game reserves of Natal.

The conspicuous outgrowths of skin or 'warts' from which the animal derives its name help distinguish between the sexes: the male *(above)* has two pairs, while the female has only one. The warthog's tusks are, in fact, its canine teeth which grow out side-ways from the jaw.

Warthogs are animals of the day and at night will commonly lie up in disused antbear holes. They reverse into the holes so that they can face any intruder. They may use the holes also as protection from the sun on very hot days, and as maternity dens. Scientists from the Mammal Research Institute have found that within such a maternity den the female will excavate a small raised area on which to place her tiny piglets, probably to protect them in the event of flooding during thunderstorms. Warthogs are largely grazers, although they do root for rhizomes, eat wild fruits and there are records of their eating carrion.

The **bushpig** *(left above)* is widespread throughout the northern Transvaal and along the east coast as far south as George. It is associated with thick vegetation and occurs in forests, reedbeds and even where there is a heavy cover of tall grass.

When foraging, individuals within groups maintain contact by grunting softly. They eat most things and are notorious for pillaging agricultural lands at night. They can scent carrion from many kilometres away and will rapidly home in on this additional food source.

A boar marks his territory by rubbing and tusking trees to apply scent from glands which open at the base of the upper canines. Bushpigs wallow in mud to help them keep cool and as a protection against biting insects.

Lion

Lions are known to have inhabited Europe 15 000 years ago and as recently as
300 BC Aristotle mentioned lions occurring in Greece. Apart from zoos, however, they
have been long gone from Europe and today lions only occur in India and Africa, although they disappeared from North Africa around 1920. They were exterminated in
the Cape by the 1860s and from most of Natal shortly thereafter. Because of their
habit of taking domestic livestock and their reputation as man-eaters, lions have
always been in direct conflict with farmers and today are seldom found outside game
reserves. Lions are, however, great wanderers, and have been known to turn up far from
their expected distribution range.

Lions are known as a 'lazy' species, having short bursts of activity and long periods of
relaxation. They are particularly loath to exert themselves during the heat of the day
and tend to lie around in groups under shady trees. Although they are terrestrial, lions
do climb and can be seen draped along the branches of trees, possibly to get the
maximum benefit of breezes or to escape annoying insects.

The mane that dignifies the male of the species has a twofold function. It serves as a
sexual signal, attracting females, while also making the lion appear larger and thus
warning off potential rivals. It also protects the head and neck areas during fights.

Lions frequent a wide range of habitats, their most important requirements being an adequate supply of prey, and some shade in which to lie up during the heat of the day. They are well adapted to life in arid regions and occur from the Kaokoveld in Namibia as far down as the Skeleton Coast where they have recently been reported raiding seal colonies.

The social behaviour of lions has been extensively studied. They live and hunt in prides of up to 30 or more individuals and occupy home ranges which vary greatly in size, depending on prey availability. Lionesses form the nucleus of lion society, being far more active than the males in hunting, which they frequently do in pairs. Males, however, will defend the carcass against other predators; spotted hyaenas will not lightly approach a kill if a male lion is present, whereas they will pluck up courage to drive off lionesses.

While lions are catholic in their choice of prey, they tend to select larger antelope to satisfy the hunger of

the pride with fewer kills. A pride will usually kill every three or four days, depending on the prey taken and the size of the pride. Males take little part in the hunt, but are quick to feed once the kill is made, taking their fill before allowing the lionesses and cubs a look in.

Courtship in lions is an intense and fascinating process with very little aggressive behaviour occurring, unlike other mammals. The number of young born will depend on the condition of the lioness, but is usually about four. Cub mortality is invariably high and is principally caused by starvation, when the adults leave insufficient food for the young. It has been estimated that in the Kruger National Park only half the cubs born will survive, and the mortality rate is even higher in the Kalahari. Lions compensate for this high cub mortality rate as, if they are in reasonable condition, the females come on heat again soon after milk production ceases. Females may reproduce up to an age of about 15 years.

ment of distances, and its teeth are as efficient as they are impressive. The canines deliver the killing bite and tear through tough hide, while the razor-sharp molars and rasping tongue make short work of flesh.

Prey is frequently carried away or dragged up into trees to prevent it being snatched by hyaenas. In areas of Namibia where hyaenas have not occurred for decades, leopards have adapted accordingly and no longer bother to cache their prey in trees, consuming it on the ground instead.

The leopard is of average size among the big cats but it also varies in size depending on where it is found. In the Judean Desert for example, where the leopard was thought to be extinct before its rediscovery in 1972, it is small, only about half the size of the Kruger National Park leopard which, in comparison, is far larger than that found in the mountains of the western Cape.

Leopards are solitary in habit and have no particular breeding season. Litters usually consist of three cubs which remain hidden until they start to follow the mother at about two months of age. Predation on leopard cubs, particularly by other leopards and spotted hyaenas, is very common.

Leopard

Leopards are widespread in South Africa and in no danger of extinction. Because they prey on a wide variety of mammals from mice to animals twice their size, and because of their secretive, nocturnal habits, leopards have adapted to a wide range of habitats. Unlike other large predators, they are not only found in game parks and reserves and many still roam in the wild, on farms and near cities. They are a problem, however, as they are inveterate poachers of domestic stock and, as such, are ruthlessly hunted. In areas where food is plentiful they can rely on wild animals; for example, they are found in the Magaliesberg on the outskirts of Pretoria, where dassies are probably their main source of food. In the lowveld, impala are their most common prey.

A highly effective hunter, the leopard makes full use of bushes, trees, long grass and dappled cover, its spotted coat providing perfect camouflage as it stealthily stalks its prey, body held close to the ground. Sometimes a leopard will ambush its victim from a tree, dropping on to the unsuspecting animal's back from the vantage point of a strategically placed branch. It is an animal marvellously adapted for hunting. Close-set eyes allow binocular vision for accurate judge-

Small Cats

There are 28 species of small cats in the world and of these only four occur in South Africa. One of these, the **African wild cat** *(centre left)* was tamed about 3000 BC in Egypt and is thought to be the ancestor of today's domestic cat. Ironically, it is the domestic cat that presents a very real threat to the conservation of the African wild cat. Well able to survive in the wild, the domestic cat interbreeds very easily with the similarly sized African wild cat which, as a result, has disappeared in its pure genetic form from many regions. The pure form of the species is a lithe, long-legged creature, rich red behind the ears and with a black-ringed, blunt-ended tail. Like most cats it is a nocturnal hunter, with prey ranging from mice and snakes to hares and young steenbok.

The **small-spotted cat** *(bottom left)* was previously known as the black-footed cat. The current name was chosen to avoid confusion with the larger African wild cat which also has black feet. The small-spotted cat, regarded as an endangered species in South Africa, has a distribution confined to the arid central parts, particularly the Karoo. It is nocturnal and feeds on small mice, gerbils and spiders in particular. Known to be vicious and aggressive for its size, it has been suggested that the small-spotted cat may kill lambs, but this is highly improbable and arises from a mis-identification of the predator, for the offender is far more likely to be the African wild cat.

The long-legged, beautifully marked **serval** *(top left)* is one of our most attractive cats, but unfortunately it is seldom seen because of its nocturnal habits. It shelters during the day in stands of long grass, underbrush or the reedbeds frequented by its most common prey, the vlei rat and multimammate mouse. It hunts on the edge of vleis, searching among the vegetation in water up to ten centimetres deep. Water is an essential habitat requirement of the serval and its wide distribution range incorporates the wetter, eastern parts of South Africa.

On the other hand, the secretive and solitary **caracal** *(right)* can tolerate far drier conditions and is widely distributed in the central and arid parts of South Africa. This heavily built cat with its characteristic ear tufts has become a problem on farms where numbers have increased considerably with the extermination of jackals, a common predator of caracal kittens. Fast and powerful in action, the caracal is a nocturnal hunter and has been implicated in mass killings of livestock, particularly sheep and goats. It will prey on mammals up to the size of the common duiker, but its favourite prey is the rock dassie.

Cheetah

South Africa has been in the forefront of the conservation of the **cheetah,** mainly owing to efforts of the De Wildt Cheetah Breeding Station of the National Zoological Gardens, Pretoria. Many unsuccessful attempts were made to breed this species in captivity before scientists found that, in most instances, male infertility was the cause and that when fertile males were used, the problem was overcome.

During experiments in releasing captive-bred cheetah into the wild, it was found that while a certain amount of their hunting behaviour is instinctive, other behaviour is definitely acquired from their mothers. For example, the captive-bred cheetah attacked and caught small giraffes, unheard of in the case of wild cheetah. They even attempted to attack a buffalo which is way beyond their ability as, with their comparatively weak jaws and teeth, cheetah are restricted to hunting the smaller and medium-sized antelope. The cheetah is reputed to be the fastest land mammal, and when giving chase can sprint at speeds of up to 95 kilometres an hour for a distance of 100-300 metres. It is certainly superbly designed for speed, having a small head, deep chest and long legs. It uses its long, heavy tail as a rudder to balance its movements when catching prey. The cheetah differs from the other big cats in that it invariably hunts by day and seldom scavenges, preferring fresh meat.

Up to the age of about three months, cheetah cubs have a mantle of smoky grey hair concealing the spots that will later appear. This is a camouflage device designed to offer them some protection while they are still vulnerable to predation.

Honey Badger and Striped Polecat

The **honey badger** *(this page)* occurs throughout South Africa, except in desert regions. Nocturnal and usually solitary, it is aggressive if threatened and has a fearsome reputation for attacking not only man but other carnivores as well. The honey badger's black and white body is a warning coloration to other animals. If an aggressor persists in annoying it, the honey badger will exude a foul-smelling excretion from its anal glands in an attempt to drive off its attacker. With its long, knife-like front claws, thick skin and odour mechanism, it is not surprising that the honey badger

has few natural enemies. It is well known for liking the honey and larvae of wild bees but mostly feeds on reptiles and rodents which it excavates. In the Kalahari the honey badger is frequently followed closely on its foraging sorties by chanting goshawks which snap up any escaping prey. The badger can raid hives with impunity as it is protected from bee-stings by its well-padded feet and thick fur. It is also partial to geckoes and other reptiles, mice and particularly scorpions. As shown here the honey badger is an adept climber and has been seen raiding the nest of a vulture 15 metres above the ground.

The **striped polecat** *(opposite)*, like the honey badger, has conspicuous black and white colouring to warn other animals that it is best left alone. Should a possible predator not heed the warnings when the striped polecat fluffs out its long hair, curves its tail over its back and stands on its hind legs, it is liable to be sprayed with a highly persistent, unpleasant musky fluid. The striped polecat is a solitary, nocturnal animal, preying mainly on mice and insects, but also taking snakes, birds and frogs. It is a purposeful hunter and will track its prey by following a scent or by stalking.

African Civet and Small-spotted Genet

The **African civet** *(below)*, which belongs to the same family as the genet and the mongooses, is characterized by very distinctive black and white markings. Colour patterns vary considerably, with no two individuals being identical, but certain features such as the pattern combination of black, grey and white on the neck, head and ears, and the black on the lower parts of the legs, are common to all.

Civets are nocturnal, generally solitary creatures. They are confined largely to areas of the northern and eastern Transvaal where there is surface water: well-watered areas provide good cover in the form of trees and shrubs which, in turn, provide the fruit and insects important in their diet.

The **small-spotted genet** *(left)* occurs in savanna woodland throughout South Africa. It is a short-legged species with a characteristic jet black band which arises just behind the shoulders and continues down to the tail. When threatened, the genet raises this band into a high crest. While it is largely insectivorous, the small-spotted genet will also feed on birds and mice and can be a nuisance in the fowl-run. Although considered a terrestrial species, it will climb trees either voluntarily while hunting or under stress, reaching the outermost branches and hiding in thick foliage or the fork of a branch.

Opposite: Suricate (see overleaf for text).

Mongooses

Of the 31 species of mongooses, 21 occur in Africa and 11 in southern Africa. Four are dealt with here.

Suricates *(previous page)*, largely restricted to southern Africa, are certainly one of the most attractive of the mongooses. Suricates are diurnal, very sociable animals, and live in colonies. When foraging in packs they chatter constantly, and post guards to watch for birds of prey and other predators while other members search for food. They live in burrows, taking over warrens from ground squirrels or sometimes sharing the warrens with the squirrels or with the yellow mongoose. Suricates often sunbathe, sitting on earth mounds near their burrows. The mounds make good observation posts and if anything interests the suricates, they stand up on their hindlegs, using their tails for balance. They are largely insectivorous but will also take some reptiles and small birds when the occasion arises.

The **yellow mongoose** *(top right)* shows many colour variations, ranging from tawny through yellow to red depending on season or geographical distribution. Although usually seen singly, like this yellow mongoose yawning as it emerges from its burrow, it is a gregarious species and often lives in colonies of up to 20 individuals. It is a good digger and will burrow out underground tunnels and chambers, or take over those of the ground squirrel. Predominantly diurnal, its diet is much the same as that of the suricate.

The **banded mongoose** *(above)* only occurs in savanna woodland in the Transvaal and Natal. It is very gregarious, and packs of up to 75 individuals live in warrens or holes in termite mounds. Packs will attack predators and competitors, particularly when young are threatened. Like other mongooses they include eggs, insects, scorpions and reptiles in their diet and also enjoy wild fruit.

The **dwarf mongoose** *(right)* is the smallest of the South African mongooses. Very similar to their banded cousins, the dwarf mongoose lacks the stripes and at a distance appears black or very dark brown. Packs of up to 30 occur, often taking up residence in a disused termite mound.

Hyaenas

Of the four species of hyaena occurring in Africa we are fortunate in that three, the **brown hyaena** *(opposite)*, the **spotted hyaena** *(right and below)* and the aardwolf *(see page 97)*, all occur in South Africa. The brown hyaena is endemic to southern Africa, being replaced north of the Zambezi River by the striped hyaena.

The brown hyaena, a distinctive animal with a long shaggy coat and white mantle around the neck, is widely distributed throughout the arid regions of South Africa. Farmers fearing livestock loss frequently persecute this species – unjustifiably, for this hyaena is not an adept hunter, and research in the Kalahari has shown that only six per cent of hunting attempts met with success. Even then, the largest animal brought down was a springhaas. The brown hyaena hunts rodents, birds, reptiles and insects, but is primarily a scavenger and with its keen sense of smell has been known to locate corpses many kilometres away. The pair shown opposite are scavenging from a gemsbok killed by lions.

Brown hyaenas are particularly well adapted to life along the cold west coast where they associate with seal colonies, preying on cubs and eating the washed-up corpses of the young seals which drown before they can swim.

Like its spotted relatives, the brown hyaena has extremely powerful jaws which cope easily with bones, hooves and horns. Both species can readily digest these items to recover the protein found in them. When meat is scarce the brown hyaena will feed on vegetable matter, especially wild melons and cucumbers which are also a source of water.

The spotted hyaena also occurs in areas inhabited by the brown hyaena but where the two compete, the brown hyaena generally will be excluded. This is because of the larger size of the spotted hyaena and the fact that it hunts in packs, whereas the brown hyaena usually forages alone.

Because they kill farm livestock, spotted hyaenas have been exterminated throughout most of their former range, and now only occur in national parks and game reserves. While brown hyaenas can also be a problem in this regard, it is usually only individual brown hyaenas that learn bad habits and so their presence passes unnoticed on many farms, whereas a pack of spotted hyaenas soon makes its presence known. In its defence, studies done by the Mammal Research Institute in the Kruger National Park have shown that spotted hyaenas, long accused of preying on wildebeest and zebra calves, took comparatively few considering the number available to them, spending instead some 40 to 50 per cent of their time scavenging, particularly from lion kills.

The spotted hyaena is a legendary animal. In the days of Aristotle it was thought to be hermaphrodite – a fallacy believed in some quarters even in recent times. This is a result of the species' very spartan social system in which the females dominate the clans, and because it is impossible to distinguish between the sexes as the external sexual organs of the females resemble those of the males. Only when females are suckling young and their teats become prominent, can they be distinguished at a distance from males.

Bat-eared Fox

The aptly-named **bat-eared fox** is widespread in the more arid regions of South Africa. During the recent three-year drought this species was found to have extended its range into areas that it had not previously inhabited. These movements are probably related not only to habitat but also to its catholic diet which allows it to adapt to a wide range of conditions. Some 90 per cent of its food consists of insects (70 per cent of these being harvester termites) and it also takes scorpions and small mice, reptiles and even wild fruit when it is available.

When foraging, bat-eared foxes appear to meander rather aimlessly but their large ears are pricked, alert to the slightest sound of moving prey. To fix the exact position of the noise, they 'point', with the ears almost touching the ground, and then begin digging using the long nails on the forefeet. The ears function not only as a 'radar' to locate prey, but also act as radiators, helping to lose body heat.

Although bat-eared foxes are largely nocturnal, they may frequently be seen during the day, particularly when it is overcast, or if food is scarce when they will be forced to spend more daylight hours searching for it.

The pair-bond is very strong and the foxes are probably monogamous. There is a definite breeding season: the arrival of the young follows the rains, a time when insect numbers are at their highest. This ensures a plentiful food supply when the young are being weaned. A litter of four cubs is usually born in a hole in the ground which the foxes may excavate themselves or which may have been vacated by antbears or springhaas. Both the male and female are attentive and protective parents. During the first excursions from the nesting burrow they will, at the first hint of danger, pick up the cubs in their mouths and carry them back to the safety of the burrow.

Cape Fox and Black-backed Jackal

The **Cape fox** *(below)*, with its soft silvery grey pelt and bushy tail, is the only true fox occurring in South Africa. This solitary, nocturnal animal inhabits the more arid regions, frequenting open country or semi-desert scrub. Prey mostly comprises a variety of small mammals, up to the size of a rabbit, and although there have been records of their attacking lambs, this occurs so seldom as to be of little importance. **Black-backed jackals** *(right)* have not been studied in any great detail in South Africa. Apart from scavenging carrion they are known to be extremely cunning predators, hunting hares, rodents, birds and sometimes newborn and small antelope. At a kill or when scavenging, the jackals observe a strict pecking order and as shown opposite, squabbles break out before they settle down to feed, with the loser adopting a submissive attitude. Although the black-backed jackal usually goes about alone or in pairs, it occasionally groups to form small family parties. They are socially very co-operative and help one another a great deal: for example, cubs from the previous two litters will assist the parents by acting as helpers with the current litter.

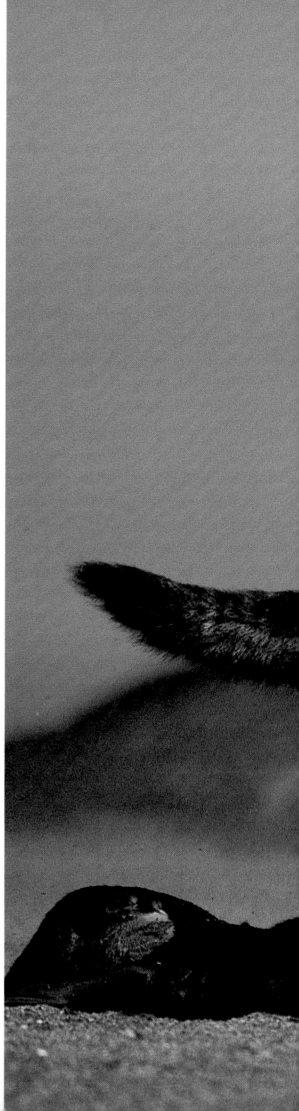

Wild Dogs

Wild dogs have evolved a highly specialized pack system, the chief function of which is to obtain food. Being little bigger than a jackal, a lone wild dog would lose its prey to the more powerful predators and would, in all probability, starve to death. But together, in a pack of 10 to 15 members, wild dogs form a ruthless hunting machine. They have great powers of endurance and a useful turn of speed, having been recorded at speeds of up to 66 kilometres an hour over two kilometres.

The pack system enables them to attack larger animals, such as

wildebeest and zebra, as well as waterbuck, impala and reedbuck. As their eyesight is better than their sense of smell, the dogs tend to frequent fairly open country and to hunt during the day. Prior to the hunt there is much excitement between members of the pack: twittering and squealing, they hold their tails high, rub noses and lick each other on the lips but, once on the hunt, the wild dogs are quiet. The hunt begins when the dogs course after the herd and separate their victim from the security of the group. They then proceed to chase it, sometimes for several kilometres, finally bringing it down. The way

in which they do this does not endear them to the general public as the victim is literally torn apart while still alive.

Wild dog pups are well looked after by members of the pack. They guard the young at the breeding hole, and regurgitate food for them. This is in response to the ritual begging ceremony in which the young whine, nudge and bite the corners of the adults' mouths to encourage them to bring up the food. Pups first hunt with the pack when they are about two and a half months old, and at a kill they are the first to eat.

Pangolin, Antbear and Aardwolf

The **pangolin** *(above)* derives its name from the Malay *peng-goling*, meaning the roller, from its habit of curling into a ball when defending itself. An unmistakable mammal, its armour of heavy brown scales is necessary for defence as it is both toothless and slow-moving. Solitary and nocturnal, the pangolin's diet consists mainly of ants which it catches with its extraordinarily long, sticky tongue.

The **antbear** or aardvark *(opposite)* has a long, flexible snout and a sticky tongue which it uses to trap its food, predominantly ants and termites. Antbears may travel up to 16 kilometres a night searching for new termite mounds. When foraging they zig-zag over the ground listening for the movement of their prey under the soil surface. Proficient diggers, they excavate extensive foraging holes and multi-chambered burrows which may later be used by other mammals, notably warthogs, porcupines and hyaenas.

The **aardwolf** *(left)* is a small hyaena weighing approximately 10 kilograms but, unlike other hyaenas, the aardwolf does not eat carrion or hunt, its prime prey being termites. Its teeth are small and peg-like and it is doubtful whether they could deal with flesh. The aardwolf digs the termites out of mounds using its powerful forefeet, and then laps up the insects with its broad, sticky tongue.

Squirrels

The **tree squirrel** *(opposite page)* is associated with open mopane and acacia woodlands, where the trees provide it with food and the abundance of tree holes it requires for nesting and breeding. During the day it can be seen foraging for flowers, fruits, seeds and leaves, ever alert for predators. If it senses danger it makes for the nesting hole, leaping from tree to tree, sometimes covering distances of over two metres in a single jump. When a female comes on heat she makes a specific call which attracts males, but it also induces other females to come on heat. As a result the births are synchronized, with many baby squirrels being born within a short time span and thus swamping potential predators.

The **ground squirrel** *(this page)* is a purely terrestrial species, commonly seen in the more arid regions of South Africa. It is gregarious and frequently occurs in association with suricates and yellow mongooses with which it occasionally shares burrow systems. They appear to cohabit peacefully but the yellow mongoose will prey on sick or injured ground squirrels.

Ground squirrels are diurnal and in hot weather are often seen with their long tails fanned over their heads as sunshades. When alarmed, the squirrels may wave their tails up and down as a visual warning to others in the group, while simultaneously calling. They have a variety of calls ranging from a growl of aggression to a high-pitched whistle or scream of alarm. Predominantly herbivorous, they will take insects when these are available.

Scrub Hare, Rock Dassie, Elephant-shrew and Springhaas

The ubiquitous **scrub hare** *(left)* occurs in such diverse habitats as the dense wattle plantations of Natal and the semi-desert conditions of southern Botswana. They are predominantly nocturnal but, in areas where they are not disturbed, they may be seen foraging at dusk. Adults vary in size, with specimens from the south-west being almost twice that of those from north-eastern areas. Scrub hares spend the day-light hours lying up in shallow depressions at the base of shrubs or other vegetation which, together with their drab coloration, provide some camouflage against predators.

Rock dassies *(opposite, top)* are widely distributed, inhabiting rocky hillsides, ravines, krantzes, or even rock piles adjacent to roadways. They are heavily preyed upon in some regions, being the prime target of leopards and caracal and a favourite prey of the black eagle. Their habit of basking in the sun renders them very vulnerable to attack, but to assist them in seeing the eagles as they stoop out of the sky, dassies have a special membranous eye shield which covers the eye when they look into the sun, thereby enabling them to see possible attackers. Numbers are strictly limited by the available shelter as once they cannot escape under rocky ledges they become even more vulnerable to predation.

The **bushveld elephant-shrew** *(opposite, bottom right)* is one of seven species of this insectivore occuring in southern Africa. Their habitat requirements range from rocky koppies to wooded areas and sand. Elephant-shrews derive their name from their trunk-like snouts which they constantly twitch up and down, sniffing the air. They show a preference for harvester termites and their tapering, pink tongues are so long that they can reach the top of their muzzles to clean the fur after a meal. Elephant-shrews are fast movers, showing a fine turn of speed when racing for cover, and are capable of great leaps, as their hind limbs are far longer than their fore limbs.

The **springhaas** *(right)* is actually mis-named as this animal is neither a hare nor even a typical rodent, and defies classification at this stage. It looks like a mini-kangaroo – short front legs, long powerful hind legs on which it bounds along in leaps of up to two metres, and a long black-tipped tail used for balancing. Springhaas are nocturnal, lying up during the day in the burrows which they excavate using the strong claws of the forefeet. They are mainly solitary although they may gather at good feeding grounds. They fall prey to a wide range of predators, not the least of which is man.

Porcupine and South African Hedgehog

Porcupines *(top, and bottom left)*, the largest rodents found in South Africa, have long fascinated man and many myths surround their habits and activities. For many years even some scientists believed that porcupines shot their quills at adversaries. This is a fallacy: porcupines in fact protect themselves by charging backwards to ram an adversary, leaving their 40-centimetre-long quills embedded in the enemy. This action is only taken if the aggressor does not heed the porcupine's warning of grunts, foot stamping, and raised and rattled quills. As they are nocturnal, porcupines lie up during the day either in disused antbear burrows which they modify, or in burrows they make, or in rocky caves. Once holed up they are almost impossible to remove as they erect their spines, thus anchoring themselves against the sides of the hole and at the same time presenting a sharp barrier of spines to the intruder. Porcupines are herbivores. They can be very destructive feeders and are frequently a problem in vegetable gardens as they are particularly fond of potatoes and other root crops. In the wild they debark trees, thereby killing them. The South African porcupine is known for its habit of collecting bones and it was long believed that it gnawed on these to sharpen its teeth. However, recent research at the Mammal Research Institute has shown that the porcupine may consume the bony material to rectify a calcium or phosphate deficiency in its diet.

Porcupines form a strong pair-bond, and they appear to be monogamous. One or two young are born, and are covered with soft spines which harden very quickly.

The fact that the **South African hedgehog** *(bottom right)* is now an endangered species is due in no small measure to the increased use of pesticides which poison their food of earthworms and other invertebrates.

The hedgehog occurs in many habitats, preferring grassland and woodland areas that are not too damp and that provide sufficient cover for resting up during the day under leaf litter, bushes or in holes. The resting places are changed daily, with the only semi-permanent abodes being those used for hibernation and nesting.

Covered with short, sharp spines, the hedgehog's defence against predators is to curl itself into a tight, prickly ball. However this is insufficient protection against the powerful talons and scaly feet of birds of prey such as owls.

Cape Clawless Otter and Cape Fur Seal

The **Cape clawless otter** *(left and below)* is well adapted to life on land and in water. Today it is found only in the more remote and protected areas such as along the coast and in the rivers and lakes of the Wilderness and Tsitsikamma areas, where this secretive, nocturnal animal is occasionally seen hunting crabs, octopus and slow-moving fish. Although not a marine mammal, it is sometimes seen out at sea if there are open river mouths in the vicinity. When hunting underwater the otter relies on sight and its long, sensitive whiskers to detect movement and vibrations. As its name implies, this otter has no claws on its blunt digits. Unlike other otters, its feet are only slightly webbed and its tail is the main source of propulsion when swimming.

The **Cape fur seal** *(opposite page)*, the only fur seal that breeds in this region, is widespread and inhabits coastal areas and offshore islands from Port Elizabeth to Namibia.

The young of Cape fur seals are born very seasonally in November or December. Each year the male fur seals are the first to arrive at the breeding colonies, followed some weeks later by the pregnant females. Seals mate again soon after the birth of the pups, and gestation lasts for nearly a year. During the first few days of a pup's life the maternal bond is strong, but the mother spends increasingly more time away from her pup, which joins a nursery group. Females often carry the pups in the manner shown opposite. New-born pups are vulnerable to predation both by jackals and brown hyaenas at seal colonies along the west coast. They are also the subject of much controversy as they are clubbed to death by man for their pelts. It is ironic, however, that had man not regarded this pelt production as a renewable resource, there is little doubt that he would have exterminated fur seals a long time ago.

Dolphins

Dolphins and whales belong to a group called the cetaceans and are among the most highly modified and specialized of all the mammals. While they are totally aquatic and never come ashore, they retain the attributes of mammals, such as breathing air and suckling their young. They lack hair but are insulated against heat loss while swimming in cold water by a thick layer of blubber under the skin.

Twelve dolphin species occur along the South African coast, two of the best known being the bottlenose and dusky dolphins. The bottlenose dolphin is the most common in our coastal waters and is the species popularly kept in oceanaria, as its apparent capacity to learn and its tractability in captivity make it the ideal candidate. The widespread distribution of bottlenose dolphins is mainly a result of their catholic diet of small fish and squid. When feeding, schools of up to 200 individuals will form a line and drive the fish before them in a well-organized capture technique.

Like all whales, these dolphins have a wide vocal range, from distress calls and whistles to squeaks, grunts and claps. They also echolocate: by rapidly emitting a number of high-pitched squeaks through the blowhole they can determine the position of an object. The 'echoes' bounce off the object and the reflected soundwaves are received by canals in the lower jaw which are connected to the ear. The progress of a school of bottlenose dolphins is marked by their exuberant activity as individuals leap out of the water or surf close to the shoreline.

Dusky dolphins, so-called because of their colouring of deep grey backs, light grey sides and white bellies, are also gregarious. They have strong social bonds and, should a member of the herd be wounded or ill, others will attempt to help by pushing it to the surface to allow it to breathe. It is believed that in winter dusky dolphins migrate from the cold south to the warmer waters around South Africa, returning to the cooler waters in summer.

Whales

In recent years the conservation of whales has captured man's imagination to a greater extent than that of any other species. Having exploited them for centuries – some species virtually to the point of extinction – man is, at last, turning to conserving all whales.

The right whales found along South Africa's coastline were given that name by early whalers because they were the 'right' whales to kill – being relatively slow swimmers they were easy to harpoon, and because of their abundant blubber, they seldom sank after being killed. Right whales were hunted not only for their oil but also for their baleen which was used during the last century to make the 'whalebone' stays of women's corsets. Instead of teeth, the so-called baleen whales have as many as 400 sheets of bone-like baleen which grow down from the roof of their mouths. When feeding, they open their strongly curved jaws and draw in enormous quantities of seawater containing squid, crustaceans, fish and krill (protein-rich shrimp-like creatures). The whales then close their lips and raise the floor of their mouths, expelling the water through the sieve-like baleen plates but retaining the food which is then swallowed whole.

Right whales have an extensive vocal repertoire. One of these calls, a low-frequency moan, travels far underwater and enables the whales to communicate over great distances. Two species of right whale frequent our waters, the rare pygmy right whale which reaches a length of about six metres, and the **southern right whale** *(below and opposite)* which achieves a length of about 18 metres.

Southern right whales were saved from extinction by being afforded universal protection in 1935. Regular aerial surveys conducted since 1962 have shown that their numbers have increased by six to seven per cent as a result of this protection and in the 1984 census no fewer than 270 whales were counted between Cape Town and Port Elizabeth. Sixty-four of these were calves.

This species is now the most common whale along our coast and is particularly noticeable when the females come in to calve *(see mother and young opposite)* in the early summer, using bays from Cape Town to Port Elizabeth. They are also frequently seen 'breaching' as shown below, when they leave the water in spectacular backward leaps, falling back into the water with a thunderous crash. The gestation period in these whales is about a year and although the calves normally have the same coloration as the adults, there have been instances of white calves recorded along our coasts.

Southern right whales have a unique feature in the wart-like protrusions situated on the front of the head before the blowhole. These callosities, clearly visible as white patches on the whales shown here, are composed of heavily cornified skin and are infested with colonies of barnacles, parasitic worms and lice. Scientists use the callosities to identify individual whales.

Index

Common name	Scientific name	Average weight of adult male	Diet	Habits	Main feeding time	Gestation	Number of young at birth
Aardwolf (page 97)	*Proteles cristatus*	9 kg	termites	solitary	night	unknown	2-4 cubs
Antbear (page 97)	*Orycteropus afer*	53 kg	termites and ants	solitary	night	7 months	single young
Baboon, chacma (page 63)	*Papio ursinus*	32 kg	omnivorous	troops	day	6 months	single infant
Badger, honey (page 83)	*Mellivora capensis*	11,5 kg	omnivorous	solitary	night	6-7 months	2 young
Blesbok (page 29)	*Damaliscus dorcas phillipsi*	70 kg	herbivorous grazer	herds	day	8 months	single lamb
Bontebok (page 29)	*Damaliscus dorcas dorcas*	61 kg	herbivorous grazer	herds	day	8 months	single lamb
Buffalo, Cape (page 32)	*Syncerus caffer*	750 kg	herbivorous mainly grazer	herds	day	11 months	single calf
Bushbaby, lesser (page 65)	*Galago senegalensis*	160 g	omnivorous	family groups	night	4 months	2 young
Bushbuck (page 40)	*Tragelaphus scriptus*	42 kg	herbivorous mainly browser	solitary	night	6 months	single calf
Bushpig (page 67)	*Potamochoerus porcus*	62 kg	omnivorous	groups	night	4 months	3-4 piglets
Caracal (page 78)	*Felis caracal*	14 kg	carnivorous	solitary	night	2½ months	2-4 kittens
Cat, African wild (page 78)	*Felis lybica*	5 kg	carnivorous	solitary	night	2 months	2-5 kittens
small-spotted (page 78)	*Felis nigripes*	1,6 kg	carnivorous	solitary	night	2 months	1-3 kittens
Cheetah (page 81)	*Acinonyx jubatus*	54 kg	carnivorous	solitary	day	3 months	1-5 cubs
Civet, African (page 84)	*Civettictis civetta*	11 kg	omnivorous	solitary	night	2 months	2-4 young
Dassie, rock (page 100)	*Procavia capensis*	3,5 kg	herbivorous	colony	day	7-8 months	1-6 young
Dog, wild (page 95)	*Lycaon pictus*	27 kg	carnivorous	packs	dawn/dusk	2½ months	7-10 pups
Dolphin bottlenose (page 106)	*Tursiops aduncus*	190 kg	carnivorous	schools	day/night	12 months	single calf
dusky (page 106)	*Lagenorhynchus obscurus*	90 kg	carnivorous	schools	day/night	9 months	single calf
Duiker, blue (page 46)	*Cephalophus monticola*	4 kg	herbivorous browser	solitary	day/night	4 months	single lamb
common (page 47)	*Sylvicapra grimmia*	18 kg	herbivorous browser	solitary	day/night	3 months	single lamb
Eland (page 18)	*Taurotragus oryx*	700 kg	herbivorous browser	herds	day/night	9 months	single calf
Elephant, African (page 43)	*Loxodonta africana*	5 500-6 000 kg	herbivorous	herds	day/night	22 months	single calf
Elephant-shrew, bushveld (page 100)	*Elephantulus intufi*	46 g	insectivorous	unknown	day	8 weeks	1-2 young
Fox, bat-eared (page 90)	*Otocyon megalotis*	4 kg	carnivorous (mostly insects)	solitary/ family groups	night/dawn	2 months	4-6 cubs
Cape (page 92)	*Vulpes chama*	3 kg	carnivorous (mainly mice and insects)	solitary	night	2 months	1-4 cubs

Common name	Scientific name	Average weight of adult male	Diet	Habits	Main feeding time	Gestation	Number of young at birth
Gemsbok (page 20)	*Oryx gazella*	240 kg	herbivorous grazer	herds	day	9 months	single calf
Genet, small-spotted (page 84)	*Genetta genetta*	2 kg	carnivorous	solitary	night	2½ months	2-4 young
Giraffe (page 10)	*Giraffa camelopardalis*	1 200 kg	herbivorous browser	herds	day	15 months	single calf
Grysbok, Cape (page 50)	*Raphicerus melanotis*	10 kg	herbivorous mainly grazer	solitary or pairs	night	6 months	single lamb
Hare, scrub (page 100)	*Lepus saxatilis*	2,5 kg	herbivorous	solitary	night	40 days	1-2 leverets
Hartebeest, red (page 27)	*Alcelaphus buselaphus*	150 kg	herbivorous grazer	herds	day	8 months	single calf
Hedgehog, South African (page 102)	*Erinaceus frontalis*	350 g	omnivorous mainly insectivorous	solitary	night	1 month	1-9 young
Hippopotamus (page 52)	*Hippopotamus amphibius*	1 500 kg	herbivorous grazer	herds	night	8 months	single calf
Hyaena, brown (page 88)	*Hyaena brunnea*	45 kg	carnivorous	clans solitary feeder	night	3 months	1-5 cubs
spotted (page 88)	*Crocuta crocuta*	60 kg	carnivorous	clans	night	3½ months	1-2 cubs
Impala (page 37)	*Aepyceros melampus*	50 kg	herbivorous grazer/browser	herds	day	6½ months	single lamb
Jackal, black-backed (page 92)	*Canis mesomelas*	8 kg	mainly carnivorous	solitary or pairs	day/night	2 months	4 pups
Klipspringer (page 49)	*Oreotragus oreotragus*	10 kg	herbivorous browser	solitary or pairs	dawn/dusk	5 months	single lamb
Kudu (page 17)	*Tragelaphus strepsiceros*	230 kg	herbivorous browser	herds	day	7 months	single calf
Leopard (page 74)	*Panthera pardus*	60 kg	carnivorous	solitary	night	3½ months	2-3 cubs
Lion (page 69)	*Panthera leo*	240 kg	carnivorous	prides	dusk/night/ dawn	3½ months	1-4 cubs
Mongoose, banded (page 86)	*Mungos mungo*	1,3 kg	omnivorous	troops	day	2 months	2-8 young
dwarf (page 86)	*Helogale parvula*	270 g	carnivorous (mainly insects)	troops	day	2 months	2-4 young
yellow (page 86)	*Cynictis penicillata*	700 g	carnivorous	colonies	day	unknown	2-5 young
Monkey, vervet (page 65)	*Cercopithecus pygerythrus*	5,5 kg	omnivorous mainly herbivorous	troops	day	7 months	single infant
Nyala (page 14)	*Tragelaphus angasii*	108 kg	herbivorous mainly browser	herds	day	7 months	single calf
Oribi (page 48)	*Ourebia ourebi*	14 kg	herbivorous mainly grazer	solitary/pairs	day	7 months	single lamb
Otter, Cape clawless (page 104)	*Aonyx capensis*	13 kg	carnivorous	solitary/pairs	dawn/dusk	unknown	1-2 young
Pangolin (page 97)	*Manis temminckii*	7 kg	ants and termites	solitary	night	unknown	single young

Common name	Scientific name	Average weight of adult male	Diet	Habits	Main feeding time	Gestation	Number of young at birth
Polecat, **striped** (page 83)	*Ictonyx striatus*	1 kg	carnivorous	solitary	night	1½ months	1-3 young
Porcupine (page 102)	*Hystrix africaeaustralis*	17 kg	herbivorous	solitary	night	3 months	1-2 young
Reedbuck (page 40)	*Redunca arundinum*	80 kg	herbivorous grazer	small herds	dawn/ dusk/night	8 months	single calf
Rhinoceros, **black** (page 59) **(hook-lipped)**	*Diceros bicornis*	850 kg	herbivorous browser	solitary	day/night	15 months	single calf
white (page 61) **(square-lipped)**	*Ceratotherium simum*	2 100 kg	herbivorous grazer	small groups	day/night	16 months	single calf
Roan (page 22)	*Hippotragus equinus*	270 kg	herbivorous grazer	herds	day	9 months	single calf
Sable (page 22)	*Hippotragus niger*	230 kg	herbivorous mainly grazer	herds	day	8 months	single calf
Seal, **Cape fur** (page 104)	*Arctocephalus pusillus*	190 kg	carnivorous	colonies	day/night	12 months	single pup
Serval (page 78)	*Felis serval*	11 kg	carnivorous	solitary	night	2½ months	1-3 young
Springbok (page 39)	*Antidorcas marsupialis*	41 kg	herbivorous grazer/browser	herds	day	5½ months	single lamb
Springhaas (page 100)	*Pedetes capensis*	3 kg	herbivorous	solitary	night	2½ months	single young
Squirrel, **ground** (page 98)	*Xerus inauris*	600 g	herbivorous	colonies	day	1½ months	1-3 young
tree (page 98)	*Paraxerus cepapi*	200 g	herbivorous/ omnivorous	pairs/ small groups	day	2 months	1-3 young
Steenbok (page 50)	*Raphicerus campestris*	11 kg	herbivorous browser/grazer	solitary	dawn/dusk	5½ months	single lamb
Suricate (page 86)	*Suricata suricatta*	730 g	carnivorous (mostly insects)	colonies	day	2½ months	2-5 young
Tsessebe (page 27)	*Damaliscus lunatus*	140 kg	herbivorous grazer	herds	day	8 months	single calf
Warthog (page 67)	*Phacochoerus aethiopicus*	80 kg	herbivorous	family groups	day	5½ months	1-5 young
Waterbuck (page 24)	*Kobus ellipsiprymnus*	260 kg	herbivorous mainly grazer	herds	day	9 months	single calf
Wildebeest, **black** (page 31)	*Connochaetes gnou*	180 kg	herbivorous grazer	herds	day	8½ months	single calf
blue (page 31)	*Connochaetes taurinus*	250 kg	herbivorous grazer	herds	day	8½ months	single calf
Whale, **southern right** (page 108)	*Balaena glacialis*	70 000 kg	small crustaceans	solitary/pairs	day/night	11-12 months	single calf
Zebra, **Burchell's** (page 55)	*Equus burchelli*	320 kg	herbivorous grazer	herds	day	12 months	single foal
Cape mountain (page 55)	*Equus zebra zebra*	250 kg	herbivorous grazer	herds	day	12 months	single foal